A PUNK ROCK FLASHBACK

LEE GIBSON

Copyright © 2013 Lee Gibson

Printed by Createspace/Amazon 2015

This Book is a work of fact.
The people and places within these pages are all real.
This book is based upon memories – sometimes perceptions were skewed.
Sometimes other people helped with the recall.
This book is as true as can be.

CONTENTS

Foreword

Part 1 –
Up North 1978-82

Part 2 –
Fanzine Interviews

Part 3 –
Down South 1982-88

'At age 50, every man has the face he deserves.' George Orwell

FOREWORD

This book was written by pure chance, inspired by random events. I'd been living in a studio flat in Hackney, east London, with my son, Felix, for seven years. My landlord suddenly dropped a bombshell and wanted to increase my rent by 80% - this was because of the Olympics; there was much profit to be made from foreign visitors. I was just one of thousands of people affected in such a manner and forced to move out because the Government had refused to put a stop to such greedy actions – as a result, I hated and loathed the London Olympics – I thought the hype was pure evil and I never was much of a flag waver.

As I was packing up my belongings I stumbled across some old photographs. A torrent of memories hit me and their power reduced me to tears. I'd just finished writing a novel, Mercury Falling, and was about to turn 50. It seemed like a good time to write a memoir covering a specific ten year period of time. This book took 14 months to write – a heavy meditation.

Whenever I mention someone in the text I only use their first name and the first initial of their surname in order to protect the innocent and the guilty alike. I would especially like to thank all the folks I interviewed back in the day for being so generous with their time; Mark E Smith, Poison Girls, Crass and Andy T, extra thanks to Andy for providing his notes on the Crass Perth gig.

Thanks and appreciation are also due to some of the folk up north, Carole D., Morgan D., Steve H., Steve W., Gary W., Geoff S., and Paul C. for their comments, photographs and assistance in reconstructing some of the timeline for Part One.

As for the Southern monkeys, hello to Gerard E., and thanks to Val D. and Joseph P. for photos and images. Extra thanks to my son, Felix, and also Tony "The Gravedigger' E. for proof-reading the final manuscript – your support and lack of bullshit means more than you know. Finally, thanks to Kim C. for permission to include her biographical essay; 'Merlin'.

Lee G.
London – August - 2013.

Part One: The North
1978-82 – Some Kind Of Disorder

CHAPTER 1

When the Sex Pistols released 'Anarchy in the UK' in November, 1976, I was still at school, aged 14. I was the second youngest kid in my year. If I'd been born in September instead of July, I would have been one of the oldest kids in the year below; with all my mates. Instead, I was cast into the year above and didn't know a soul. It's funny how things work out - The joke of life.

At the time, in '76, I was busy either disrupting the classroom due to lack of interest and motivation, or otherwise bunking off school, throwing stolen school canteen cutlery onto railroad tracks from above Yarm viaduct – hoping to cause a disaster (got caught by the headmaster), hanging around the local abattoir by Yarm river, watching guys fill metal skips with severed cow's heads that they said were all destined for McDonald's, shoplifting sweets from a nearby garden centre, eating take-away chips, hiding out at my pals house while we were supposed to be doing a cross-country run (we'd always muddy-up on the way back to school), or otherwise fighting bullies who were usually older and meaner than I ever was. In other words, like thousands of other children of my blank generation, I underwent a normal Northern upbringing in the late seventies. Nowhere to go and nothing to do – 'No future' written large against a blank grey sky.

I grew up in the small village of Longnewton, just off the A66, four miles between Darlington and Stockton-on-Tees – a kind of no-man's-land surrounded by fields, streams and woodland, a local sulphur factory and a Ministry of Defense base that we used to sneak into to collect spent and live ammo from the firing range. The railway line from Stockton to Darlington was the first ever built in the UK.

Don't get me wrong, there were a lot of things that I liked about growing up in the countryside – free to roam, free to play war games through isolated forests – free to build dens in lofty tree branches and to build secret dens underground. Yet, even in a small village, I had to contend with bullies that were older than me, bullies who derived a certain sadistic pleasure in taunting me and then beating me up with their fists that felt like steel when I responded to their taunts. I guess I was easy to reel in. An easy target, being tall and skinny, or 'wiry', as my dad called me. Even at that age I knew that I didn't quite fit into the moulds being prepared for me. I always felt like an outsider; a square plug in a round hole. I just didn't fit anywhere. It took me a long, long time to appreciate that fact about myself and to finally learn how to celebrate my own individuality and answer to no-one. My path is my own, as your path is yours.

I'm not going to waste time ranting about my childhood or my parental upbringing, or whatever physical 'heavy discipline' I endured – my whole generation had to suffer similar things, and the truth is that our parents loved us and did what they thought was best, and half of them went through worse things than we did – they were just blinded by their own upbringing and all the social conditioning that governed their own parents upbringing and so on and so on, and these days I get on great with my pensioner parents, I have done for decades now – we understand each other better than we ever did and they are lovely when they interact with my son, Felix (15 at the time of writing).

This is not going to be a book about blame, just a book about how it was for me and how random events unfolded in my little random life and some of the weird events I experienced and some of the wonderful people I met. My anger has been consumed and dissolved by time and reflection. This is just my fucked-up life in a fucked-up world, as honest as I can tell it, and as best as I can recall it due to years of drinking and years of determined substance abuse. I'll enclose a few quotes from my peers when I can to back me up, because this story is for real. I have no axe to grind – I'm just a fifty year old man looking back through the magic mirror of time, reflecting, while my lungs still work and my kidneys ain't collapsed – while my heart still beats and pumps blood through my veins...while my brain still functions – ha-ha.

It was the 70's, and things were pretty grim all round. The future felt like a black hole – what future? Opportunities and career options were limited. On my last year at school, 1978, that I rarely attended, I already knew that only three paths were available to me. 1. Join the army. 2. Work in a factory. 3. Go to borstal or jail. I didn't know what I wanted, but most certainly none of the above.

Many of my school friends had already been locked away in a local D.C. Two of my friend's dads worked at Kirk Levington Detention Centre as screws and as a result, my pals were ostracized by many of their peers, like it was their fault that their fathers worked for the system. All my pals smoked, to look hard and cool, but most of them could barely write their own names. I didn't smoke as a child – I suffered from severe asthma as a kid and when an attack kicked in I could barely climb a flight of stairs and as a result I had a fair amount of time off school due to that suffocating illness. However, these days I smoke roll-up cigarettes, and I've smoked a whole lot of other shit between then and now, with no regrets and a lot of good times...if my experimentation and dabbling has shortened my life, well, I simply don't care. I'll take it on the chin. What will be, will be; besides, like many people of my generation, I never thought I'd make it to age 21, so in my book, I've done ok. Better than expected. (Note – I stopped smoking in October 2012, opting for e-Lite's).

At school, music never interested me much – I never could understand the recorder/flute thing? The only person who looked cool back then playing a flute was David Carradine in the Kung-Fu TV series. I only attended art because the teacher was a soft hippy who didn't give a damn and I was rubbish at it anyway. In English my teacher was a closet Communist - I read what I was told to read, that was it. Not bad books when I look back on it – '1984' and 'Animal Farm' by George Orwell, and 'A Clockwork Orange' by Anthony Burgess are the only ones I recall, but I hated English, like I hated all classes – they all felt like jail to me.

If I ever wrote an essay, my Commie teacher would make me read it aloud. At that time, hitting puberty in my year when the oldest guy in my year already possessed a hairy chest, I was shy and felt very self conscious. However, perhaps my English teacher was trying to encourage me, but I didn't take it that way – the last English lesson I attended I grabbed him by the throat, slammed him against a cheap wall and threatened to punch his face in – respect to him, he stayed calm and actually suggested I stay on to the 6th form! That was something I just could not imagine myself doing – I simply wanted out.

Now, as a 50 year old guy, and as a father, I think I should have taken his advice, but I never attended his lessons again and dedicated myself to bunking off, although I sometimes used to hide out in the library, avoiding lessons and bullies alike, and I got right into Sven Hassel novels; World War II books written from the point of view of a German soldier. Sven Hassel actually applied to join the SS but he was rejected. His novels are bloody and violent, and anti-war. I guess Sven was a mixed-up dude. Still, who wasn't mixed up in that era – let's face it, just before the Americans sided with us in WWII, they were also making plans to invade England and to side with Hitler; so much for our 'special relationship'. The Yanks butt-fuck us every time, whenever it suits them.

I felt weak and disempowered at school, out of my depth, like an alien. I hated the system and daily brutality. I saw a compass point shoved into another kids face. I saw a teacher kick a kid in the belly and the kid spewed up – complaints were made but the teacher got away with it Scott free, just like a cop would in a demo. I saw a girl fight; they both had Coca-cola ring-pulls wrapped on their fingers like savage rings; their faces got sliced and after the fight they both looked like chopped tomatoes; I had a headmaster with a withered, deformed arm – a girl had passed out in class – two of my mates clocked him through the staff-room window, he had his good arm down her pants – they went back to school that night and spray painted all over the external school walls – 'Gammy is a Child Molester' – they were never sussed and never caught, and neither was Gammy – the fucker might still be there, with his good arm down a fresh set of panties, for all I know. I felt trapped at school; caged in. I felt powerless, always watching my back, but if ever a bully came at me, I usually beat them up, mostly out of fear – like a closet Knights Templar. For all I was 'wiry', I was sometimes full of surprises.

Twice a week, for three months or so, after maths, two guys from my class were always waiting to beat me up. I never knew why. Maths was always a long, long hour of fear. I'd face the two guys, or rather they would back me into a corner and we would fight – just with our fists – no boots or knives or guns, and obviously I always lost – then, one day, instead of fighting them, I simply put my hands up and said 'I'm not doing this anymore' – to my amazement, they backed off, and within a few weeks we became good friends – I guess it was their way of saying 'Hello'. Is that just a Northern thing? I doubt it.

*

The first thing I heard or saw concerning punk rock manifested in the daily newspapers, with their tales of moral outrage accompanied by images of teenagers wearing black bin-liners as outfits, safety pins pierced through their lips, cheeks and ears, the female punks wearing heavy black mascara. I didn't pay much attention; it had nothing to do with me. I just thought they looked rather odd and a bit wild.

The first punk rock song I heard was 'God Save The Queen' in 1977 by the Sex Pistols; a bunch of guys from London, half of whom were ex-art-college students – they were the first wave of punk rock. Many of the original punk bands were ex-students. The second wave of punk, circa. 78-79, were a mix of college types, working class, unemployed and guys who were musicians in prog-rock or heavy metal bands who decided to shorten their hair and the length of their songs in order to jump onto the latest bandwagon; careerist, ex-hippies with little soul.

Andrew A, a year older than me, with long blonde hair and the usual Wrangler's denim jacket/jeans outfit of a wrecked 60's dope-smoker, played the Pistols single to me. At that time we were both into David Bowie and Patti Smith and had no taste for many of the sounds that dominated the scene - he read the only music news-rags around at that time; NME and Sounds. I heard that Pistols song and Bang! The dull, vacuous music of my childhood and the music that dominated the charts and Top of the Pops were suddenly very dead – at least six feet under.

TOTP was a bloody sad joke – a one half hour show a week was all the music that got fed into people's homes via the TV that shut down before midnight. We only had two or three channels – all of it shite. TOTP with its fuzzy videos with dancers wearing silly outfits, all designed to give 'pops' a little sexual simulation, hence the show's title. The songs of that time were generally flat, mind-numbingly dull, mundane, inane and always mimed and sometimes just plain insane. The 'stars' wore the stupidest outfits and long hairstyles – everything they sang about had nowt to do with real life and what was going on for the average kid who bought their records. The 'stars' were rich and they were famous and far removed from reality due to their cocaine addled lifestyles, but the kids buying their records lived on the exact opposite end of the scale – they lived on the wrong side of the street – the wrong side of the fence – the wrong side of town – the wrong side of the social divide. A musical rebellion - a jolt in the arm – was way overdue. If the Sex Pistols hadn't arrived, my entire generation would have been terminally enslaved, and life in the gutter would never have been so much fun. We won't even mention Jimmy Savile.

The next day I went out and bought the Sex Pistols 'God Save the Queen' 45-inch vinyl. I was 15. Money was tight. It was the year of the Queens Jubilee – there was a street party where I lived, but I stayed home alone, playing electric guitar (I didn't even know how to play a simple chord), very loudly, and very badly, so loud it made the windows of the house vibrate. I figured that if I was making the windows of the house shake, then I was definitely doing ok.

I know the Sex Pistols made it to number one in the charts, but a conspiracy was already underway. Some charts show Rod Stewart as number one, but I specifically recall walking into WH Smith's and seeing a black, blank panel covering the number one spot. I knew I'd found something...maybe my thing...without a doubt, the Sex Pistols had kicked the door wide open. There was no going back…only forward...into no future – low on hope but high on attitude.

I was still at school when the Pistols played Middlesbrough Rock Garden under the name of Acne Rabble in '77. The rumour on the streets first started with the word that S.P.O.T.S. (Sex Pistols On Tour Secretly), were going to play the Rock Garden. They were forced to do secret, clandestine gigs around the country as every local council had automatically banned them from playing. England at that time, just like now, was very Conservative. I knew about the gig, but I was under curfew and not allowed to go; my mum ruled the house with a velvet fist.

At school I had to wear a uniform – when I started wearing a leather, metal-studded, dog-collar, I was threatened with expulsion and had to stop wearing it. If I got expelled, I'd have to face father-wrath and I chose to avoid that at all costs. I painted my school haversack with the words 'The problem is you'. I bought the Sex Pistols album, 'Never Mind the Bollocks', but when my dad heard it, he ripped the record off the turntable and he broke it in half. The next day, I went and bought another copy, but I could only play it when my folks were out of the house. This was clandestine music. Secret music; mine, not theirs.

I fell in love with this new angry music and its songs that barely lasted three minutes. I bought random singles by random bands whenever I could and started listening to Radio Luxembourg and to John Peel; like many kids my age, listening late at night underneath the bedcovers after curfew. I bought 'Go Buddy Go/Peaches' by The Stranglers. I saw a weird black and white hand drawn 7" single cover of a strange looking guy wrapped in a chain and padlock by some band I'd never heard of called The Fall, and picked that up as well. By the time I picked up their second single, 'It's the New Thing' – I was hooked on that particular Salford band for life.

We only had one music shop on Stockton High Street – HMV - a guy called Blank Frank worked there – he was in a local band called Blitzkrieg Bop, they were formed in 1977 and named after a song by the Ramones. Blank Frank was always helpful, letting me put up notices about our band's forthcoming gigs, etc, in the store by the counter. Later, he worked with another guy, Ian I., who was also in a local band; Bombay Drug Squad – he used to make me laugh when a customer wanted to buy some tripe pop music - he would argue with them and try to talk them out of making their purchase – he eventually got fired for his endeavours. Right then, I didn't know another soul who was into this new punk vibe. I was alone on what started to feel like a one man mission. 'Punk Rock', the media called it, 'Teenage Uprising' is perhaps more accurate, but all tags become body bags in time, especially when the media wrap their insipid tentacles around it; they sure know how to build 'em up and knock 'em down.

I wanted a piece of punk. The whole vibe hit me like 10,000 volts – like an electrical shock I'd been waiting for through all my redundant, bullied, smashed-up years at school. I knew I was a full part of the nowhere generation. I was angry and frustrated by the restrictions of the time that boxed me in like some kind of state-owned animal. I wanted to be on the outside of the machine, even if I didn't quite know what that would mean – young, blind, foolhardy and looking for an out...any way out of the box of restraint and constriction of what I had been told were the limitations of my life in the industrial wasteland of north-eastern UK. I wanted to kick the sick junk habit of social conditioning and now was the time.

*

I left school aged 15, just a few weeks before I turned 16, in 1978, and walked straight into a job on a small industrial estate – the factory was run by a friend of my dad's (a touch of nepotism – just like Hollywood;-). My apprenticeship as a sheet metal worker was supposed to last four years. I managed to stick it out for nearly two of them. The job was a nightmare, building huge metal sea-containers, the kind you see on ships or stacked up like giant Lego blocks on the docks. I was pressurized by the foreman every Friday to do overtime on a Saturday – I never worked a single hour of overtime. In the factory is where I first started writing, usually poems/lyrics to songs I guessed I'd never sing. I'd hide in the toilets and basically write stuff on toilet roll paper while the older guys, mostly the welders, smoked dope and injected pure alcohol into their veins or jacked-off to pornographic magazines. The factory floor consisted of men. The only women in the place worked in the office, out of sight.

My best pal in the factory was Eric M. (Maz). He was a year older than me – he was right into Northern Soul. We used to hit pubs in Darlington on a Friday night after work – then he would want to hit a nightclub, but due to my punkish clothes we were usually turned away. I didn't mind – I've never liked clubs very much, I always preferred old men's pubs, spit'n'sawdust suits me just fine.

One day a week I went to technical college. I only had three pals there; Soapy, who had long stringy hair and was a street urchin into all kinds of music who chose not to dress in any particular style, then a guy into Northern Soul and all the clothes that went with it; more pockets and buttons on his flash trousers than you could count, and Eddie, whose job was putting all the stickers and tags and labels on the inside of freshly built buses – he was into rockabilly and had the tight jeans, black leather jacket and greased-up hairstyle to go with it. We were the oddballs in college – an urchin, a Northern Soul guy, a Rockabilly dude and punked-up me, all hanging out together because everyone else was plastic. To be fair, I think we all appreciated our differences and we each respected our different tastes in music. Back then, it seems that the music you listened to defined who you were – like a musical identity.

At college, I attended classes in the morning, but in the afternoon I would drift off to watch a horror movie alone at the cinema. I've never had a problem going to the cinema alone – it's just me and what's onscreen – just me and another world, although watching John Carpenter's 'Halloween' alone in a totally empty, old style Odeon cinema in Darlington was quite a scary experience. Despite my obsessive, weekly movie habit, I somehow managed to pass the exam with a Distinction, but it didn't really mean a damn thing to me.

I had a friend called Andy D. who I knew from school and he lived nearby. He was also getting into punk. We used to hang out in a brick bus shelter at night, melting candles and making wax hands by dripping hot wax onto our skin. We also bought a jar of Indian ink and used a safety-pin to tattoo our skin – blue dots on the knuckles, that kind of thing – it hurt a bit and our hands swelled up. The pain and the swelling didn't matter – we thought we were cool; pseudo rebels with nothing but idle time on our hands.

Sometimes at night we would enter the village church (we knew where the caretaker hid the key) and ring the church bells. My grandmother, on my mother's side, was an official church bell ringer. My granddad was the village gravedigger. My grandfather on my father's side was killed during an air raid at Biggin Hill air-base during WWII where he worked as an ambulance driver – ironically killed the first time he ever used a shelter in a raid. My grandmother on my father's side died a year or so later – as a child she had been an orphan.

As a result of their deaths, my father was abandoned by his elder brother and sister; they moved to America. My father became an orphan when he was seven years old and moved from Kent to the North East to live with a sadistic aunt – he survived his ordeal and managed to raise a family – he deserves a bloody medal for his endurance, and for the fact that he didn't kill the wicked bitch. Personally, I'd have cut her throat and pissed on her fucking grave. He left her house aged 14 and stepped alone into the world.

Andy D. and I decided to buy some cheap guitars and amplifiers. We messed around – we were both rubbish guitarists and didn't know the slightest thing about chords, notes or progressions. It didn't bother us. It was fun making a racket. We started talking about forming a band – definitely more fantasy than reality. At that time I think we were into football hooliganism as much as anything else.

(It has always been in my nature to be something of a dabbler – Jack of all trades and master of none – and since it was the 70's we had to check out the football scene. Andy D. and m'self used to go and watch Middlesbrough (The Boro), although we were selective about which games we went to see. Whenever Boro played Leeds you knew it was going to kick-off – I once saw Leeds player Billy Bremner head-butt a Boro player, so the potential for violence and a bit of excitement was taking place both on and off the pitch – and we would always be there for sure. We used to wear our red and white scarves tied on our wrists, but unlike all the other Boro scarves in the football ground, ours were covered in safety pins – at that time we were the only punks in the stands; the Hollgate End.

We never really got caught-up in any actual fisticuffs – half of the football hooligan scene was just male posturing, like chimps in designer gear snarling at each other, taking a quick dig at someone, then backing away before they became ensnared in a shit situation. Saying that, I did see people getting bricked or hit over the head with a fence post ripped out of someone's front garden, and sometimes 6 onto 1; hooligans were that hard. I thought most of them were cowards and morons. Most gangs were usually made up of nine wannabe's for every tenth psycho who would lead them into the fray. Most times it was more vocal than violent. It was a way to let off steam and get chased by the cops and tell stories later.

I must confess that I found it very easy to trigger off violent episodes at football matches. On several occasions I would stand next to the metal, blue-painted fence that separated the Boro fans from the Leeds fans. Then I would start hurling abuse and spitting at them, jibbing them up. In a minute or so, the away fans 'firm' would be squaring up, like a pack of raging, angry pit-bull motherfuckers. They would scale the fence and it would all kick-off. By that time, I'd moved away from the 'front line' – I just got off on the power of manipulating the whole thing, then watching it all happen – sometimes the fighting spread right through the football ground like a bushfire. That was my rush.

At the end of a game it would spill out onto the streets – we used to get chased by cops on horseback and then duck into my mate's auntie's pub and drink while people ripped into each other or got arrested. I sussed back then that the more people you put together, the stupider they tend to be. I think that fact holds up to this day. I think I did two seasons of football matches and that was it. Shortly after that, football took on a darker persona and people started using Stanley Knives and craft knives on each other's faces. The joy and rush of football violence has never been the same since, unless you enjoy retro-movies on the subject.)

We used to walk two miles from Longnewton village at evening time, usually six or seven of us, from our village to the edge of Stockton, to an area called Hartburn. There, we found an off-license that would sell us bottles of wine and cider, whatever. We were all well underage and the seller didn't care. It was the same with cigarettes – shop owners would sell them to anyone back then – you just had to say you were picking them up for your mum. We would start drinking booze, walking back through various estates and play areas that we weren't too familiar with, getting pissed and gradually making our way back to Longnewton, and we'd be smashed by the time we all got home. Straight up to bed and no messing about once you got home – play it low profile, keep the parents in the dark and avoid a bashing. We got away with that for a long time. I've been getting pissed ever since I was 13. Maybe it's time I straightened up? I'd ask a priest for some advice, but I don't want to get butt-fucked by a God-dealing monster - know what I mean?

One night, around the time I was getting into punk and starting to dress that way (i.e. – straight jeans - not flares, short hair - not long), our village crew were staggering back home through a large play area in Hartburn. It was dark. I was drunk and singing/shouting 'Anarchy in the UK' at the top of my voice. As we crossed through the area I noticed two guys sitting high up in a tree. I later found out they were hiding from us because we looked like a gang – I guess we were, in our own way, but we never really thought of ourselves like that, and we certainly didn't act like that either – we were good natured kids and never picked a fight or took advantage of numbers – it simply wasn't in our nature – never been in my nature either; I never pick a fight. Saying that, however, I did pick one fight at school with a guy who was much bigger than me and he smashed the shit out of me faster than it took me to write this sentence!

I walked over to the tree and that's when I first met Andy M. and Pete M. (not related), they were both punks. We immediately clicked. They both remember that moment as well. Years later, we'd end up living in the same shared, communal house in Stockton, doing drugs and attending gigs together, getting busted, and even living together in East London in various places, as well as working together on building sites all across London and once in Vienna.

It seems our paths were destined to cross. At that time, you made instant pals with anyone who looked like a punk – it was almost like recognizing yourself in someone else – like a magick mirror. Without a doubt, anyone who was getting into punk in those days was already equipped with a punk radar set. It took just a few seconds to clock one another, to approach, chat, and from that moment on become casual friends; there were so few of us – we were always outnumbered and outgunned, but, somehow, we were all on the exact same wavelength-frequency. At the time, it seemed like the natural flow of events, but now, looking back, it seems uncanny. I know I'm not the only one who took such casual meetings and friendships for granted – it was the flow of life, but getting older, I realize now how unique that time in life was, it's like we were all fire balls being spat from the same volcano that was erupting through every village, town, and city, enveloping the entire country, before it eventually crossed the entire planet – probably excluding North Korea (they think Michael Jackson is still alive). We were all intrinsically connected by a vibe; a vibe of awareness – like

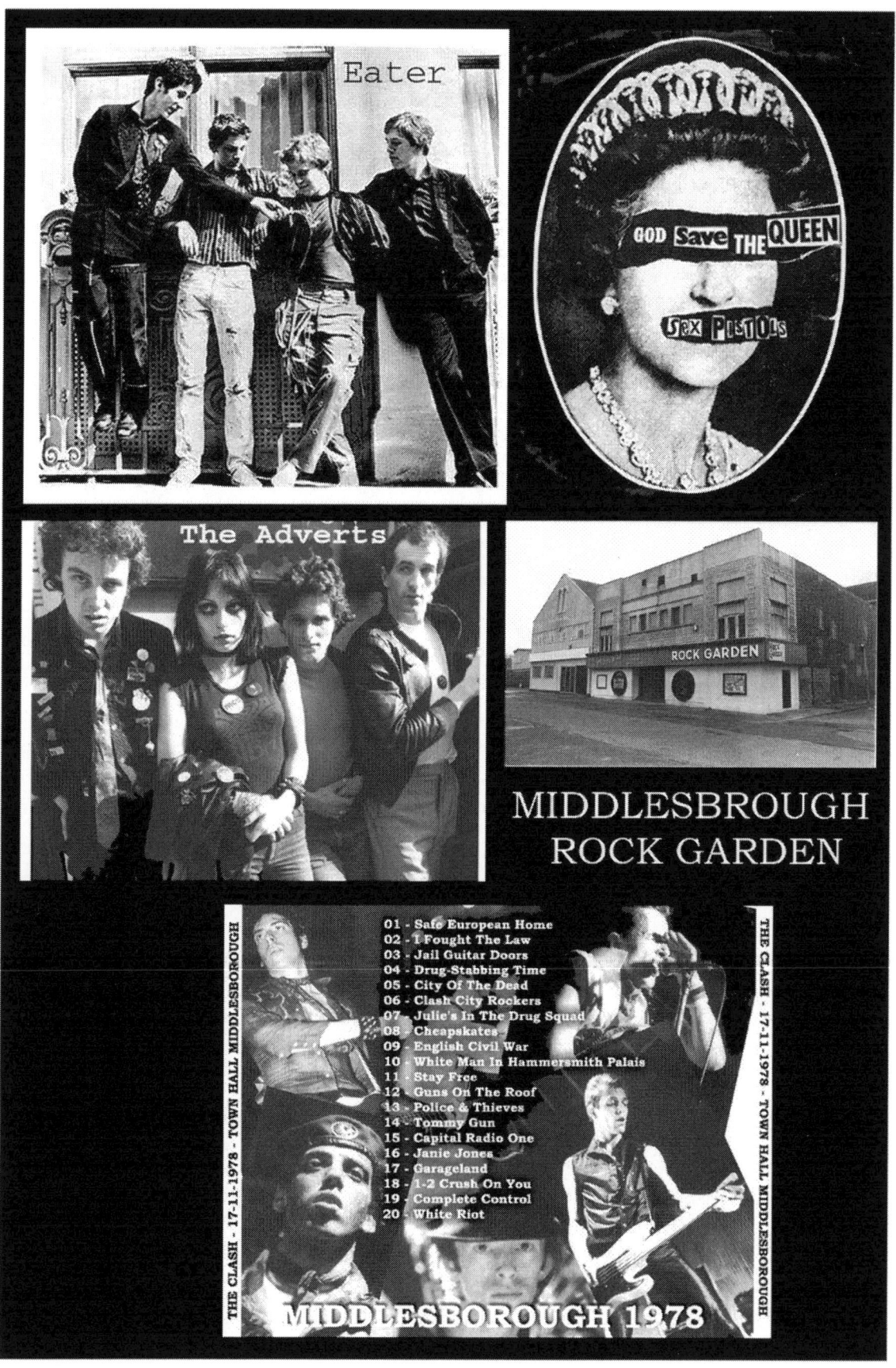

a psychic link of rebellious consciousness – we were all tuned-in - grooving on the same outcast wavelength – the rejects of society were beginning to unite and at the same time we didn't even know it. I guess we were all caught up in the flow of our age and a surge of rage – bright-eyed and looking for something new to relive the terminal boredom.

I don't think anyone understood that at the time. I certainly didn't. I wasn't that aware. I was acting on pure reactions and pure instinct, scarcely aware that I was listening to my soul or to my higher self - we all just reacted to that whole process on some deeper, generational, instinct of connectivity, plus the fact that there was nowhere else to go and no-one else to be. You had to be yourself and front it out, making it up as you went along. It's funny how nothing much has changed in thirty years. If anything, those times are very much like these times, but now the lost generations walk our streets with knives and guns. Go figure.

The funny thing about every punk being a solitary born rebel, which is what actually happened to every single punk – self included – is the fact that at the same time we were also actively seeking out fellow minds that were travelling along that same wavelength – seeking justification or mutual support for our own sense of being. It was like we'd all received the same message – we were attuned – generationally connected to a vibe, or perhaps with energetic forces from outer space, or driven by astrological forces, who knows? We were all ready and willing to challenge the status quo and the corrupt powers-that-be and to forge our own paths in life – daring to break the mould of regimented normality and to burst the bubble and say 'Fuck you! Fuck you all!'

(Now, my generation have had children – self included – and I hope we have given them a voice – their own voice – which is what we felt we had been denied and what we were really fighting for back in the day.)

Now, of course, I realize that we were all caught up in a rebellious tidal wave – an ongoing flow that progressed from the beatniks in the 50's, to the hippies of the sixties, to pub rock, to punk rock and ska, to post-punk and new wave, to New Age – and hopefully the wave of the rebellious child will never stop until the world begins to treat its children with a fresh, open-minded respect. The Aeon of Horus, the child of force and fire, has well and truly arrived, as predicted in 1904 by Aleister Crowley (more on that dude later, perhaps).

The youth vibration first started back in the 1950's, with beatnik writers like William S. Burroughs and Jack Kerouac, with the early days of rock'n'roll, and even before that, with the blues and with the banjo-hillbilly stuff. 'Rebel Without A Cause' with James Dean and Dennis Hopper, was probably the first film ever to acknowledge that teenagers had feelings, that they had problems - they were confused, ignored by their parents and the establishment; they had the right to fight for their right to be heard and to even exist. Pop-media eats itself, and continually evolves, throwing one fresh layer of expression and revolt upon another. It's a vibe. It's a pattern. It's a wave – like when Punk Rock washed over the UK – and sometimes, that wave transforms into a fucking tsunami.

CHAPTER 2

When I was sixteen I went to my first gig at the Middlesbrough Rock Garden. The band was called Eater. I bought their single 'Thinking of the USA' in June 1977 ('Thinking of the USA, dreaming of the CIA'). They were about my age – Andy Blade, the singer, was 16 – the drummer, Dee generate, was 15, they were one of the youngest London punk bands at the time and they feature on the Roxy-Live album, recorded at the 100 Club in Oxford Street. Other bands on that LP, one of my favourites from that time, include Wire, Slaughter and the Dogs, Johnny Moped, X-Ray Spex and The Adverts.

You had to be 21 to get into the Rock Garden, but the bouncers didn't check for proof of age or ID – they just liked getting stuck in at the end of the night, once the skinheads had done their fair share of physical damage.

The Rock Garden was hardly a garden at all. If anything, it was more a concrete garden, with concrete floors and skinheads with concrete skulls, head butting people in the face. Things frequently got very intense, heavy and bloody in that venue – skinheads and punks mixing it up. It was all plastic glasses and the few tables and benches in the place were all firmly bolted into the concrete floor. The Boro skinheads were always nutting people, sensing easy victims because the rest of us came from Thornaby estates, Stockton estates, Norton estates, Billingham estates, and lanky me from the little village in Longnewton. For example - a woman once got raped in the toilets. A guy in a fight outside fell into the road and had his head crushed by the wheels of a bus and that was when the place eventually shut down, but before that incident, it was the best and only place to see touring punk bands who ventured to the North-East from London and Manchester.

Like most Northerner's, then and now, I had an inbuilt dislike and mistrust of London; the heart of Government and power, the source of corruption, where decisions were made that fucked-up our lives and kept us all skint and living on the breadline, sometimes way below it.

I remember the Eater gig, 22nd September, 1978, just a few months after I'd left comprehensive school. As a young and enthusiastic fan I got there really early, sometime in the afternoon, just hanging around, waiting for them to arrive. When Eater pulled up outside the venue in a small hired van, I introduced myself and helped them to move their gear from the van, into the venue, and onto stage. It was my first roadie experience and to be quite honest, I felt like I'd been initiated into a secret society.

Eater were very friendly blokes, funny and devoid of ego, totally up for having a laugh. They got me into the gig for free and bought me several beers – we were about the same age. They actually got me pretty drunk - we all got pretty drunk. I definitely dug the whole idea that the barriers between bands/performers and the people who came to see them were instantly broken down. Eater were the first Londoners I'd ever encountered and we got on just fine. However, when they played, I thought they were awful – the sound levels were so cranked up you could barely tell a drum beat from a bass line from a guitar stroke, never mind hear Andy's vocals - it was like white noise – the sort of music that guys in orange coveralls listen to these days in Guantanamo Bay. I wondered if every gig was going to be like that, but thankfully they weren't.

As it was something of a hassle for me to get to the Rock Garden, not to mention the acute levels of violence that I had to skate around, plus the fact that I didn't know anyone else there, I was selective about the bands that I went to see. I only went to see bands that I really liked – bands like The Adverts (September 1978), The Lurkers (October 1978), who were like a soft-core UK version of the Ramones, with great riffs, but with lyrics that were weaker and not half as odd-ball or disturbed as the Ramones, The Fall (October 1979), Gang of Four (November 1979), plus Crass and Poison Girls (October 1980) – my last visit to the concrete 'Garden'.

*

Around that time, 1978-79, I discovered a pub called The Teessider – it was a rough, deadbeat, ramshackle place just next to Thornaby Bridge that crossed the River Tees. The metal structure of the bridge still has bullet holes in it from cannon shells fired by Nazi aircraft in WWII – so big you can put three fingers into them. The Teessider was based opposite a dole office, and although the place has since been knocked down, it retains a certain legacy. Local bands from Norton, Stockton, Thornaby, Billingham and Middlesbrough played there. It was free to get in – the place was a two room dive – it was chaotic, and at that time, one of the few places where punks and skins could get together and strut their stuff. Drugs were probably a part of that scene, but what I saw around then – it was just cigarettes, glue and beer.

I started going to The Teessider alone, every Friday night after work, drinking lager underage and gradually getting to know other people on the scene. I'm not even sure how I found out about the place, but as soon as I started hanging there, I began to feel a sense of belonging – like these people were part of my tribe – it offered something fresh and relatively wholesome to me after the general misery of school and the loathsome, lonesome, daily grind of the factory fuck-up.

*

The Factory, with its overhead cranes shifting twenty tonnes at a time, and the crane brakes continually failing – the crane would never stop when it should – it would just gradually grind to a halt (on that note alone the place would have been shut down), plus a small, oppressive foreman, like a little Hitler, that I constantly wanted to punch out.

This little fuck with his stupid moustache used to try and pressurize me into working weekend overtime. I always refused. He even went so far as to lean into me, step on my work boot with its external steel-cap, and tell me I was putting my job at risk. I never hit him, nor did I ever work a single hour of overtime. I just clocked-in, did my shift, wrote lyrics and stuff in the toilets, clocked-out, and got the hell out of there.

I never trust or believe anyone who says they have waltzed through life and say they have no regrets. I think that's bollocks and utter, phony bullshit. We're here to learn, and since no-one is perfect, we all make our mistakes and our bad judgments. Sometimes we let our friends down, or we let ourselves down – we tell lies, when maybe we should have told the truth – we tell the truth, when maybe we should have told a lie. Through the errors of our ways, we learn how not to repeat them, at least some of us do, anyway. Isn't that the point of existence?

I have a few regrets and one in particular is not smacking that little Hitler bastard in the mouth, or at least giving him a good crack in the shins with my metal-capped boots. At the time I was scared of losing my job, and what that might entail – but I should have kicked the bastard anyway. So, yes, I have a few regrets and Little Hitler will always be one of them.

I trust people who have fallen from the wayside, I trust people who are strong enough to admit to their imperfections. I trust people who are trying to improve themselves, regardless of what happened to them or where they came from. I trust people from all walks of life, just so long as they are real and not self-deluded or self-promoting. I usually give the latter short thrift – verbally, I usually cut them down with a single, sharp sentence. Oddly enough, the fakers usually know when I've sussed them out and they creep back into the shadows of their own illusions, where they belong. I guess, like most people, I'm like a two-sided coin; I got my generous, polite, truthful and helping hand. The other side of the coin I don't even want to talk about. Of course, a coin actually has three sides, if you include the edge upon which it can stand – maybe that's my Zen side?

In the factory I was frequently getting red-eyed (not stoned on marijuana) but catching a 'flash' from an arc-welder's torch; the light when a welder lit-up was so bright it literally burned a layer of skin from the eyeball if you caught it from the side, at the edge of your vision, and it took days to recover from.

In the tube-shaped, cylindrical sea containers, made of thick aluminium which I used to mark out on huge flat sheets, before cutting them on a machine (that once severed off a guy's hands), then roll into shape on this huge machine and weld it all together. I had to climb inside the container, wearing ear-muffs and hold a heavy hammer up against the weld, while a guy on the outside hit the weld with another heavy hammer, flattening it out. Then the aluminium container was welded to a steel skeletal box-frame. The entire process was hard, hot, and sweaty work. Same shit killing me every fucking day.

Before I started there, one guy had cleaned out the dust of a container using a pipe attached to an oxygen cylinder. He ended up getting torched – a human fireball – that was the end of his apprenticeship and his life. Another guy had his arm severed when a piece of sheet metal slipped loose from an overhead, overloaded skip. No wonder some of the welders were jacking-up with alcohol. I was a year and a half into this apprenticeship and I'd had just about enough of it. Surely there must be a better life? I wanted fun, not this endless, soul-destroying, mind-numbing crap and monotonous, tedious graft, especially on an apprentice's wage. The idea of being actively unemployed began to appeal to me, more and more, with each and every passing week.

I could not imagine or picture myself doing this job for the rest of my life, grafting in a North-East factory where health and safety was nothing more than a vague notion – more theory and empty chat than actual practice.

*

One night at The Teessider I got talking to a guy who sang for a band called Vermin – they did a song called 'Murder in the Manchester Morgue'. Like me, he worked in a steel factory. I can't recall his name and Vermin seem to have disappeared off the north-eastern punk-net map. I showed him some of the poems/lyrics that I'd been writing in the toilets at work. He liked what he read and said I should get up and sing them. That's exactly what I did. I took the microphone – there was no stage, it was just the cigarette burned carpet on the floor of the pub. I asked if anyone fancied playing the bass, the guitar and the drums. Three random guys I didn't know from Adam volunteered. One guy was a skinhead; I knew that he was called Varney but had never spoken to him before. He had a huge V tattooed on his forehead; obviously making him unemployable. Anyhow, he stepped forward and sat behind the drums for the first time in his life. It was complete chaos. It was totally liberating. We did three songs, if you could call them that – 'The British Press ('is a fucking mess/controlled stories that try to depress/ but I won't read 'em/'cos I don't need 'em/and neither do you/do you?')', 'Borstal', and a lovely ditty called 'Church', with it's rousing chorus of 'Fuck the Lord and Jesus Christ'. Even though the songs were musically incoherent and I was shouting and ranting, certainly not 'singing', a few people liked it. It was that kind of scene. Anything was better than another 20 minute piece of self-indulgent crap from the likes of Pink Floyd, ELP or Deep Purple, or another spineless, mindless trivial pop song about being in love. Personally, I wanted songs of anger and revolt. I was stepping out, carefree, and sincerely not giving a fuck. I was on a path, certainly not a cycle-path (they didn't exist back then), maybe a psycho-path?

*

At the factory, a guy a bit older than me, called Mike, sporting a short Mohican haircut, worked in an outer building that was the industrial equivalent of a metal saw-mill. Mike looked like Travis Bickle; the Robert De Niro character in the Martin Scorsese movie, Taxi Driver; a film that would later impact my life when I had an intense, rather psychotic period as a speed-freak.

During that cold winter, his place of work was absolutely freezing – even inside the main factory, snow used to pour down upon us through gaping holes in the corrugated metal roof. Despite the cold, I used to seize every moment possible to hang out with Mike; the guy had a cool attitude.

Mike said he liked playing drums – I only ever did the one 'gig' with him in Darlington and it nearly cost us our lives. We managed to wangle our way into a rock'n'roll social club that put on Teddy Boy bands only; we weren't dressed overtly as punks – in fact I never went for the punk rock uniform of black leather jacket and jeans; I preferred baggy old-mans suits with turn-ups at the ankles, bought from Oxfam, where I bought most of my clothes, or Doc' Martens, straight jeans (which were highly anti-fashion at the time as people were wearing flares), a granddad shirt (a shirt with no collar), and braces – I've never been a designer-gear kinda guy, but I shifted between the punk and skinhead images. That night, we both deliberately dressed down.

The entire crowd in this club were Teddy Boys. However, these 'boys' were all guys in their 50's reliving the old days, a bit like me right now, I guess. They were dressed in their smart, colourful draped jackets, straight pressed trousers and suede 'brothel creeper' shoes, with their hair slicked back into a style that was known as a duck's arse.

We sat drinking beer for a while, watching the retro rock'n'roll bands take their turns. They were rather polished and tight, no doubt working a regular circuit – they were proper musicians. We waited for our moment, and as one band finished their set and walked off stage, we made our move. We jumped onto the stage. Mike started bashing the shit out of some guy's expensive drum kit. I grabbed the microphone and launched into 'Church', repeating 'Fuck the Lord and Jesus Christ' over and over again. I think we managed to play for a full two minutes before the entire crowd were on their feet – don't get me wrong, this was not a crowd in a state of holy illumination or mystical, rock'n'roll rapture – they were in a state of pure outrage and hate, with sheer murder written in their crow-feet eyes.

We jumped off the stage and ran out of the club with about twenty duck's arses chasing after us – we even had to shove a bouncer out of the way to make our escape. This was getting serious – these guys were chasing us through the ill-lit back streets of Darlington, intent on giving us a serious kicking, or worse. We turned a corner and barged our way into a nightclub. Mike was pretty tough and he pushed two bouncers over while I slammed the night-club doors shut behind us and dropped the bolt. It was a lucky escape. The duck's arses gave up their pursuit, although the bouncers were threatening to have us both arrested for assault, which was kinda funny as the guys were huge. They didn't call the police. They didn't beat us up. Actually, they showed us some mercy and they let us wait fifteen minutes before kicking us out onto the street. Thankfully, the coast was clear and we burst out laughing. The 'gig' had been a total success; we'd managed to upset the apple-cart and ruffle a few feathers, and most importantly, lived to tell the tale.

Mike got sacked a few weeks later due to lack of attendance and I never saw him again.

After that, I was still hiding out in the toilets at work and writing lyrics on sheets of bog-roll and I was back down to having only one guy at work I could call a mate; Maz – he was into Northern Soul but that was ok by me, at least he was into something! We often went boozing in old men's pubs in Darlington together and I'd crash at his mum's house on a sofa after a healthy after-work drinking session on a Friday night. We couldn't go to any nightclubs because of the way I dressed – I was always refused entry by the black-suited bouncers and in Stockton and Darlington, you didn't mess with them; they really enjoyed their work.

I only went to one gig in Darlington, to see two Darlo punk bands – it was a bit odd, to be honest. The first band played covers of Clash songs. The second band played covers of Sex Pistols songs. I thought it was a waste – better off doing something of your own, something original, not cover-jobs.

I feel exactly the same way today about vacuous TV shows such as The X-Factor – if artists could play their own self-created pieces of words and music then I might be interested, perhaps true talent, real emotions and the spark of genius would see the light of day. However, X-Factor, despite its commercial TV success, is just a karaoke gig - it missed the spot by a thousand miles, it missed the spot by a fucking light-year - its only tiresome purpose is to drag another generation into a self-serving musical sewer/ghetto with no spark of life, thought or individuality. X-Factor and its creators need a bullet to the head, or at least 10 years in a North Korean camp.

*

Around that time Andy D., who gradually became known as Adolf Fuck, and me, who became known as Jesus Idiot or Mr. Yak, started booking a local youth club so we could make a racket with our guitars. We decided that if we could get an anti-band together it would be called 'The The And'. It's ironic that a decade or so later a band with the name 'The The' became rather successful.

A few weeks after my first random Teessider 'gig', a similar thing took place. Adolf was there; ready to display his non-musical skills. Morgan D. had decided to take a leap and drum for us – he wasn't a punk at all, but I didn't care about appearances, though I wasn't into the prog rock music that he liked. We had Tom on bass guitar – thinking about it, I'm sure Tom played bass on my first impromptu gig at The Teessider. Kie-Eye also joined us that night playing guitar - we had our line-up.

A quote from Kie-Eye - *'I remember seeing you about and especially in The Teessider. I remember one night particularly when I'd gone along, probably with 50p in my pocket to watch some band or other. You were sat with Mandy. That was the first time that I was aware that you and her were going out together. The both of you had been having some conversation about a band that you wanted to form and I think it was Mandy that had mentioned that I played guitar. It all stemmed from there really, you asked me to play and I had no hesitation in agreeing. I was overawed with you, your belief systems and the stuff you wrote about in your songs. There was a conflict going around in my head and I was trying to work out how someone like you could be so outwardly angry. My upbringing had stifled me.'*

This time I was fully prepared; I was armed with a can of Heinz Baked Beans, which I opened during a 'song' before pouring them all over my head. I have no idea what kind of statement I was trying make, it just seemed like a good idea at the time, as they say.

A quote I found on the net from an old friend, Bungy, who attended most of our gigs – *'Lee Gibson was definitely the main man from The The And. Remember seeing them at The Teessider when the said Mr Gibson opened and then poured a can of baked beans over his own head! Needless to say they were then invited to leave the premises.'*

I loved The Teessider and its mad bands such as Bombay Drug Squad, Vermin, Tick-Tick, The Filth, Discharge (a skin-head band who were a right bunch of hard, mad bastardo's), No-Way, The Extreme, The Sines (a three-piece band who were a bit mod and a bit like The Who/The Jam), The Vultures (they had a single out that I really liked, but one day I was walking alone into Stockton and three guys came up behind me and kept trying to trip me up. Two of those guys were in The Vultures. The tallest of them eventually leapt on my back, but I did a quick swivel-turn and threw him into the road, in front of the oncoming traffic – he didn't get ran over, but I wouldn't have minded if he did. After that, they left me alone. I still liked their music, but as people, I thought they were utter wankers), also Those Responsible, Billy Oblivion, and The Amazing Space Frogs, to name but a few.

A quote from Kie-Eye – *'Do you remember us turning up one night at the Teessider believing we had a gig, but apparently no-one else knew about it? We used the room anyway to run through the set and we kept getting interrupted by the women coming from the other bar to use the toilet. I remember one of them saying 'I can play better tunes on the hairs on me fanny'. We then spontaneously played House of the Rising Sun to appease her but you were having none of it and you told us to shut the fuck up and play British Press, or whatever.'*

A similar recollection from Morgan - *'There was one time we were playing at the Teessider, I think somehow it was a rehearsal, rather than a gig. So part way through two "Wifey" types came through, one was very drunk, on their way to the toilet, when they returned, the drunk one started talking with us/you, asking what kind of music we played, needless to say you tried to explain, then she said "You're fuckin' shite - I could play better music on me fanny hairs!" I always remember that line - so Lee are you gonna stick that in yer book, hahahaha.'*

*

Around that time I became known as Mr. Yak. The name came about more by accident than design. I had a huge pet toad that I used to carry around in the baggy pockets of my baggy, 1950's style, Oxfam suit – I found him in a pond at the MOD site we used to play in, along with huge Salamanders that were going extinct in the UK at the time. I made a large badge with the name 'Mr. Yak' written on it. I think people assumed that it was my name, but it wasn't. Whenever we sat in a cafeteria drinking tea, I would get Mr. Yak out of my jacket and let him hop and bop free around the table – it was usually worth a giggle and I'm sure Mr Yak was always glad to get out of my Oxfam pocket in order to roam free.

Adolf Fuck was moving more and more toward the Nazi-skinhead gangs that we knew in Stockton – they were in the National Front and he eventually left the 'band', but we remained friends. I got on OK with the Stockton skinheads, although their racism confused me more than anything as they all loved reggae music, essentially performed by black artists from Jamaica. I never really cared much for reggae unless it was played by The Clash, but I didn't mind a bit of two-tone-ska – I thought ska did a whole lot to brings skins, punks and black people together in those times when the right wing were just itching to exploit the poverty of our lives for their own ends. If ever they got into power, we were the first people they would shove into their ovens if they ever got a chance to build them upon English soil; this green and pleasant land.

At that time there were few black people around where I lived, and just a few Asian families who lived in one street, for security and harmony, I guess. In my school, with 1,200 pupils, there was only one black guy and two Asian guys in my year – one of the Asian guys, Timothy, was a friend of mine. After school we used to go to a nearby industrial estate and raid the skips of a Commodore factory. They made the latest high tech gadgets; pocket calculators the size of your outstretched palm – clunky shit compared to the micro-alien technology that is currently taking over our lives. Tim would grab various discarded and rejected pieces of software and hardware and then assemble them into working products. He was genius with putting that electro-shit together. I simply acted as the lookout because he knew which components he was looking for and I didn't have a clue. We always had to be quick, before security guards chased us off. Sometimes they had dogs. Timothy would build build the calculators and we'd sell them at school. Quite simply, racism never made a damn bit of sense to me – didn't then, doesn't now - the colour of someone's skin was never my

enemy – it was always the bastards in control, or the bully boys who thought they were in control – the truth is, any sense they have of control is a fucking illusion – like someone once said, 'Anyone can kill anyone'.

I guess Ghandi and John Lennon and Malcolm X know that to be true and I suspect that's what JFK heard on his last phone call from the FBI/MAFIA/CIA before they blew his brains out and scattered them onto Jackie's lap, way back in the sunny 60's Dallas motorcade, back when acid/LSD was still cool on the streets and when the black-budget government had just started to play with it, back in the year I was born – The year Marilyn Monroe died.

At one time, Adolf warned me that he'd heard the Thornaby skinheads were planning to beat me up, but the Stockton skinheads, despite their NF influences, and perhaps because of their reggae influences (or maybe the mutual respect I paid them daily on the streets), said that they were covering my back and they told the Thornaby skins to leave me alone, and thankfully, the Thornaby nutters did as asked – they could have easily turned me into dog-meat and laughed while they did it.

I didn't hang out with the Stockton skinheads, I just happened to be hanging around Stockton town centre all day long just the same as them - we just used to nod 'hello' in acknowledgement, obviously our mutual low-life existence paid off. We were all low-life scum that no-one gave a fuck about.

Back then I never really judged them as a group and on the Stockton streets I saw and dealt with them as the individuals that they were – I always thought gang members were looking for an identity, just like me and all the kids I knew from the ramshackle estates, looking for somewhere to belong; needing to belong somewhere because they'd been rejected or neglected, kicked-out, kicked-around and abused all their fucking lives. I understood their anger, the rage….man….it was like 'Gimme a gun…put Thatcher in my sights…put that cunt who played it like a man in my range, the bitch who sucked Reagan's dick, I'll blow her away! She is anti-woman! Can't you see that? Her dildo is a nuclear silo. Plain and simple.'

Obviously I could never condone such violent attitudes, but I was pissed off when the fucking IRA couldn't even do a decent Brighton bomb blast. I guess the IRA, like most terrorist organisations, are better off when they are dealing in drugs (and knee-capping anyone who steps on their drug-dealing turf – like all freedom fighters they have their 'interests' and they have their 'concerns'), guns and whores and looking after their own business, just like gangsters anywhere all around the fucked-up world, they don't give a fuck about creating a change that would ever benefit the regular Joe or his wife or their children. The truth is; these people are exactly like the politicians they oppose or serve, they ain't no good. Just like the CIA. Just like Al Qaeda Airlines. You buys your ticket and you takes your chances. Sometimes you need to stay grounded, baby, otherwise the airplane of freedom you think you're riding is taking you straight into a steel and concrete structure. A fireball and burning, falling bodies ain't the way to move forward on the path of human evolution or to magnify our stellar born selves.

Anyway, these days, you can't judge a skinhead by his hairstyle– quite often, the guys with cropped hair, Doc' Marten boots and green bomber jackets are gay. No doubt half of them were gay back in those days as well. Who cares? I have always dealt with people one to one; I hate group discussions , I don't do re-hab or A.A. – like I said before, the more people you put together, the more stupider and dumb-ass they become. You can count on that.

*

By this time I was spending my free weekend time just loitering around Stockton High Street, along with other kids who would sooner be roaming about than spending time at home. I was sort of rehearsing with The The And; Me writing the lyrics and howling, Morgan on drums; glasses, curly hair, tweed jacket and still learning to play, he had an erratic, kinda mad style, plus Kee-Eye on guitar and Tom on bass. Tom came from a tough estate in Norton – he was partial to sniffing glue from a plastic bag but was keen to play bass – I think he robbed somewhere to get the money to pay for his instrument – his older brother was always in and out of jail and accepted it as a lifestyle – they were both sweet guys, just victims of the system. This was our line-up for the rest of our gigs. We were an eclectic bunch of people – each one of us from a completely different background.

Quote from Morgan, (who I've recently been in touch with via Facebook, or Facefuck, as I prefer to call it) – *'Ok, now here's a thing - you were instrumental in turning my musical direction around. I was a very dyed in the wool Rock/prog rock merchant - One time you came to the house and lent me a bunch of albums, the 2 albums that stood out for me were Wire – '154' and 'Entertainment' – Gang of Four - 154 is Still one of my top 3 albums of all time and I still love GoF.'*

We rehearsed in Morgan's parent's attic once a week on a Sunday afternoon, although Tom was sometime so out of it on glue that he never turned up. We gigged at several youth clubs on tough estates that no band had ever played before.

Quote from Kie-Eye – *'We played at a community centre in Eastbourne - that was rough.'*

Yes it was, scary, but somehow worth the while.

Although our songs were ragged and raw, some of the young kids really liked it and turned up at subsequent events – we had a following of maybe twenty people the next time we played The Teessider with Tick-Tick; a band who were smart, intellectual and rather delicate compared to the likes of The Filth and Discharge – whose vocalist, Scrubber, would sometimes slam his head into a wall and knock himself clean out. We certainly had more energy and attitude than talent and made no apologies for that and I think some people dug the audacity of it – it was the nature of the times.

*

After nearly two years in the factory I handed in my notice – I could do that shit no more. As a result I had a blazing row with my father. I wasn't exactly kicked out – I just didn't stay at home very often after that.

I ended up sleeping over at Mandy's house. Mandy H. was my first lover. She was a college student and her folks let me sleep on a sofa in their living room. When Mandy went to college, and later to work as a dental technician, I would leave the house and spend all day walking the streets until she finished work. Finally, I was on the dole and free to loiter, to think, and to write. Finally, I'd achieved that strange, off-beat, punk dream – I was a drop-out – a social reject – a social failure – 'No Future' had arrived – no future and no coin in pocket.

Mandy's elderly father was very deaf, essentially due to his time spent in tanks, fighting against Rommel in WWII. He used to sit real close to the TV so that he could hear it. Mandy's mum used to sit in the kitchen at the other end of their large house, doing crossword puzzles – she was in Mensa. Mandy used to wear a long skirt, and no panties, and simply straddle me on the sofa at the back of the living room where we would have sex while her old man watched TV in an armchair just a few feet in front of us. Sometimes her mum would come into the living room to ask if we wanted a cup of tea – fortunately the door had frosted glass so we could see her approaching and stop our thrusting. I used to hang the used condoms on her next door neighbours rose bushes – once again, I don't really know why. I was a stupid kid, I guess. Maybe I was a bit of a twat?

Two weeks after quitting my apprenticeship I received a phone call from my father. He informed me that my work pal, Maz, was dead. He'd been crushed to death in the factory, doing what would have been my job. My pal was gone, and with it, what little faith I held in the 'system' totally evaporated with the bright light of his soul. I might have been angry at the world before, but when Eric was crushed to death I pretty much declared war on the world of oppression 'till the day I die.

I was devastated, let down, sad and gutted, and angry with the entire world. I never attended his funeral, although I did communicate with him a few years later via the Ouija-board during a family séance – I'll explain that one a bit later, maybe. His death somehow empowered me with a determination not to compromise my values and gave me strength to follow my own path. His death still haunts me now – it could so easily have been me – should it have been me? Perhaps in a parallel universe I'm dead and he's alive? Maybe Maz is a messed up writer and I'm six feet under? Either way, he knows that I miss him.

*

Shortly after leaving my job I began to have trouble with my feet. My toes were curling up and were growing increasingly painful; a result of wearing steel-capped working boots; a thing called hammered toes. I ended up in hospital where surgeons put me under and literally hammered three toes on each foot, completely shattering the bones. A metal rod was pushed up the middle of each toe to keep the healing bones in place. The first time after the operation, when I put my feet on the hospital floor, I screamed in agony – the worst physical pain I've ever endured. As a result of the operation I spent three months in a wheelchair; a punk on wheels – a 'raspberry ripple' as my Cockney pals might say.

To be honest, those three months were something of a blur. I was only 17 but me and my fellow punk-skin street urchins would get drunk and I would literally be legless – it didn't matter how pissed I got; I was in a wheelchair and didn't have to walk anyway. Sometimes, in the shopping centre, we used to sniff liquid Zoff (an Elastoplast remover bought from Boots) from our jacket sleeves – it made your head go fuzzy and light and made your feet feel like blocks of ice. We also bought tablets designed to thicken the blood. If you took a handful, everything went into slow motion as your blood slowly crawled through your veins – it was like moving through syrup in a dream - obviously, take too many and everything would stop, for all time. For most of us there was no risk. After all, what did we have to lose? I think that same short-term mentality flows through all the gang-bangers who currently prowl our streets day and night – they're like vampires on a short lease.

My pal Granty would ram my wheelchair into the backs of people's ankles. They would turn around, with an angry yelp of pain, but when they saw me sitting in the wheelchair they would instantly apologize. We did that a lot. We also used to buy pigs' eyes, with the accompanying eye-socket flesh still attached, from a butchers shop, and stick them on the palms of our hands, then hold them up in front of people just to freak them out. Sometimes, when we were pissed, Granty would push me in my wheelchair between the traffic in Stockton High Street, running full pelt between the moving cars. I liked Granty a lot – he was a sweet natured kid who came from an unbelievable, shockingly bad home – I'd like to say that he didn't give a flying fuck, but I know that he did.

Granty grew up in a tough house; I went there often just to hang out with him and to write graffiti on his bedroom walls. His parents didn't give a shit; they were total alcoholics and heavy betting-shop-junkies. His home life was truly shocking to me and totally diabolical. They had a pet Alsatian dog that his father chained-up in a garden shed where he starved the poor beast to death. The carpets in the living room resembled soil. There was a blue milk crate with a pint of milk in it and half a loaf of bread – that was the only food in the house – and a TV set that also stood on a crate. Granty's younger brother and sister, four and six years old, walked around half naked and caked in dirt – today, we would call this child neglect or child abuse – back then, it seemed that no-one gave a good-god-damn. Back then, on those estates, neglect was the norm.

A quote from Kie-Eye - *'Wasn't Granty the one that lived in Swainby road, whose dad used to walk up and down with a handcart collecting scrap?'*

Granty got sent down for shoplifting. Six months later, when he got out, he wasn't the same guy I used to know. He got glued-up one night and took a razor and slashed himself all over the chest and stomach – he needed over 80 stitches. For some reason, local media caught hold of his self-abusive story. He liked the limelight and two days later, he took a razor and re-opened all his fat, worm-like, stitched-up wounds that spread all across his chest and belly. Needless to say, Granty is dead – another spark snuffed-out by a society that simply doesn't give a fuck about its children or its youth, even now, things have not really changed for the better. Now, kids smoke crack and they carry knives and guns. They need to get into books and get into their own heads in a positive, self-affirming way. I truly believe that reading books can save minds and souls – they saved mine.

Sometimes my fellow urchins would steal my wheelchair and go play with it on the ramps of a multi-storey car park and I would have to sit and wait for them to return it; they always did. They were good urchins. They were the lost, the forgotten and the abandoned; they were the flowers in your dustbin and they were my friends of many different strokes.

Whilst sitting on the bench, usually with a few other street kids (I was never left alone during my period of disability), I would watch as a skinhead guy called Durnan forced a young girl to jerk him off by the lifts, to one side of a staircase that led to the multi-storey car park situated above the shopping centre, even as regular shoppers – regular people - were passing by. He wasn't the smartest specimen of the human species; in pubs, guys would fill a pint glass with their collective piss or phlegm – he would drink it down, then everyone would buy him a beer.

The multi-storey car park was all concrete and late at night we were free to roam (this was before the era of CCTV), riding down the slopes on stolen shopping carts. It was the place to sniff glue. I never went down that particular avenue but nearly everyone I knew at that time was on it. I once talked Craig R. down from the edge of top level – he wanted to jump, or fly, I wasn't sure which, but I stopped him falling into his glue-addled dream. The way I see things, if you're out of your mind and think that you can fly like a bird, or like Superman, then try taking off from the ground first, that way, if you don't take off, at least they won't be scraping your remains off the pavement. I watched as another guy, cannot recall his name, a rockabilly guy who thought all his teeth were falling out – he was glued-up to the eyeballs and thought he was catching his falling teeth in the open palms of his hands. All he was catching was streams of his own frenzied dribble. It was a disgusting, pitiful sight to behold – he was so gone. Then again, like the rest of us, he had nowhere else to go – that was our common bond. Some of the glue-heads I knew began to suffer from severe hallucinations and experienced what they thought were cross dimensional visions, sending out beams of light from their minds to destroy some kind of alien entities that were intent on taking over our little corner of the universe; I always assumed that they were witnessing the gradual dissolution and terminal destruction of their own brain cells – like an apocalypse viewed from within.

*

After the death of Maz I started writing more and went on to create my first fanzine, writing under the pseudonym of Jesus Idiot. It was called 'A Movement with No Name'. All typed out on a hefty manual typewriter – computers and the digital age were still a long way off. Mandy's older sister, Vanessa, worked in an office for the Shell Oil Company, where she stealthily printed and stapled 50 copies together for me. Looking back, the title sounds like some kind of bowel problem. Maybe it was? In a way, I was trying to get rid of, and to express, all the confused anger and shit going round in my head. I sold all 50 'zines on the streets and at a few local gigs, then started work on issue number two. This time, Vanessa printed out a 100 copies. I sold them just as fast. They were cheap; twenty pence per copy. From the get go they were never about making money – it was all about the mangled Word. Individuals I'd never met began to correspond with me, I also began communicating with other fanzine writers from all around the country – a network was developing – like a matrix that crossed an entire generation – a long time before the dawn of the internet and electronic social networking sites such as Facebook – this was grass roots and unprecedented since the 60's hippy era.

*

One night, after The The And had played at The Teessider pub, Mandy, Morgan and myself were standing together in a shop doorway waiting for a bus. Two nightclub-type guys in designer disco-fuck-up clothes approached us. One guy spat in my face and then his pal punched me in the face. Right then, a cop car pulled-up into the bus stand. The cop got out of his vehicle and simply leaned against the roof of his car, arms folded, idly watching, with no intention of intervening. I took another punch in the face. Still, the cop did nothing. Encouraged, the guy who'd spat in my face tried to kick me in the stomach – I grabbed him by the heel and flipped him to the ground, appreciating the astonished look on his face; I totally suckered him, but I didn't step in and follow it up – the cop was still standing there, watching me. Then the cop lifted his face and walked straight up to me. He waved the two night-club fuckers away, and then he threatened to arrest me for disturbing the peace!

A quote from Morgan: *'I also remember that time we were talking one night at the corner of John Walker Square and some twonk had a go at you, he swung a kick at you and you grabbed his foot - you totally immobilized him - very deftly done.'*

That was my wake up call to the Stockton Police Force – it was the start of a whole different story of harassment and corruption that I had to endure. I guess in London at that time, the cops were prejudiced against black and Asian people – up North, they hated punks – everyone hated punks. You had to be careful. I had to be careful, not only of straights and squares and cops, but skinheads from out of town.

I was in WH Smiths once, wearing straight jeans and a baggy pink/purple mohair jumper, scanning books. Out of nowhere, without warning, someone smacked me in the face and sent me crashing to the floor. By the time I got to my feet, there was no-one around willing to take responsibility or follow the matter up. A crowded store, yet no witnesses - that's just how it was.

Sometimes, even walking through Stockton High Street, one of the widest High Streets in Europe, day or night, cars would suddenly bounce up over the kerb and try to run me down, just because of the clothes I wore. This happened, not only to me, but to other punks as well, on a regular basis. It's like my generation, who had chosen to step out and be different, who chose to question and threaten the status quo, were walking around with a target on our backs – uneasy times, for sure. (It's rather funny that at the time of writing Manchester Police have just announced that perpetrators of 'hate crimes' against Goths and punks and other 'alternative culture' people will suffer heavier penalties – somehow it all seems thirty years too late. All violent attacks are acts of hate and inner-rage.)

We were often the target of gangs and dim-witted, mob-minded, discotheque motherfunkers who were drunk and storming through the streets like members of the Waffen SS. They wanted to kill us for daring to step outside the box; for daring to be different; for daring to be ourselves, or at least for trying to find out who we were and where we belonged in the grim world of state control, despite the fact we never knew who we were; strangers to ourselves.

*

Shortly afterwards, I was standing by the window of the HMV store with two other punk friends. We were just loitering and chatting and not causing anyone any problems – we never did. Suddenly, a police van pulled up, several cops rolled out and we were all shoved against the store front window, cuffed, arrested and forced to spend all night in the cells – there's nothing quite as tedious as a night in the cells.

We were charged with causing an obstruction and refusing entry to people who wanted to get into the store. This was a blatant police distortion of the truth, to put it nicely, and although HMV never pressed any charges against us, the police did.

When we appeared at Middlesbrough Magistrates Court, several weeks later, we all went dressed in our usual punk attire. Legal-aid refused to represent us. In court I accused the police of lying on the stand (big mistake – like a Judge or Magistrate would ever entertain such a wild idea). I said that we were being targeted and victimised just because of our appearance. Needless to say, despite our innocence, and because of our outward image, we were found guilty and fined accordingly. Case closed. One more stain on my State File.

*

I'd been arrested a few times previously for the usual juvenile, bored teenager stuff that happens everywhere all the time, be it in a village, a town or a city.

When I was 14 I was arrested for damaging a millionaire's bungalow as it neared completion. Me and a few pals were playing hide and seek in the empty building, but accidents happened, like people falling through ceilings, or falling from the top shelves of a walk-in wardrobe, or me setting a door on fire while my younger brother, Wayne, counted to a hundred in a bathroom while we are ran off to hide. It turned out that we'd caused over £10,000 worth of damage.

We got the late night knock at the door and the police carted me and my brother away. Due to our age, and the fact it was our first offence, we both received a caution. When we were eventually released from Stockton Police Station, my dad put me and my brother in his car and started to drive. It was the middle of the night and Dad was frighteningly furious, he was shaking with an inner-rage and he didn't speak a word for the entire journey. He eventually drove into an industrial estate where all the offices and factories were closed and all the lights were off; we were in a dark zone for sure. He pulled the car over and told us what he was feeling; he said he wanted to murder us both and dump our bodies by the side of the road. We sat in silence for a long time, and then Dad started the engine and drove us home.

The next day, Dad woke me and Wayne up and told us to gather up all our toys, gadgets and action figures and take them into the garage that we'd help him build at the side of the house. He closed the garage door behind us and then gave us both a hammer. He then ordered us to smash all our toys to pieces. At first we were reluctant to do so, but then we got into it and started to enjoy destroying all our possessions, ripping the limbs from Action Men, tearing them apart and breaking everything that my father and mother had worked so hard for. I think Wayne and I ended up snickering, totally missing the point that he was trying to get across to us about destroying other people's property. Years later, mom told me; 'That day in the garage, you broke our father's heart.'

See what I mean about having regrets? Who can experience this life and not have any? Maybe in that alternative universe I got murdered in that desolate industrial estate? Maybe I deserved it? Anyway, I'm not going to spend much time here going into that Philip K Dick – Alice in Wonderland rabbit hole perception; I just thought it was worth a mention, is all.

Obviously I'm something of a slow learner. A few months later I was arrested for writing 'Fuck Off' on a store window in Stockton High Street during a lazy Sunday afternoon. I was caught bang to rights; I had blue magic-marker all over my hands – I'd make a crap criminal; inept mastermind. My accomplice at the time, who also wrote similar mindless stuff, was Andy D. aka Adolf Fuck. When my parents came to collect me from the police station I called a police officer a 'pig' and my mother promptly slapped me around the mouth; 'Don't call them that!'

The strangest thing about that incident is that our cell door was left open during the entire time we were detained. I wonder how things might have turned out if we'd decided to do a runner. Obviously, if it was in the USA we'd have got a bullet in the back – I'm not quite sure how that scene worked in North East Ghetto England. Was that cell door left open by accident by some dopey cop, or was it left open by design by some smarter cop with a hidden agenda? The question remains and hangs in the air like stale cigarette smoke.

Later, in Teesside Magistrates Court, when a barrister, or whatever his official title might have been, asked me, in a very posh voice without any trace of a Northern accent, if I, Lee G. wrote 'Fuck Off' on the store window, Adolf and I couldn't help but snicker and snigger – the words just didn't sound right coming from this posh guys mouth. We laughed. I admitted my crime. Our parents in attendance were disgusted. We were found guilty of criminal damage and fined accordingly - £30 as I recall - Paid back £1 a month because I was on the dole.

*

Without doubt the heaviest case I ever faced in court involved a fractured skull, a broken face and at least three broken ribs and none of them were mine. There were almost a dozen witnesses against me. In my defence I had two friends. I was facing two years in prison. The stakes were high and I was frightened for my life. I'd been frightened for my life for the previous six months...so full of fear I never thought it would go away...I couldn't see beyond it. Fear was a wall I couldn't climb over. I have suffered sporadic nightmares from the day it took place until now; I think I will carry that nightmare with me until the day I die – despite my innocence and the fact that I was a victim, I think the events that took place back then have stained my soul ever. If I was in a jovial mood, I would call this my sack of woe.

The saga began when a friend (Raz) and I went to a youth club in a nearby town. As we were leaving a gang was waiting for us and we ended up running a gauntlet of fists and boots. It just so happened that my father happened to be driving past. He pulled up and we jumped into the back of the car. A face pressed itself against the car window, a face I didn't know, and said: 'Gibson, you're a dead man.' I think I was targeted for being a punk.

Later, word went out that this gang seriously wanted to fuck me up. In Stockton High Street they tried to run me over in a car, and for a few weekends in a row a gang of ten bikers or so would rove up and down the village looking for me; I was hiding in the village cemetery with my mates. I had to be constantly on the alert, watching my back. A few of the gang members were my age, but most of them were a year or two older. They had something of a reputation – one particular trick they were fond of was picking on some random person and throwing them through the plate glass window of a storefront. They were mostly ignorant, nasty bastards who had probably never read a book between them.

One night in the village I was helping to run a disco event at our local youth club. The gang turned up looking for me, four car loads of them, and soon made their intent as clear as day. One of them, who had just been released from prison for stabbing a police officer, walked up to me and brandished a Bowie knife in my face.

I remember dancing that night, despite my fear, to Hong Kong Garden by Siouxsie and the Banshees – 'harmful elements in the air/cymbals crashing everywhere'.

That night I had a few friends who were willing to back me up, including one of the guys who used to beat me up at school a few times a week (he came armed with a flick-knife), but we were seriously outnumbered. Outside the youth club I was surrounded. A fight was going to happen. There was no way out. So I singled out the leader, the guy who seemed to hate me with a vengeance, the guy who'd told me I was a dead man. He agreed to fight me one to one at the bottom of a street. As we set off walking, his gang were slowly following. I knew that he intended to grab me so that they could all have their jollies. I was frightened beyond words. I saw a hefty stick laid by the side of the road and I picked it up. I chased him down the street, with his mates not too far behind me and a few of my mates and my brother behind them. The guy rounded a corner then turned on me. I hit him. He screamed and grabbed me around the waist, his blood soaking my clothes. I hit him again and he sank to his knees. I hit him again and the stick broke in two. He collapsed to the ground and I kicked his ribs in.

As the gang rounded the corner I climbed over a high wire chain-link fence and vanished into the woods. I watched, helpless, as a very tall guy grabbed my younger brother, Wayne, pushed him against the fence and smashed him several times in the face.

There was nothing I could do. I ran through the woods and circled through the surrounding fields of the village and made it home. I stepped over the threshold and vomited.

It wasn't long before two police detectives turned up at the house. I admitted hitting the guy, who I will only identify as 'W'. I was taken to Stockton police station, questioned and charged with malicious wounding. 'W' had a fractured skull, a broken nose, two black eyes and several broken ribs.

The court case was a long one. I attended Teesside Magistrates Court 6 times over a period of 6 months; a very stressful time for our whole family. I was facing 2 years in prison. In court, I saw the police photographs of 'W''s injuries for the first time. He looked a mess, but I could not muster any sympathy for him. He was the one that created the entire situation. I was just responding to his threats and trying to survive.

The longer the case went on, the more the truth gradually began to emerge. 'W' had over a dozen witnesses (his gang). I had two pals. Various members of the gang, under questioning on the stand, revealed that they had previously attacked me and Maz, that they had been hunting me down for months, and they also revealed their intent and purpose that night; they were going to 'Get Gibson'. Four car loads of guys had travelled a few miles to beat me up. Thinking about that fact, how much damage might they have inflicted upon me if they'd gotten a-hold of me? I have no doubt that they had cold-blooded murder as entertainment on their minds.

During the court case I was still being threatened. One afternoon I was standing at a bus stop in our village of Longnewton. A blue car swerved around the corner and screeched to a halt beside me. I recognized two gang members and I legged it. They got out of the car; both armed with iron bars, and they ran after me. They chased me for almost 2 miles.

I ran like I was running through a bad dream, where the air feels thick like syrup, like running in slow-motion. I ran through the youth club grounds, through a famer's yard, across fields and into the church cemetery. I crawled through an underground drainage pipe half-filled with rancid water, then across more fields, across a schoolyard and through the streets until I eventually managed to reach a girl friend's house and avoided them; otherwise

I'd be dead. Someone had seen the pair set-off after me and called the police. They were both arrested.

Anyway, after the sixth hearing at court I got a 2 years suspended sentence, and so did 'W'. His gang's notoriety was their undoing. I only ever saw the guy twice after that. One time was in his neighbourhood. I was at a wedding with my family. I was pissed outside some pub. I didn't clock him and he didn't clock me, but my dad saw him and didn't say anything to me until later.

The second time I was working night shift as a hospital porter in A & E at North Tees hospital when I saw 'W' sitting with the big guy who'd beaten up my brother – the big guy's face was badly lacerated and his blood was pooling on the tiled floor – he'd tried to throw someone else through a shop window, but the tables had been reversed on him. 'W' recognized me. He drew a finger across his throat. I didn't bother letting any hospital staff know that there was an emergency in A & E. I simply locked myself in the staff room and continued reading a Stephen King novel - so fuck if the guy bled to death? Maybe it was time he did? I got a serious bollocking at work for that, but no regrets on that one.

The guy who was still giving me death threats was killed a few years later in a hit and run incident, but that knowledge did nothing to appease my personal nightmares that continued, off and on, for more than a decade. The levels of fear that guy put me through are simply beyond forgiveness – fuck his corpse!

*

I only worked at the hospital for nine months. It was a job that I enjoyed and it was entirely different to The Factory; I actually felt like I was doing something useful. I used to cycle to work for my rotational shifts and for a few weeks I had to cycle past this small Gypsy camp. Every time I passed, these two huge dogs, Afghan Hounds, would chase after me, trying to bite my ankles. After the first time it happened I always cycled with a couple of hefty rocks in my pockets to ward them off.

It was in that hospital that I saw my first dead bodies. I had to lift the body of a dead patient from the hospital bed they'd died in and place them on a trolley. The trolley was fitted with a hinged, box-like, coffin-like lid that we raised over the corpse. We then put a sheet and a pillow on top of it and wheeled the body away. If anyone saw me pushing the trolley they would naturally assume that I was going to collect a living patient, not ferrying a dead one down the corridors to the morgue. Being in a morgue was a little creepy, but the mortician was even creepier. He used to keep his bottled milk and his sandwiches in the freezers that were used to store the dead.

We had one porter who, when moving a body, would place one of those 'laughing-bags' on the trolley. He had a seriously warped sense of humour – moving a laughing corpse! He got caught out and fired on the spot. I saw so many peculiar things there that I was sorely tempted to write an expose for the local newspaper, but I bottled-out. Two instances will suffice.

Two porters wheeled a patient who had died of a heart attack to the morgue. As they went to lift him onto the 'slab' they dropped him and his skull smashed like a melon on the hard tiled floor. How the hospital authorities explained that to the deceased's relatives I have no idea.

One day I arrived at work for the 2pm to 10pm shift. As I walked down a corridor a disgusting smell hit me like a wall. It was the distinctive and repulsive smell of a rotting human corpse. A few days previously, two porters were moving a body, but as their shift was coming to an end, they simply shoved the trolley, along with the body, into a storage cupboard, where it proceeded to decay in the warm temperature of the room.

After a period of nine months I was made redundant from the hospital, essentially due to government spending cuts. I was back on the dole.

*

Mandy's mother was the Chief Traffic Warden in Stockton – I always got on well with her even though she knew I was anti-establishment and she was Tory thru'n'thru, (she let me crash on the sofa and probably knew that I was having sex with her daughter), and she warned me that undercover police officers were buying copies of my fanzines and were leaving them lying around the station for other officers to read. She informed me that some officers liked some of the things I was talking about, (domestic violence, street violence, unemployment, arms dealers, animal testing for beauty products, punk music, anti-politics, anti-war and to be honest, pretty much anti anything you could name at the time), but she also warned me that many of them wanted to see me put behind bars – innocent or guilty wasn't their concern.

I was beginning to learn about Freedom of Speech and at the same time, in my naive state of youthful optimistic trust, I thought I could write whatever I wanted – but God knows, I was making so many typing errors that it seems shocking to me, even now, that they would pay the likes of me any attention at all.

Certain phrases flashed through my mind, especially The Party's slogans in George Orwell's novel, '1984' (written in 1948); 'War is Peace', 'Ignorance is Strength', 'Freedom is Slavery', plus the highly cynical and ultra-nasty Fascist slogan that arched over the gates of Auschwitz in cold metal script; 'Work will set you Free'.

As The Clash sang, many years later on the song 'Know Your Rights', from their album 'Combat Rock' – *'You have the right to free speech, as long as you are not dumb enough to actually try it.'*

CHAPTER 3

I only saw The Clash play live once, in November, 1978, at Middlesbrough Town Hall on their 'Sort it Out' tour. It was £2.50 a ticket and they were brilliant, total high energy. The gig was packed. I recall one of the huge wooden town hall doors being ripped off as people left the gig. That was possibly one of the best gigs I ever attended. They had a huge backdrop composed of flags of the world. They played twenty songs, ending with 'White Riot'. There's a bootleg recording of that gig out there, with Middlesbrough spelt incorrectly as 'Middlesborough', and I would really like to hear it.

Paul Simonon, bass player with The Clash, mentioned Teesside in a recent interview in The Guardian 24/5/13 – 'What was really good about the beginning of the whole punk thing is you would leave London and go to Teesside or anywhere up north and there'd be kids turning up who'd got their shirt and cut the sleeves off or splattered it with paint and done something themselves.'

Most bands that I went to see in the early days I really appreciated and enjoyed. Music was like oxygen. One band I didn't like was The Skids, from Dunfermline in Scotland. I heard they were doing a free afternoon gig at the Rock Garden (March 1979), so I decided to go. To me, they were a bunch of poseurs, although I liked their song 'Into the Valley'. I stood right at the front, spitting at the vocalist, Richard Jobson (who eventually became a TV presenter for a while – so I guess my instincts were right). They stopped playing at one point and asked people to stop spitting at them. Eventually, a few of their mates from Scotland grabbed me and threw me out. That is the only time I ever spat at a band – it's a disgusting habit. Spitting in someone's face is a big 'diss', as the kids on 'da' streets say nowadays.

The The And only played one gig in Middlesbrough, at a pub called The Empire, supporting Those Responsible and Frenzy Battalion; a Middlesbrough band who had a guitarist who played a bit like Keith Levine out of Public Image Ltd. A handful of people from Stockton and the estates of Hardwick and Norton, where we'd played at youth clubs, turned up to support us. We played new songs, such as Rebellious Housewife, TV Brain, Killing Babies, Public Toy, Sell-out, Speech of Youth, Maggie's Military Men, Don't Waste My Time, and Pigs in Blue. A few photos of that gig have survived the decades. Kie-Eye recently handed me a tape cassette recording of a The The And gig.

I started writing and corresponding with a few people and bands that I was getting into – Mark E Smith of The Fall, Swell Maps, Robert Smith of The Cure, Lance d'Boyle – drummer with Poison Girls. I also corresponded with individuals who wrote to me because of my fanzines, and I wrote to the writers of other fanzines around the country as well.

*

There are certain moments in one's life that are pivotal, like pebbles dropped into the pond of life – they cause ripples and repercussions that change your path and your direction forever. For example, finding certain 7 inch vinyl singles by chance – finding music and ideas that tune you into a new frequency, a new energy level, a different wave-length, a different way of thinking and being, like finding a damn good novel. You never notice such key moments when they occur – they are only ever revealed in hindsight; through the looking glass – the moment has already occurred and there is no turning back, no rewind.

*

There were three bands, apart from the Sex Pistols, who gave me a kick start in my teenage rebellion years; The Fall, Crass and Poison Girls, all discovered at random.

On the rather desolate upper level of Stockton's indoor market, a friendly hippy guy ran a little store called Green. He sold T-shirts, booklets on anarchism, vegetarianism, etc, and hippy comics like The Freak Brothers. He got a bit of hassle from the cops. I liked the guy, and when I wrote a poem about the bombing of Hiroshima (which I wrote in Stockton library one rainy afternoon when all my mates were glued up and not really worth talking to), he pinned it on the wall. It was at the Green store that I noticed the first single by Crass. I picked it up for 'pay no more than' 45p. Shortly afterwards, I also bought The Feeding of the 5,000; an 18 track, 12 inch 45rpm vinyl EP. I bought it by mail-order from Rough Trade Records in London. A few months later, I started writing to Crass.

('The Feeding of the 5,000' was actually the first release by Crass on Small Wonder records. However, workers at the pressing plant refused to handle it due to the alleged blasphemous content of the song 'Asylum'. '5,000' was eventually released with the offending song removed, replaced by two minutes of silence, entitled 'The Sound of Free Speech'. Crass formed their own independent record label, Crass Records, and released the offending track as 'Reality Asylum'.) The iconic Crass symbol, designed by Dave King, displays the Cross entwined by a two headed serpent, Ouroboros, suggesting that all power will eventually consume and destroy itself. Ouroboros is traditionally depicted as swallowing its own tail.

Around that time I also stumbled across a 12 inch vinyl EP called 'Hex', by Poison Girls. The eight tracks were titled 'Old Tarts Song', 'Crisis', 'Ideologically Unsound', Bremen Song', 'Political Love', Jump Mama Jump', 'Under the Doctor', and 'Reality Attack'. ('Hex' was later re-released on Crass Records.) I began writing to Poison Girls, mostly corresponding with Lance D'Boyle (drummer and creator of their magazine 'The Impossible Dream'), little knowing back then that I would eventually spend seven years living with the band in Leytonstone, East London, as well as collaborating with them on a live show called 'The Naked Addict', although we only performed twice as Poison Girls broke up.

*

Ever since buying the first single by The Fall, who hail from Salford, near Manchester, I've been a fan. Their first album, 'Live at the Witch Trials', despite the title, is not a live album. It was recorded in one day and is a challenging stroke of genius that still stands upright today. Their second album 'Dragnet' was recorded in three days and had just been released – October, 1979, when I first went to see them play live.

I always thought there was something occult about The Fall and the lyrics of M.E.S. – his writing was very evocative and surreal – conjuring images and characters through his unique lyrical style. One thing I especially liked about The Fall was they didn't make singles from album tracks – they always released something new, so you were never ripped-off. Compare that to whatever band you can think of; they always release one, two or even three singles from the album, thus short-changing and exploiting the listener/fan/buyer. Due to my own experiences in The Factory, I was instantly fond of a song of theirs called 'Industrial Estate'-

Yeah, Yeah, Industrial Estate
Well you started here to earn your pay
Clean neck and ears on your first day
Well we tap one another as you walk in the gate
And we'd build a canteen but we haven't got much space
And the crap in the air will fuck up your face
Boss can bloody take most of your wage
And if you get a bit of depression
Ask the doctor for some valium
Yeah, Yeah, Industrial Estate

The Fall have continued to be a hardworking, prolific band, releasing, on average, a studio album every year (29 studio albums in total, so far, plus well over 60 live albums), and they continue to gig all over the UK and the rest of the world. As M.E.S. frequently says in interviews, 'The Fall are a working band'.

I'd previously sent Mark E Smith a copy of one my fanzines and a brief letter, dated 15th October 1981, where I asked him what the E stood for. I've still got a copy of his brief reply –

'Dear Lee,

Enjoyed mag, like the eclectic feel of it, the way y'can find great things in the corners of it etc. We've left Rough Trade and have 1-off 45 deal with Camera Records who'll release 'Lie-Dream of A Casino Soul/Fantastic Life' on 1st week in Nov.

Enclosed is tour dates and we'll guest list you from Newcastle onwards if I don't see you.

Was showed 'Guardian' thing and it beats me how those people can laugh at the 'Mirror' and even the 'Sun', def. a case of over-education.

Anyway, much rushing and things, see ya.

Edward.'

When The Fall played Middlesbrough Rock Garden – Sunday, 4th November, 1979, they received a very mixed response, to say the least – the gig was heavy. Here are a few quotes I've found on some Rock Garden related websites regarding that gig -

From Funtime Franckie – *'I saw The Fall there in 1979. Remember a gang of skinheads being there hitting anything that moved...The skinheads were going up to everyone asking where they were from, and if they didn't like the place they nutted them. I was only 15 so when they came up to me I was expecting a right kicking. When they asked me where I was from I replied South Bank. They just nodded at me and moved onto the bloke next to me and nutted him. Phew.'*

Anonymous wrote – *'I can vouch for the violence at the venue having being threatened by skinheads on more than one occasion…they never quite managed to attack me but others weren't so fortunate, particularly the post-punk crowd. I was there the night of The Fall bloodbath and remember Mark E Smith taking the piss out of the UK Subs.'*

Mark Hammonds wrote – *'Ah yes, that famous Fall gig…it's seared into memory. Skinheads daring you to dance. The dangerous walk to and from the bar/toilets. The bloody noses around the place. Horrible night. I sort of lost my interest in concert-going after that, oddly enough.'*

That gig was heavy, for sure. The skinheads didn't bother me. In fact, I remember dancing, in an act of foolish defiance/bravado, down their tables as The Fall played, obviously careful not to spill their pints of beer so that they didn't spill my blood. During the gig Mark E Smith seemed happy to wind up the crowd. He said 'I hear the UK Subs played here last week', and received shouts from the audience; 'Fuck off!' The UK Subs played there a lot; they were one of the Rock garden's favourite bands. I found a few of the things M.E.S. said during that gig on a Fall-fan website:

'One, one…aaaaaaah! Futuristic aides on long legs…good evening, we are The Fall. Northern white crap but we talk back…we were spitting, we were stepping. Cop out, cop out! As if from Heaven. You can get wise at half the price…get wise at half the price. We are The Fall…as if from Heaven.'

(In response to crowd requests) *'I know it's been hard going so far, but you've got to face up to it one day. This one was a hit for me and the lads in Tibet, it's about drinking. Jukebox!'*

'This next one is epic. Okey dokey!'

'There's no requests tonight, sorry. We'd like to finish off with a religious song, seeing as it's Sunday." Before playing 'No Christmas for John Quays' (i.e. Junkies).

I continued to exchange a few letters with M.E.S. and when he informed me that they would be playing the Rock Garden on Saturday, 15th November, 1980, I asked Mark if I could interview him for my fanzine. He agreed to do so after the gig was over. I'd never interviewed anyone before and I was a little nervous, so when Gary Widdowfield from Tick-Tick, also a Fall fan, found out about it, he asked if he could help me with the interview. I was glad of his help. Tick Tick, as I've recently been informed by Geoff (Tick Tick), also supported The Fall that night and I recorded their set for them. Quote: *Just read your last message. You can't remember us playing with the Fall? Ha ha ha, you're not serious are you? We played that night you interviewed MES! I even think it might have been you that recorded our show, fucking up the recording of Hand Over Fist!'* (Note – I'd written to Geoff recently trying to get hold of Hand Over Fist, my fave Tick Tick song and now I do recall that I did indeed fuck-up some of said recording – I think I had my hand over the mic.)

I'll put the Mark E Smith interview in Part 2 for those who might want to read it.

*

There was an upstairs art-house real-ale bar in Stockton called The Dovecot. It sold Old Peculiar and traditional ales, but more to my liking were full green bottles of Grolsch lager with its flip-top that you could seal, thus keeping your drink alive. Downstairs they showed movies – that's where I first saw Neil Jordan's punk film 'Jubilee'; a dubious effort. I first met Lorraine L. there and eventually she asked if Mandy and I would like to move into a shared household – sharing it with Lorraine, Ian I. who worked in the HMV and sang in

Bombay Drug Squad, and Salla, a guitarist in local band Basczax (bass & sax), who appeared on a compilation EP with Joy Division. We jumped at the chance and were finally free from living at home with our parents – saying that, my dad did help me move my gear and he built shelves and stuff for us and was generally supportive.

When I left home and moved into the house I made the decision to become a vegetarian, and still am to this day – to the day I die. I was concerned about the systematic slaughter and abuse of animals and decided to take a step toward being responsible for my own actions. Within a few months a handful of us formed a Stockton-based Animal Aid animal-rights group. We met once a week, discussing possible tactics. Everything we did with the group was within the law. We'd receive boxes of leaflets from Animal Aid and we would hand them out on the streets, trying to raise people's awareness and make things change for the better. Surely the less suffering we have in this world then the more chance we have for a better future? Maybe I'm wrong? But that's what I believe. There's too much arbitrary suffering being caused in the world today – by scientists and by greedy, heartless, gutless, lying government's right across the planet.

Take cigarettes, for example, dogs are fastened into revolving chambers and forced to smoke hundreds of cigarettes a day, like we don't know that smoking is bad for us! I smoke, that's my fault, my addiction, my responsibility. I don't need dogs to smoke a pack of twenty to prove the point. Add the fact that the deaths related to cigarettes and alcohol, plus drunk drivers and their innocent victims, amount to more dead people a year than drug-related fatalities in the last five years and you start to see that things don't quite add up. Their equations are skewed. They always have been and I fear that they always will be.

One major campaign we did as a group was directed against Boots, the chemists, objecting to the fact that all of their beauty products were tested on animals in laboratories. Take shampoo, for example, in the labs they would pour their new product into the eyes of rabbits and study how their eyes dissolved as the chemicals burned through them, and usually the animals received no anaesthetic, no doubt to save costs. This process happened every time a new product was being prepared for the 'market' and included soap, lipstick, mascara, you name it. This vile process continues to this day. As a whole, the group shied away from taking direct action, so I undertook a few clandestine, non-violent, direct action events on my own initiative. Ya gotta do what ya gotta do.

Millions of animals suffer every year for the cosmetics trade, and if we consider all the animals that are slaughtered for the meat 'trade', we're stepping into the billions. A veritable Auschwitz supplying people with meat, when the majority of meat eaters would be afraid to cut an animal's throat, skin it and gut it before eating it, let alone bear witness to its obvious fear or hear its death cries and witness the gush of blood – this is the problem with living in a pre-packaged era. Half the kids these days who eat their take-away meals of chicken wings couldn't even draw a chicken! They've never even seen a cow and they think milk comes from the moon. I do despair for our uneducated, ill-informed, mesmerised children. They are almost as pre-packaged as the animals they eat and half of the processed food they eat is almost as plastic as the X-box that swallows their childhood time.

At night I used to venture out with several tubes of super-glue. Super-glue was designed during the Vietnam War to treat the wounded. If a grunt was gut-shot, the medic would just slip on a pair of surgical gloves and liberally smear a handful of super-glue across the wound to stop the poor guy's guts from spilling out into his lap. I would put super-glue into the locks of stores like Boots, and on every lock in the Stockton shopping centre that contained several butchers' shops, just to fuck them up a little, week after week.

We were relentless with our Animal Aid campaign against Boots – similar actions were taking place in every town and city around the UK. It took a long time to get through to them, they were very slow to change and wise up, but today, all of Boots beauty products are not tested on animals – good for them. It makes sense. Who wants to buy a beauty product built upon torture, suffering and death?

All of this took place a long time before we had Linda McCartney meat alternatives or The Beauty Shop.

Our little Stockton group of Animal Aiders also raised enough cash to hire a 35mm film and projecting system to show a very heavy film about the sick, yearly event of Seal-culling. The film is massively graphic and includes scenes that depict baby seal skulls being smashed in with metal picks by heartless guys who are only there for the profit. The film includes a sickening scene where a baby seal has its brains smashed out, and is then skinned whilst partially alive, followed by a scene of the pups mother trying to nudge her skinned and bloody baby back into life. We were able to hire a place in Middlesbrough and show the film to anyone who cared to see it for free.

I also took part in a peaceful demonstration against the proposed plan to build a nuclear power plant in Hartlepool. The big issue was the fact that the plant was going to be built next to a whole series of chemical, paint and fuel factories that were all connected and spread right into the heart of the North East. Yeah, we marched and we sang songs and we waved banners, and yeah, they built the nuclear power plant anyway, like we always knew they would. What does the voice of the people matter when you've got contracts and government deals and secretive backhanders going on all over the place?

*

We hadn't been living together for long when I decided to hitch-hike to Bradford to see The Fall. They were playing at a club called Palm Cove. I was a little apprehensive about it as I'd never hitched a ride in my life. Ian offered me some white powder to snort before I left the house, saying it would help me through. I didn't even know what it was, but snorted it anyhow. That was my first use of amphetamines, or speed, as it was more commonly known. It took me about three lifts in cars and HGV trucks to get to Bradford – I chatted amiably with the people who had stopped to give me a ride. Looking back on it – I wonder if I was jabbering with all the enthusiasm of a crazy man!

The Fall gig rocked and I sold all the fanzines I was carrying with me and Mark E Smith let me in for free, but we did have a misunderstanding. I'd published his interview in two issues of my fanzines and had gladly posted him a copy of them both when they were hot off the press. MES said he'd never received either copy and gave me this piercing, withering look of doubt. I felt bad about that because he mistakenly doubted my integrity. As a massive Fall freak there was no reason on earth why I wouldn't send him the finished articles – obviously someone intercepted them along the way. My feelings hurt, a sense of trust broken, I never wrote or spoke to Mark after that. Despite that hiccup I am still into The

Fall. That particular night in Bradford The Fall were excellent, they were using two drummers and the sound was immense. Two songs, 'Crap Rap/Spectre vs. Rector' and 'Cary Grant's Wedding', from that gig appeared on 'Totales Turns'; The Fall's third album, a rough live compilation.

I had nowhere to spend the night, but got chatting to a punk called Dave who lived in Leeds. He asked me if I had anywhere to stay – I told him I'd clocked a flat rooftop across the road, above a car showroom that I reckoned I could access and roll out my sleeping bag for the duration of the night. Dave said I could crash at his bedsit. I took a leap of faith in a random stranger and after the gig we took a train from Bradford to Leeds. He was older than me, and I was a bit apprehensive, but everything was cool. After that, anytime I hitched to Bradford or Leeds, I would stay at his place. He was a sincere, kind fella who just liked helping out random punks from out of town.

Despite not writing to Mark E Smith anymore, I hitched across country to see them play in Wigan, at a place called The Trucks – the stage had a scaffolding type structure, and due to all the sweat and spilt beer, blue sparks were flying everywhere. I'm amazed no-one was electrocuted. I also saw them play in Manchester, and years later, when I moved to London, I must have seen them at least a dozen times over the years. The first gig I ever took my son, Felix, then aged 6, to see, was The Fall in Islington – we sat with Mark's mum and his sister Pauline – I recall asking them if I'd be able to film a Fall gig – his mum replied: 'Mark can be awkward. He doesn't like being filmed.' A guy off The Fall official, now unofficial, website, kindly sent me a recording-desk CD copy of the gig for prosperity. As a rule, Fall fans are cool people, smarter than most – they read books.

When I found out The Fall were going to be playing at Hackney Empire in 2010 – I wrote to The Fall asking if I could film them. The Empire does not allow photography or filming to take place. Mark's third wife, Elena, who plays keyboards in the group, thought it might be a good idea, but Mark finally said 'No'. However, not to be deterred, I filmed a few songs covertly and posted them on You Tube, they can be found, along with other stuff I've done, under the user name 'lee3813'. (I've also posted some of my art and other stuff on You Tube under 'leeG777G').

*

The first time I saw Poison Girls and Crass play was at Middlesbrough Rock Garden, October 11th, 1980. I was keen to attend the gig and through mail correspondence I'd arranged to do an interview with Poison Girls after the gig was over. Things didn't quite work out as planned because that particular gig was even more violent than 'The Fall bloodbath'. As usual, it was the skinheads knocking fuck out of people.

As always with the Rock Garden I attended the gig alone. I got there early and chatted briefly with Vi Subversa before the gig started. Vi was friendly, witty and somewhat culture shocking to me, she was about the same age as my mum! That night, both bands received a hostile reception from the mass of skinheads who frequented the Rock Garden. Poison Girls managed to get through their set, but when Crass started playing all hell broke loose. Due to their stance as anarchists, the neo-nazi contingents made every effort to disrupt Crass gigs and to intimidate and assault Crass fans. The skinheads tried to storm the stage and I recall Phil Free, bass player with Crass, jamming the end of his bass guitar straight into the chest of a skinhead, sending him flying. It was a very scary gig and I'd had enough. I eventually kicked open the emergency exit doors just to get the fuck out of there in one piece. Stockton is only a few miles from Middlesbrough, but sometimes it could be a long walk and felt light-years away.

Afterwards, I wrote a letter to Poison Girls explaining why I wasn't around at the end of the gig. They wrote back to me and suggested that I send them some written questions in the post, which I did. At their house in Leytonstone, East London, they recorded their responses to my questions and recorded them on tape cassette and sent the tapes up to me. I always thought that was a very generous act, plus the fact that they took me seriously, despite my young age and my relative naivety. I published their interview over two issues of my fanzine, the first part coinciding with the second part of my interview with MES in Protesting Children Minus the Bondage #2, and in Anathema #1. The Poison Girls interview is included in Part 2 for those who might like to read it.

After the violent gig at Middlesbrough Rock Garden, I also wrote to Crass and arranged to visit them at their communal headquarters in Dial House, Epping Forest, to do an interview.

As I was skint and on the dole, I couldn't afford a train ticket or a National Express coach ticket, so I decided to hitch down to London, a journey of about 250 miles. I only had a few quid in my pocket – not the best way to go travelling around the country – it was a shit or bust situation.

When I arrived in London, after a fluid six-hour sequence of lifts from complete strangers, including a stoned, long-distance heavy-goods vehicle driver who was actually driving barefoot like some kind of hillbilly freak, I was dropped off near Oxford Street in central London.

I then realized that I should have paid a little more attention to planning my route. I was about 20 miles from Epping. I only had a few quid in my pocket. I rang Dial House and was advised to just 'bunk' the tube, and so I did – it was before the Oyster card system so I just jumped the barrier and when I got to Epping, the station was unmanned.

I stayed with Crass for a few days, half mesmerised; it was like a different world and made quite an impression upon me. Crass were very organised and focused on what they were doing, whereas I was still making things up as I went along – ha-ha, no change there. The people in Crass treated me so kindly, without any fakery or bullshit, I felt like I'd stepped into an alternate universe. It kind of flipped me out. It was the first time that I really glimpsed the possibilities of alternate ways of living, something different from the usual family set-up and all the restrictions that invariably come with that package.

I did the interview with Penny Rimbaud, Andy Palmer, Eve Libertine, Pete Wright and Steve Ignorant (who only made one comment, although it was a humorous one). Eventually, it was just me and Penny chatting as the other band members drifted away to get on with other things. Recorded on a cheap cassette recorder, we talked for over two hours – Penny talked a whole lot more than me, I just threw him the odd question and he would get right in depth, and we kind of worked it from there. If anything, I was young, naive, curious and questioning society and I found his conversation enlightening. After that, I started following them all over the country whenever they did a tour – often going from one gig to the next, all over the UK, sometimes on the road for a few weeks at a time.

Like the previous interviews mentioned, the Crass interview is enclosed in Part 2. In total I only ever did five interviews for my fanzine; Mark E Smith, Poison Girls (once by mail, once face to face), Crass, and Andy T. Looking back, I see that I only wanted to interview people with integrity; people who might teach me a thing or two about a thing or two, though I wish I'd interviewed The Mob as well.

*

Hitching could be a great way of travelling around for free, but it wasn't always easy. Sometimes, especially trying to get out of Birmingham, I had to wait hours for a ride. Getting out of Birmingham was pure hell. I saw Crass play there once and people were throwing chairs at them from the balcony above. I had a small two-man tent with me and a sleeping bag. After the gig I just wandered around until I found a small park, not too far from The Bullring, as they call their central shopping area. I just pitched my tent and crashed out. I was awoken the next morning with hot sunbeams blinding me and someone's dog pissing on my tent. At least I wasn't killed or set on fire by random Brummie rogues.

Like anyone else who has done their fair share of hitch-hiking I've had swift lifts and slow rides, sometimes not making the destination at all and sleeping rough. I've stood in freezing cold rainstorms, holding out a thumb that was turning blue. Other times, I've melted like an ice-cream beneath the Sun. The best times were when the rides flowed like a cool Zen stream, one ride after another, and I'd reach a town with several hours to kill before the gig started. It was like a Jack Kerouac thing, long before I even knew about his books and the Beatnik lifestyle. I'd sit in town centres or in cemeteries and just write. It wasn't long before I was helping Crass and Poison Girls unload their gear into the venue – getting in for free – then helping them pack up their gear after the gig. It felt good to be involved in something real. I guess I was a cheap roadie/devoted fanster-monster.

I got lifts from long distance truck drivers who always quizzed me about the punk attitude and lifestyle – generally they appreciated my rebellious stance. I got lifts from guys heading back to their military bases, even though they were not supposed to give civilians a lift. I got rides from salesmen, from women who wanted to give me a lift because their sons were students who also hitched about just like me. I got lifts from people who were on a long journey and were just glad of a bit of company, people who would also buy me a meal and refuse my offer to pay. I got lifts from all walks of life - all good people.

I only ever had one dodgy ride – some older guy gave me a lift down the A1. He started jabbering about Jesus and God and for the first time I wondered if I'd finally thumbed a ride with a serial killer – I'm sure there's more chance of that happening now than there was then, which is probably why you don't see so many hitch-hikers anymore – everyone is afraid of everyone else and our moral decline seems more pronounced than ever. This ranting guy stopped to pick up another young kid who was also hitching. The kid climbed in the back seat. The religious mania continued and the guy was really starting to piss me off. I was starting to think he might end up killing us both, like a double whammy, maybe dump our bodies on the hard shoulder. After a few more miles I put my hand on the door and told him to pull over, thinking, 'Fuck this, I'd rather walk'. The guy complained, but I was insistent, ready to smack him in the mouth, if need be, hoping I wouldn't have to jump out of the speeding car. The guy pulled over. As I started climbing out of the passenger seat, the kid in the back seat said 'Don't leave me here!' He got out as well. We had a brief chat, agreed that the guy was completely nuts, and then put 500 yards between us so that we could both carry on with our respective journeys. I can't remember which one of us got the first ride.

I hitch hiked all over the country to see Crass and Poison Girls play. Places like Leeds, Bradford, Wigan, Swansea, Birmingham, Manchester, Cardiff, Cambridge, Liverpool, Nottingham, Todmorden, Hebden Bridge, Irvine on the West coast of Scotland and across to Perth on the East side. I always hitched alone, usually carrying little coin in my pocket, with a rucksack full of fanzines (actually getting by from selling them in order to buy food and beer), a small tent and a sleeping bag, a bit of food, and, of course, a pen and a notebook. I loved arriving at a strange town and finding somewhere to sit down and write.

Irvine was my favourite trip. I got there several hours before Crass and Poison Girls were due to play and walked out of the town. I found a crumbling, rickety-old timber built pier, and settled down, the waves beneath my feet, the sun in my face, writing whatever popped into my head. The coast of Irvine used to get a warm oceanic drift from the Gulf Stream (don't know if it still does); it had palm trees growing along its shoreline - Palm trees in Scotland, how weird and wonderful is that? Man, just sitting there on that ramshackle pier, it was so much better than writing on toilet paper in the crummy toilet cubicles of the scummy Factory. Yes, I was skint, so what? I was about to see two bands that I really dug. I felt free...like time had stopped...time was irrelevant and I totally got the Zen flow of the whole moment. I sucked it deep into my soul and because of that solitary, magical afternoon, writing, with the gentle wind, the warm sun and the lulling waves for company, I will always love the Scottish town of Irvine.

*

After the gig in Irvine, people who were hitching on the tour made their separate ways across Scotland, heading for Perth. I had some difficulty hitching all the way to the east coast and had to take a coach for some of the journey. The Crass Perth gig is as infamous as 'The Fall Bloodbath' at Middlesbrough Rock Garden. It took place at the Lesser City Hall on July 4th, 1981.

The gig was recorded through the mixing desk by Andy T and later released as a CD; 'Crass: You'll ruin it for everyone'. The album title came from the words shouted from the stage by Steve Ignorant to a group of National Front skinheads who were beating people up. These days the CD is something of a rarity and the last time I looked on Amazon it was selling new for £53.00, and used for £34.99.

Trouble started almost as soon as the gig began when about 30 NF skins turned up with nothing but confrontation and physical violence on their minds. I recall that there were at least two police officers standing at the back of the Hall, 'keeping an eye on things'. Yet when the skinheads started wading into the crowd, kicking and punching men and women alike, the police did absolutely nothing to intervene. I recall me and Andy T asking the police to leave, saying that we'd take care of it. The officers were only too happy to oblige. Talking to Andy recently (June 2013) he said he recalled the fact that their leader wore a red Harrington jacket. I don't remember that specific detail, although I'm sure it's spot-on, and

I've asked Andy to contribute a few lines toward this piece on the Perth gig. (True to his word, he's sent me a copy of a piece he wrote for the sleeve notes that accompanied the live album mentioned above and I'll include it after this article on Perth.)

I recall seeing Nil (Poison Girls) sat on the edge of the stage with a bloody, broken nose. I recall seeing young punks getting punched to shit. I recall seeing punkettes getting nutted. Andy T and I decided to take some direct action.

The atmosphere was very heavy, and very threatening. Crass repeatedly asked people (the skinheads) to stop fighting. In reality it was more of a co-ordinated gang assault than a fight.

By the time Crass started the second song of their set, Nagasaki Nightmare, things really exploded (excuse the pun). Eve Libertine halted the song and shouted 'Stop it!' Steve Ignorant said 'Stop fighting, please, stop. Stop fighting. Stop fighting.' The song resumed for about fifteen seconds before the band stopped playing for a second time.

Steve Ignorant shouted 'Stop fighting. Stop it. You'll ruin it for everyone.' The song resumed for a third time but again it was stopped after about 20 seconds. 'Pack in the fighting or this gig's gonna get stopped,' said Steve, 'I don't want that, you don't want that. I don't want the police, you don't want the police. So let's just have a good time, hey? For fuck's sake.'

NF skins were shouting 'You want anarchy.' Steve replied 'I just want a gig, alright? Let's stop fighting, fucking hell, for like, an hour.'

The fighting continued. Penny Rimbaud grabbed a microphone, 'If you want anarchy, mate, go out on the street and start it. We're in here for our form of anarchy; you go outside for your form of anarchy. Now fuck-off out of it. Just look at what happened in London last night, mate, if you want anarchy, just you wait for to come to you and then you'll learn a little bit of what the word means, wise guy.' A riot had taken place in London – riots also happened in Birmingham and Liverpool. The NF kept shouting and Penny continued his outburst, 'Mouth and trousers will get you nowhere, so fuck-off out of it.' One NF guy in particular was very vocal, and Penny concluded with 'Ah, balls you twat! I've got a feeling these guys have to go.'

Eve Libertine shouted 'Those that don't want the gig, get the fuck out!'

The punks who'd turned up to see Crass play started chanting 'Fight war, not wars', then Penny started drumming, the chant grew louder and then Crass finally managed to finish playing Nagasaki Nightmare.

Crass played a 17 song set, but trouble was still happening by the 12th song, Big A Little A. Steve shouted 'Pack it in. Pack it in' Then he started to sing 'Fight war, not wars', joined by the crowd and then the song got underway.

Andy T and I set to work from the back of the hall and slowly but surely worked our way toward the stage where Crass were playing. Every time we saw a skinhead hitting someone we stepped up behind them, and then punched them in the face from two sides at once. Generally they dropped like the sacks of shit they were. We hit a lot of NF guys that night and handed out black-eyes like they were free fanzines.

After the gig, when we'd kicked the NF out, they were waiting outside for us, ready to fuck us up, knowing that we were a long way from home.

I remember helping Poison Girls to dismantle their gear and then help to carry out their equipment. When I reached the back door, a gang of about fifteen to twenty skinheads were lurking, waiting for their moment. They all had at least one black eye. I might have seen the glint of a knife, but I can't swear on my oath that I did. I nipped back inside and explained the situation.

Poison Girls saved a lot of people from getting a serious beating, or stabbed or even killed, that night in Perth. They got each person who had travelled to see them and Crass who didn't live in Perth, to carry various items of equipment into their tour van (the old white ambulance), and then to remain on the van.

They filled the van and stacked us in like sardines, and then they drove us safely out of Perth, denying the battered NF skins their vengeance and retribution.

Poison's drove us down the A90 for about 30 miles and took us across the River Forth on the Forth Road Bridge, and then pulled to a halt. We all piled out of their tour van before a police patrol car caught them severely overloaded, and we made our way toward the next gig, cloaked by the stars and safe in the distant light of an Edinburgh night.

*

THE DAYS OF WHINE AND BROKEN NOSES – By Andy T.

Nostalgia is a long strange trip. Blurred and battered. Torn and scattered. Memories faded. Sepia toned. Edges burned. Blackened and bloodied. Screwed up. Chewed up. Spat out. Flat out and broken. Will the circle remain unspoken...?

Remember the daze..? No neither do I, I'm afraid.

Fear of the unknown tomorrow is quietly subdued by the opiate of nostalgia. Slip silently into the sea of dreams, nightmares and unrealities. Another triumph for the flaccid casualties.

Can you get enough together for one more fix?

This night in Perth was the fourth or fifth in a short tour of Bonnie Scotland. It was always an interesting place to visit. Far removed from the London smog, people weren't snowed under with gigs like the lucky folk in the smoke. You were always aware of the importance of these events. Aware of the impotence of the usual music business angles, the tried and tired cabaret circuit. Where the Clash always played to rapturous applause, and the sound of their emptiness was deafening. These tiny halls were a fertile breeding ground for those who really believed in doing it for themselves. As opposed to those who were doing it soul-lessly FOR themselves.

I always tried to attend as many Crass gigs as possible, wherever they may roam. Armed to the teeth with bread and cheese and sometimes even a map with the big blue roads on. Hitching was the usual method. A tad hit and miss at times, but lack of finance and a distinct mistrust of public transport guided me the way of the thumb. Besides which, it was a perfect way to meet all sorts of different people. Some friendlier than others, but all equally as precious. All with something unique to contribute.

Communication is our greatest asset...Our reason for living. Our reason for travelling the length and breadth of this septic isle and beyond. Hundreds of ragged individuals gathered together in darkened rooms, to celebrate a common cause. We found we had a lot in common.

Anarchy and peace...loaded words...important words with many varied meanings for everyone concerned. These gigs were a contact point for many friends inspired by a network of letters, phone-calls, fanzines and records. If we didn't think we could change the world, we knew we could always change our own minds...for the better.

About half a dozen of us were following the bands to each gig this time. The rest of the audience was mainly local to the area. A few came from nearby cities such as Dundee and Edinburgh, which were also dates on this tour. Many were seeing the bands for the first time, experiencing something new and exciting.

Another peaceful evening…or maybe not…around the end of the Poison Girls set, and during Annie Anxiety's short piece, trouble was brewing. Some scuffling and pushing was occurring around the edges of the dancing crowd. The source of the unwanted harassment was a bunch of young skinheads who seemed to take exception to the punks. They were led, to some extent, by a tall, fierce looking chap in a red Harrington bomber jacket, who had a rather unpleasant line in hating the English invaders from over the border.

When Crass began their set, the skinheads started running around, randomly attacking anyone and everyone who stood in their way. Especially those who couldn't or wouldn't fight back, either because of pacifist ideals or slight of frame. A safe haven had turned into a dangerous place to be.

Over the years we had to deal with violence at gigs on several occasions, so some of us had developed certain techniques for stopping the troublemakers. Phil, the guitarist, was particularly proud of his disabling hold that he'd perfected at an earlier gig at the Conway Hall in London. I had grown up in a fairly violent environment myself, and was used to unprovoked attacks. I have always considered myself a pacifist at heart, but have always believed that self-defence is sometimes necessary. It's not big and it's not clever, but quite often it helps…

Eve, Steve and Penny all tried to stop the violence, shouting down and arguing with the skins. The music stopped as more chaos ensued. In the audience, we started up a chant of 'Fight War, Not Wars'. An apt phrase for all occasions, which helped to bring a strength of togetherness to the frightened and fragmented crowd.

The skinheads backed off and most of them left the building or retreated to the back of the hall. They had lost the element of surprise and fear which fed their hatred. The adrenalin dissipated. Apart from a few further minor incidents, the rest of the gig went along pretty peacefully.

That days newspapers had been full of tales of rioting and looting in sunny Brixton. The streets had been very busy the night before. The last thing we wanted was a repeat performance in picturesque Perth…Violence Breeds Violence Breeds Violence…

However many-sided our form of Anarchy, we knew there no place for violent upheaval in our philosophy. That is not a constructive way to change anything. That is the way the system keeps us in check. It makes us angry, then chastises us for showing emotions. Punishes us in our confusion.

When the lights came on, after a fine energetic set, we tended to the wounded, packed up the equipment and someone made a pot of tea, probably…

Some of the skinheads stayed around for a chance to talk and make peace, albeit a shaky version. The ringleader was still the most aggressive, arguing the toss about all sorts of things. He took a lot of persuading before he finally calmed down. I seem to remember, he promised to come to the Edinburgh gig the night after, with a strong desire to cut my throat with his shiny penknife. Despite these happy thoughts the following night's gig passed without much fuss, and a jolly time was had by all…Maybe my friends in the red jacket got stuck on the Edinburgh road without a lift in sight…I know what that can feel like…

Whenever we discussed that night together afterwards, in the coldest light of day, we always had a good chuckle about it. This fact would most definitely appal those destructive "so called" journalists and assorted non believers. They harboured a warped idea of us as sad old druggies, hippies and punks who sat in miserable heaps, crying over the poor furry animals, and the rising cost of brown rice…Why should people be so surprised that we still retain a healthy sense of humour? We always had the last laugh…

The good times always outweighed the grim. Never let the bastards grind you down…everyone you encounter in this life, has some special knowledge to impart, no matter how unimportant it can seem at the time. All the time we can learn from our own experiences and those shared with others. Nothing is wasted.

To all the friends I was fortunate to cross path's with, all those years ago, who offered a smile, a conversation, a cigarette, or a cuddle, a place to crash, or even a cup of tea.

I can't recall every name and face, but I'll never forget the relentless enthusiasm, in the face of adversity, and the sheer bloody spirit of those involved.

We've mostly gone our separate ways since. Concentrating our energies into many worthwhile directions I've not kept in touch with people like I should have done. Hopefully this project will help to rectify that situation…I've also got plans to start writing again with a view to a possible album, of songs and poems. I've got a sneaky feeling the time to start something again, may we be just around the bend…Controlled insanity, indeed??...

Nostalgia is a long strange trip indeed…And the band played on…
Keep smiling…Anarchy…Love…Peace…and Earl Grey…

*

My ties with London at that time were very minimal. I was writing to maybe half a dozen people there, most of them linked to the 'Kill Your Pet Puppy' fanzine collective of writers and artists (the KYPP website is certainly worth a browse). I was definitely writing to more people from outside the Capital and to people in Sweden and South Africa during the Apartheid reign while Nelson Mandela was still in prison (I share the same birthday as him) – how they got hold of my fanzines, fuck knows? But I did get letters from South Africa saying that my fanzines we're being used as a topic in their classes at school. A voice of freedom? A study on a crazy English white man? Who knows?

As the fanzine thing grew, Vanessa could no longer print them on the sly for me as I wanted to produce 500 copies. I had to find somewhere else to publish my stuff, and pay for it. Up North, I was met with a total brick wall – no-one would deal with my stuff. There were no places that I knew of that were willing to help a young punk print his angry anti-establishment writing. I had to get resourceful and look elsewhere. I happened to be writing letters to Martin C, who lived in a squat in Stoke Newington. He suggested I try using a resource centre in Camden, London, called Centerprise, and said I could stay over at his place if I wanted as it would probably take a few days to print my fanzine.

I was 17 when I took an overnight train to London and found my way to the squat in Stoke Newington, my first experience of the squatting lifestyle. Although there was an element of squalor, it also struck me that an alternative way of living was taking place. The general vibe was positive, very energetic and supportive, something that transcended material cleanliness and comfort. Martin shared the house with a few other people, including Bob S. who was later the guitarist and driving force behind a band called Blood & Roses, and also Richard C. aka Scarecrow, who later opened an art venue called The Institute of Rot. Scarecrow is still an industrious creative artist.

I remember talking about some out of body experiences that I'd been having that puzzled me. I first had an OOBE when I was about 7 years old. I used to rise up to the ceiling and spend ages floating above my sleeping body, but never really knew what was going on. Bob handed me a book called 'Magick' by some guy called Aleister Crowley and opened it to a certain chapter that dealt specifically with the development of what occultists call the 'astral body' – the star body, and said 'Read this'. Oddly enough, I'd already featured a page on Crowley in an earlier fanzine, the article was written by Vanessa, although I'd never read or even seen any of his books before. I only included the article because Crowley was obviously such a controversial figure, then and now, plus the fact that since Vanessa printed my first few fanzines it would have been plain ungrateful to refuse her article on old Crowley.

I never really clicked with Bob, but I did like Blood & Roses (still listen to their tunes to this day), and I thought he was a smart, perceptive guy with a sly humour. The chapter in Magick was numbered XVIII, entitled *'Of Clairvoyance and the Body of Light, its Power and its Development'*. I read it and was astonished that someone else knew exactly what I'd been experiencing, and more than that, they wrote with an open mind and encouraged the reader to experiment for themselves – *'Within the human body is another body of approximately the same size and shape; but made of a subtler and less illusory material. It is of course not "real"; but then no more is the other body!'* I've always been grateful to Bob for that little Crowley moment. When I returned from London, I mentioned that book to Mandy and she bought me a copy of Crowley's 'Magick' for my 18th birthday. Thus began several intensive years of research into the various aspects and tendrils of occultism.

At Centerprise I was given a crash course in printing. Each page of my fanzine had to be lazer-burned onto a plastic sheet called acetate. If I wanted to use more than one layer to a page, for example text in black and images in red, then I had to make two separate acetates. The acetates were then attached to the drum of a hand printing press. Each page was rolled out, 500 times, or twice that for double-layered pages, and then collated, and finally stapled together and boxed up. The reason it was cheap to produce a fanzine there was essentially due to the fact that I had to do all the work myself, which I was more than happy to do – I simply paid a cost rate for the materials that I used. At least I could print what I wanted to with full control over the finished product. I would print for eight or nine hour stretches each day. It was rather sweaty work, but work of a different nature, especially when compared to the Factory. This was a labour of love, and you can never beat a labour of love; its power is limitless, infinite – it sends out waves of energy across the cosmos. Performing a labour of love is also self-rewarding in itself. In Crowleyan terms, I was following my 'True Will'.

I printed most of my subsequent fanzines at Centerprise, and I camped out on the grounds of an adjacent City Farm – just me and the farm animals in the middle of London. I didn't bother to explore London or to see the sights. The Big City didn't appeal to me at all. I simply got the work done and got out of there.

*

Back up North, The The And managed to play more gigs in various local youth clubs and ramshackle low-key pubs in Stockton and Middlesbrough. We rehearsed for minimal fees at a youth club on a tough Stockton estate called Hardwick and at a community project centre in Middlesbrough called Impasse. In all, we did 13 gigs. I don't know what it is with the number 13, but I also happened to produce 13 fanzines. Perhaps it's fitting that this book is written in 2013?

Kie-Eye: *'We played at a community centre in Eastbourne, that was rough. Do you remember that Morgan had a little van and he'd come and pick us up on Sunday afternoons? I think we had to contribute 50p for petrol. Twas the highlight of my week! Got me out of the shit-hole I called home. And we got asked for our autographs at the last gig at The Corporation Hall. I think those kids who wanted autographs are the one's I let in for free 'cos they were hovering outside with nothing better to do.'*

I organized our last gig with the help on Mandy and her elder sister, Vanessa. I fronted money to book the Corporation Hall in Stockton and arranged for us to play with four other bands. Entry fee was cheap and any profits went to a women's refuge; basically a centre for battered wives – like most English towns, there was no shortage of husbands and boyfriends who like to beat up on their partners. People helped organize food and canned booze. About 200 people turned up. The gig was a success on that level. Tom, our bass player, only had two strings instead of four. Adolf Fuck joined us, as if completing a cycle, and played a penny whistle. Kie-Eye, as she's recently informed me, refused to play the Church song ('Fuck the Lord and Jesus Christ'), and apparently I called her a 'wanker' – for that, I sincerely apologise to her. Singers can be pricks sometimes. Toward the end of our 'set' I started playing loud static from a hand-held radio through the microphone. I threw the radio - it smashed against a wall. The The And was over. Our existence as a 'band' was short and sweet.

Writing this flashback book and doing internet research on my own past, essentially to help me fill in the gaps, its kinda nice to find people who are posting stuff about us online. The The And were only a small dysfunctional ripple in what was a very dysfunctional world. I'm glad some people got the point and enjoyed our chaos. It was mad, made-up, off-the-cuff stuff. We were stepping out of the box the world wanted to put us in. I'm glad we did it. Definitely no regrets – although I do wish we'd managed to get it together to do a demo recording, a single, or even a flexi disc - that would have been a groove, but we simply didn't have the money. All in all, being in a randomly formed, ramshackle band wasn't such a bad thing to be dabbling with in those times, at our young age and in our particular environment. We stood up. We counted, if only for the simple fact that we existed and we resisted the Big Nowhere that wanted to swallow and destroy us all, wholesale. The thing I love most about The The And is that we played to people on tough ghetto estates and those kids totally got the point. If we managed to serve as a springboard or encouragement for a dozen individuals to wake-up, step-up and step-out, then our little renegade mission was a success. To inspire or to be inspired – therein lays the magickal path.

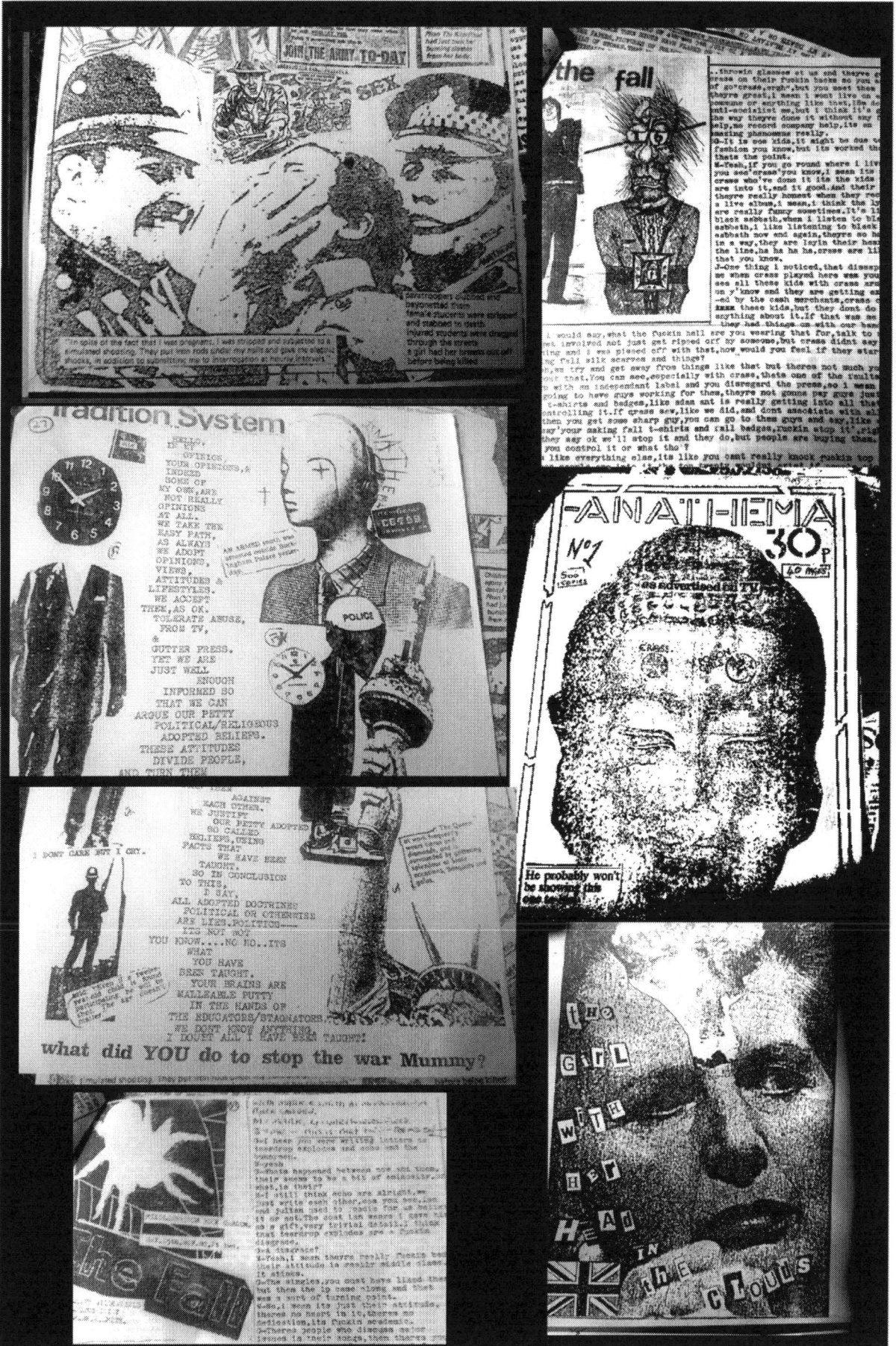

CHAPTER 4

The fanzines I created usually sold out pretty rapidly – people were hungry for something different or something that went against the grain. I sold them on local streets, in pubs, at local gigs and gigs around the country. I sold them in a few anarchist bookstores in London on a sale-or-return basis. I sold them by post if people sent me a postal order. Considering the fact that I was, and still remain, an anti-capitalist, I was doing a whole lot of selling! (Albeit for little or no profit)

As I was shifting one fanzine, I would also be in the process of creating another. Even to this day, if I am not actively involved in a creative project, be it writing, photography, painting or music, I usually feel lost and life seems to have no meaning, the spark of life seems to grow dimmer. Perhaps I'm addicted to the creative process? I certainly acknowledge that I have what psychologists call an addictive personality.

Changing the fanzine titles would become a regular pattern for me. I had it in my head that I didn't want to be known – didn't want to become a brand name, so every one or two issues the name changed – I can scarcely remember all the titles. The third fanzine was mostly full of the letters I'd received from doing 'A Movement with No Name' – letting other kids have their say, essentially because I was a little taken aback by the positive feedback that I received.

One letter I printed, by a guy called Brocky, from the Hardwick estate, called for a demonstration against police violence. I published his letter because the police in Stockton and Middlesbrough were often very heavy handed and it seemed that they were free to bash the shit out of anyone they wanted, with no-one to answer to. No doubt that was the beginning of me appearing on their radar.

By the time I was selling Anathema I was getting listed in various top-ten punk fanzine charts in several music magazines and music papers like Sounds and NME, listed alongside other notable fanzines such as Vague, Toxic Graffiti, Kill Your Pet Puppy, In the City, and others. It seemed funny in a way because fanzines were the direct opposite to what the established music press was all about. I recall a journalist for the NME, Dave McCullough, wrote a review of Anathema - someone showed it to me during a Crass tour in Scotland. Although the review was favourable I didn't like music hack's and I wrote him an angry, ten page letter, slagging off music journo's and the NME.

I was also credited in an issue of Enigma fanzine, along with a host of other people. I wrote Rob Enigma a letter of complaint, as I hadn't contributed anything to that great fanzine. Scarecrow replied and told me it was kind of an in-joke, listing all the so-called 'hip' people on the underground 'scene', and he liked the fact that I was actually the only one from the 'list' to complain about my name being used. I've always been an awkward bugger.

Here are a couple of quotes I've found online regarding some of my old fanzines that have been scanned and uploaded onto a some web-sites that are devoted to 'zines from that era in time. I had no idea that they were out there, on the web, until Andy T brought it to my attention. From the Essential Ephemera website-

'Anathema #1. 'THIS FANZINE BELONGS TO_____ ANOTHER POSSESSION FOR MY COLLECTION.' I think there were just two editions produced, both in 1982 (corrections always welcome). Anathema is a series of astute rants, essays and poetry grappling with politics, feminism, consumerism, socialisation, torture, animal rights, religion, machismo, mental health, and the occult. Great contributions from Amanda M, Andy T, and Vanessa L. Includes an excellent interview with Crass and Part 2 of a Poison Girls interview. Unfortunately this copy is missing pages 32-40.'

'Anathema #2. More cogitations from Lee on topics derisively dismissed as 'the usual issues' (generally by types who talk of right-wing this and left-wing that – blind proponents of what has become little more than an act of mass-mesmerism – an illusion of choice pitting people one against the other, divided and ruled – whilst dark market forces, whom we all ultimately serve, grin with greedy glee...), at any rate, those 'usual issues' are still relevant today and the more that air them the better. Features an interview with Andy T, poetry, collage, fanzine round-up, The Mob lyrics and pieces on factory fodder, wonky civilisation, old age, gender conditioning, personal revolution, the Falklands war, insincere celebrity and contributions from Gerard (Anabolic Steroids).'

From the Kill Your Pet Puppy Website-

'Gerard says – Does anyone know what happened to Lee who did Protesting Children Minus the Bondage?'

'Sned says – No idea what happened to Lee, then again, I never ever met him or even knew him, a fan of his/their work though. I would love to see copies of Anathema 'zine which I assume was made by Lee/Protesting Children folk. I have a really messy copy with bits missing and so on, that's all.'

'Nic says - I remember Anathema, Sned: another great magazine (and interesting to think that it was probably linked to Protesting Children: he later did that magazine Kiss the Earth where the address was 56 Brougham Road)...In fact, I remember throwing what was left of it away (after I'd cut out all sorts of bits and pieces) back in 1988...it would be great to see some of the other magazines from back then: A-Z (by Paul of This Bitter Lesson and Faction), Paroxysm Fear (by Mag of Flack), Fat Man – Little Boy, Cobalt Hate, Ability Stinks! (get your archive out Gerard!), and even A System Partly Revealed (by the Fascist John Cato)...if only because they represent a flurry of creativity undertaken without sanction by the culture around them (and ultimately inspired by the example of Crass)'

'John no last name says - I was just reading this post and thinking about how funny Lee (Kiss the Earth, Anathema, Spitting Pretty Pictures, etc), was. At the point when I was pretty much bored with a lot of people from 'the scene' Lee was always worth talking to and always had a great outside perspective. I actually often wondered what happened to Lee too, anyone know?'

I think a lot of my fanzines got destroyed by the people who actually bought and read them, afterwards cutting out various images or pieces of writing to stick on their bedroom walls. I have no problem with that. In fact, I kind of like it that they got annihilated. I do find it a little strange that they are being resurrected on the net here and there as I don't possess a single copy of any of them. I guess circles and cycles are turning, like they always do.

*

Things in our shared house in Richmond Road, Stockton, just down the street from Ropner Park, definitely took a strange turn. Sala introduced me to lysergic acid diethylamide, otherwise known as LSD, or Acid. He gave me a piece of what looked like thin card, known as blotting paper, half the size of the nail on my little finger, and suggested I pop it into my mouth. It seemed small and harmless. He told me that it was acid, but at that time I didn't even know that acid was LSD.

Anyway, I popped it and within an hour I found myself laughing for about four hours non-stop, stomach cramps, the whole works, the living room and the entire Universe seemed endlessly hilarious, colourful beyond belief and shimmering like the surface of a magical pond. If I waved my hands, they left behind ghostly, glowing vapour trails, like I could see my energy body moving through time in slow motion. I loved the vivid, electric colours, the swirling, congealing patterns, the creeping, slithering carpet and the shifting, rippling walls. I dug the whole extra-sensory expansiveness of it all. I loved the sudden shift and jolt to my usual perception, and so began my random exploration of the acid-trip as I flowed into the depths of my fickle body and dipped a toe into the glowing ocean of the cosmic mind...hit with all the usual acid questions, such as: What if the energy source behind the manifested and un-manifested (invisible/dark matter) Universe or Multi-verse is a form of creative consciousness – what if God does exist, but He/She/It is completely and utterly insane?

The macrocosm and the microcosm, the big universe and the miniscule universe of atomic particles became one and the same; creating a sense of unity, of connectedness with absolutely everything that filled me with such a genuine state of joy, all I could do was laugh. Experiencing the Cosmic Joke is a profound moment, even if it occurs outside of regular space and time. Now I knew what people said when they were out of their heads – you don't just step outside of the usual restrictions of your head, you get out of your body, too. Suddenly, I felt truly awake for the first time in my life. I was turned on. I glimpsed the magick of existence and tasted the pure folly and joy of awareness. I was in the holy state of illumination. I was a radiant Eye, like an eye of total perception, like the opening eye of Horus from ancient Egyptian times...whose eye in a pyramid is now tattooed upon my right forearm.

LSD was first synthesized in 1938 by Swiss chemist Albert Hofmann as part of a program searching for medically useful ergot alkaloid derivatives (you'll have to Google that one). LSD's psychedelic properties were discovered 5 years later when Hofmann accidentally ingested an unknown quantity of the chemical. The first intentional ingestion of LSD occurred on April 19, 1943, when Hofmann ingested 250 micrograms of LSD. He found the effects to be much stronger than he anticipated. Sandoz Laboratories then introduced LSD as a psychiatric drug in 1947. All business like and strictly legal – it was a great idea; let's trip out people with mental problems – let's spike the crazies and see what happens. At least it was better than electro-shock 'therapy' or a frontal lobotomy where they shove a screwdriver type device above the eyeball and into the eye cavity, then push it directly into the brain, wiggle it about a bit and see what happens - It certainly calmed the patient down, and at the same time destroyed their minds.

In the 1950s the C.I.A. began a clandestine research program code-named Project MK-ULTRA. Experiments included administering LSD to CIA employees, military personnel, doctors, other government agents, prostitutes, mentally ill patients, and members of the general public in order to study their reactions, usually without the subject's knowledge. The project only came to light to the US congress in 1975, however, the CIA Director at the time, Richard Helms, had already ordered all MK-ULTRA files to be destroyed back in 1972. Even so, a Freedom of Information Act request in 1977 uncovered some 20,000 documents related to the project. MK-ULTRA was an extreme act of government sponsored dark magic with no bottom or ceiling to it.

Using 'front' organizations, the CIA research was undertaken at 80 different institutions, including colleges, universities, hospitals, mental hospitals (where one patient in Kentucky was given LSD for 174 consecutive days), and prisons. MK-ULTRA had many sinister overtones. Its main focus was behaviour modification; mind control. The operation used unwitting subjects and many methods to manipulate people's mental states and brain functions, including the surreptitious administration of drugs (including LSD), hypnosis, sensory deprivation, isolation, verbal and sexual abuse and various forms of torture.

Two heavy but well researched books that explore the activities of MK-ULTRA are 'Operation Mind Control' by Walter Bowart (which is now hard to find – perhaps the CIA have been buying up all the copies? – in paperback it costs £39.99 on Amazon, and £448.88 (!) in hardback), and 'Journey into Madness: Medical Torture and the Mind Controllers' by Gordon Thomas. Read either book and then add a further thirty or forty years of CIA dabbling in the area of mind control and you could let yourself in for a paranoid nightmare, where all of your worst imaginings are actually true and barely scratch the surface!

One curious aspect of the MK-ULTRA project involved the author Ken Kesey, who wrote the novel 'One Flew over the Cuckoo's Nest' (written back in 1962, the year I was born). At the Veterans Administration Hospital, when he was a student at nearby Stanford University, Kesey volunteered for the MK-ULTRA experiments that involved taking LSD and other psychedelic drugs such as psilocybin and mescaline.

Afterwards, he formed The Merry Pranksters, who began travelling around the West Coast of America, setting up parties using music and lightshows, along with vats of free orange juice that were laced with LSD (the first rave's?). Kesey and his Pranksters were accompanied by Neal Cassady; the real-life inspiration behind the character of Dean Moriarty in Jack Kerouac's influential novel, 'On the Road'. The Merry Pranksters forged a link between the beatnik generation and the development of the hippie generation. 'The Electric Kool-Aid Acid Test' by Tom Wolfe recounts his time spent with The Merry Pranksters and provides a good insight into the vibe of those times.

At least, in this one instance, MK-ULTRA's operation of mind-control backfired and inadvertently helped to spawn an anti-establishment generation who were willing to challenge the prevalent mind-sets of parents, authorities and governments alike – the Flower Children were born – only to be snuffed out years later by Charles Manson and his 'Family'.

I must admit that I like watching interviews with Charles Manson that have been conducted in prisons over the long years of his imprisonment; I also like music by Manson and The Family. That's not to say I would actually want to spend any time with the fella. I don't know what the toxicology reports are regarding the members of The Family who brutally murdered Sharon Tate and others, but no doubt traces of LSD were in their system.

LSD has continued to be used and abused throughout the decades. Personally, it was an experience I usually enjoyed. It wasn't in my nature to suffer from a bad-trip. The only bad time I had on LSD was a short spell when I began to focus intently on my own heartbeat and became convinced that it was going to stop. It was a bad thing to focus on. I thought I was in a dying process, laughable now, but at the time…

I recall when Mandy had a very strange trip – it was her first one. She spent a good few hours on her hands and knees, moving through the living room and the garden, convinced that she was a sheep. The only words we got out of her during that time were 'Baaaa!' – it nearly drove us mad, she was totally out to pasture!

One night the whole household was tripping and someone saw a cockroach. We began hunting the critter down and in the process we turned the entire house inside out, but we never did find the wee beastie. On another occasion when my housemates had gone out for the night on acid, I stayed home alone, straight, probably writing, but while they were out I found all these weird dolls with long dresses – if you flipped them upside down the dress revealed another coloured pattern and another head. I hung the double-headed dolls by their necks all over the house, from windowsills and from the staircase, very creepy. I'm glad to say that I did manage to freak my house-mates out when they staggered in through the front door – job done.

We used to go out to pubs in Stockton tripping, but some pubs were heavy. You'd be looking around and catch some guy's eyes a couple of times and he'd march over with the usual 'What you looking at?' I saw more than a few people get glassed full in the face for committing such a harmless offence, just because some guy had a chip on his shoulder and wanted to act like a twat. It often proved easier to stay at home, in a more controlled environment, or otherwise we'd go drink in an old people's bar where folk knew how to behave themselves - some old fella would play the piano and people were more relaxed and able to have a laugh and talk about their day, their lives and the messy state of the world.

If ever someone was having a bit of a heavy trip I always had the solution, I'd just put an orange in their hand and say 'Check this out'. Suddenly, they were distracted from whatever demons were assailing them and now they held the orb of the Sun in their hands. If I wanted to mess with them in a fun way, I'd ask them to peel it. Peeling an orange on acid is a cosmic journey in itself; it takes, like, forever – even worse than skinning up or making a roll-up cigarillo.

If I chose to drop some acid I instinctively followed Timothy Leary's basic advice of three simple rules, long before I'd actually heard of them. The rules are simple, but solid advice – Right Place, Right Time, Right People. You don't want to be tripping off your face in a place where you don't feel comfortable and safe. You don't want to be exploring the heavy strata of your psyche if you're feeling depressed or emotionally vulnerable. And you certainly don't want to be tripping with people who you don't trust or who might be prone to picking your mind apart in a negative, unsupportive fashion and hanging you out to dry beneath an alien sun. Three simple guidelines that saved many people from totally freaking out and they are as applicable today as they were in the 60's.

Timothy Leary, who died in May 1996, was an American psychologist who believed in the therapeutic potential of LSD. He also coined the phrase 'Turn on, tune in and drop out'. Leary's research, originally conducted when LSD was still legal and purchased from the Sandoz labs in Switzerland, focused on treating alcoholics and criminals. Many of those who participated reported profound spiritual and mystical experiences which they claimed permanently altered their lives in a positive manner.

During what was known as The Concord Prison Experiment Leary and his associates guided prisoners through a psychedelic experience. In that particular prison the average recidivism rate was 60%, meaning that 60% percent of prisoners would re-offend upon their release and face further incarceration. The recidivism rate in Leary's test group dropped to a remarkable 20%. It wasn't long after that experiment that LSD was made illegal and Leary eventually attracted the attention of the authorities.

During the 1960's and 1970's Leary was arrested many times and held captive in 29 different prisons around the world. President Richard Nixon once described Leary as 'the most dangerous man in America', which seems laughable if one considers the fact that Nixon's government were bombing the shit out of Vietnam at the time. The CIA were also busy smuggling huge quantities of heroin from the Vietnam war-zone back to the USA on what was known as 'Air Opium', with the cynical intent of flooding black neighbourhoods with the addictive drug in an attempt to de-rail the civil rights movement.

The English poet, artist and printmaker, William Blake (1757 – 1827), quite possibly the first creator of a fanzine type magazine, self created and self printed, captured something of the essence of the LSD experience in the opening lines of his poem, 'Auguries of Innocence' –

To see a World in a Grain of Sand
And Heaven in a Wild Flower
Hold Infinity in the palm of your hand
And Eternity in an hour
*

Musicians, writers, artists and drugs and alcohol have always been firm friends. The appearance of new drugs invariably results in new forms of music and literature. You just need to take a brief overview of The Beatles to see how it works. In their early days The Beatles played fast rock'n'roll because they were taking amphetamines. When they later started to experiment with marijuana and LSD they created an experimental soundtrack to accompany their visions, to capture the vibe, the mindset or essence of it all – they used layers of music that seemed to cross, cut-through and transcend or distort time. When John Lennon got into heroin, his productivity took a swift nosedive. Only when he kicked his smack habit did he start creating new songs, touring America and playing every town where budding President to be, Ronald Reagan, was campaigning, and then the FBI started rummaging through his trash and finally Mark Chapman shot Lennon dead outside the Dakota Hotel in New York.

Mark Chapman showed all the signs of having been involved with MK-ULTRA, or a similar mind control project. Despite articles written in the mass media, Chapman wasn't a Beatles fan. He only owned one (!) Beatles record. He was out of work, but $50,000 dollars had recently been put into his bank account by an unknown source. After shooting Lennon several times at close range, the same way a cop is trained to shoot someone, Chapman made no attempt to escape; instead, he continued to read The Catcher in the Rye. Despite the huge success of that novel, the author John Salinger never wrote another book. Sometimes you have to wonder what is really going on and what dark forces are writing this insane script.

Obviously just about every band in the 1960's was experimenting with drugs and in the late 1970's the entire punk scene was fuelled on speed, hence the wide-eyed, gaunt looks and the pale complexions. Then Sid Vicious got into heroin, murdered his girlfriend and later overdosed. Smack is a crap drug. Heroin is a sedative and a soul destroyer. Taking smack is like catching a bus – you know exactly where it's going to take you; nowhere. That old saying of 'never trust is a junkie' is so true. They will lie, cheat and steal to maintain their crap buzz, doing whatever it takes to provide the next fix. I've always tried to be a drug user, not an abuser. I've always tried to be creative if under some influence, otherwise, for me, there's little point in going there in the first place.

When Ecstasy came along, so did a whole new bunch of bands, like Happy Mondays, and the whole rave scene. People just wanted to dance for ten hours at a time. It was an utterly hedonistic scene, like the final months of the Roman Empire, before the inevitable collapse.

Back in the day, the hillbilly's were drinking moonshine in order to reach an altered state and the fact remains that most of the greatest songs ever written and played throughout the history of music would not have been created if people were not dabbling with various substances. The same applies to some of the most pioneering visionary work in both art and literature.

Samuel Taylor Coleridge, the Romantic poet, used opium and in 1797, after taking laudanum and waking from a stupor, he penned 'Kubla Khan'. His addiction killed him in 1834, but it didn't kill his poem. Charles Baudelaire and Alexandre Dumas (The Three Musketeers) belonged to a club called Club de Hachichins; The Hashish Club. Robert Louis Stevenson wrote The Strange Case of Dr Jekyll and Mr Hyde during a six day cocaine binge.

Jack Kerouac was an alcoholic and a Benzedrine (speed) freak when he wrote 'On the Road' in three weeks. It took him a further five years to edit what he'd written and another five years on top of that to find a publisher. Jack drank himself to death. His good pal, infamous beat writer William S Burroughs spent decades addicted to heroin, and like Aleister Crowley and Hunter S Thompson, he probably took every drug known to man.

Sci-fi writer Philip K Dick made intensive use of speed and hallucinogens. Between 1963 and 1964 he produced 11 novels and several short stories. When Stephen King's books dominated the book-charts and he became known as 'The Master of Horror', he was using cocaine and was addicted to it for eight years. He's admitted that he can't recall writing some of his best sellers, such as Cujo; the story of a rabid St Bernard dog.

The influential crime-fiction writer, Raymond Chandler, with his stories about private eye Philip Marlowe, was addicted to alcohol for his entire writing career, during which he managed to produce 23 novels. He also shot himself in the head with a .38, but his suicide attempt failed when the bullet bounced off his skull.

Other writer's addicted to booze include the playwright Tennessee Williams, Dylan Thomas, Edgar Allan Poe, Truman Capote, F. Scott Fitzgerald, James Joyce, Ernest Hemmingway and Charles Bukowski, to name a few. We won't even start with Hollywood actors, producers and directors, nor cops, judges, politicians, soldiers serving in war zones or TV presenters and various vacuous celebrities who are only famous for their liposuction, their breast implants and their sordid publicized affairs.

Drugs also influence the technological world. Steve Jobs, the co-founder and former CEO of Apple Inc. said, *'Taking LSD was a profound experience, one of the most important things in my life.'*

There you have it – no acid, no Apple Mac...perhaps they should have called it the Acid Mac! Why not? Computers have tripped-out the entire world and changed the way that we communicate with each other across the planet. Information on anything you can possibly think of is just a few typed-keys away...it just depends on what kind of information you're looking for.

The internet, like certain drugs, has enlightening aspects, but it also has its dark caves of sickness and depravity. I guess it represents the spectrum of human nature and it feeds and supports whatever habits or interests or beliefs you may have. Things change, but nothing changes...Earth is still a school and we are here to learn, to grow and to become aware, perhaps even catch a glimpse of our own souls and transcend this grand illusion of physical existence and rise up beyond the hologram-matrix that bewitches us all through the river of time. What do we know? Really? What do we know? Could Earth be a farm?

*

After living in the shared house in Richmond Road, Lorraine L suggested we move to another, larger house. Her mother, Dot, owned two properties on Oxbridge Road. She lived in one with her husband Owen - the house was actually an old hotel, and she used it to provide somewhere to live for kids who'd just got out of detention centres, borstals and prison, some of whom were friends of mine. Obviously, Social Security paid their rent as they were all signing on. Dot was very kind hearted and very rarely received any disrespect from her 'tenants' although the local media sometimes rallied against her. Her second property, called The Gables, was just a few streets away, opposite Oxbridge Cemetery. It had a huge Monkey Tree in the front garden and the house had lots of rooms. We agreed to move.

Mandy and I had a living room downstairs, and a bedroom upstairs. Ian I. shared a bedroom with Lorraine L., and a separate living room downstairs. Salla didn't go with us – he moved somewhere else. Instead, Andy M. and Pete M. (the punks I first met when they were hiding in a tree and I was out of my tree), moved in – they had a bedroom each upstairs and shared a third living room downstairs. The Grange was a big space with a large kitchen that we all used, although we never really got it together to cook and eat on a communal level. We set up cleaning rota's and suchlike to keep on top of the place and maintain a semblance of domestic order.

One afternoon I borrowed Lorraine's 8mm movie camera and went walkabout, filming the ICI factory, filming butchers hacking up dead pigs, filming traffic in Stockton high street. I was just curious about film and wanted to have a go, filming random stuff from my day to day ugly surroundings. Two cops stopped me in the street and accused me of stealing the camera. Despite my explanation, they hauled me off to Stockton police station and put me in a cell for a few hours. Later, I was taken to an interrogation room and questioned by a female police officer. She accused me of stealing the camera. I told her who the camera belonged to and gave her a phone number she could call to verify my story. She wasn't interested and kept pushing me to confess. I guess she must have been more stressed out than me because at one point she actually broke down in tears and stormed out of the interrogation room. A minute later a huge sergeant walked in and hoisted me out of my chair. He shoved me against the wall and grabbed me by the throat, telling me that I'd better confess to stealing the camera or he was going to break my face. I stood my ground. He let go of my throat and I was taken back to a cell, where I remained until about four o'clock in the morning. I was released without any charges being pressed against me. Back then there were no night buses, so I had to walk home. The thing about that little incident that galls me the most is that Lorraine received a phone call from the police shortly after I was taken to the station. They asked her if I had borrowed her camera. She told them that I had. When she asked the police if they were holding me, they informed her that they were not. As the night wore on and I remained locked in a cell, she made several more calls to the police, and each time they said they were not holding me. Very strange, yet disturbingly true.

*

One evening there was a knock at the door. I answered and was confronted by two people who said they were Jehovah's Witnesses. Usually when religious zealots, no matter what their religion, knock on my door, I tend to greet them with a foul-mouthed tirade of satanic abuse, making sure that I've booked my seat in hell.

However, on this occasion I decided to play a different sort of game, playing it nice and a little weird. I told the 'witnesses' that I was busy, but I invited them to visit the next evening to share a meal.

The next evening they turned. We sat at the kitchen table and ate a vegetarian curry that I'd prepared, and we discussed their beliefs. They did their best to be nice, but they were severely tested because I was wearing a long blonde wig, clumsily applied make-up, huge clip-on earrings, and a bright flowery dress. All through the meal I was gently doing my best to test their boundaries and to break their minds. I was dressed as a tart, and played my role straight, and inside I was laughing my knickers off. Despite their niceness it was obvious that they couldn't wait to finish the meal and get the hell out of Satan's lair. Fair play to them, they did finish the meal. I wish I'd thought to put magic mushrooms in the curry, and maybe then they might have 'witnessed' something that would really turn them on.

*

One evening everyone in our household went to see Here & Now play at Middlesbrough Town Hall Crypt. We didn't hang together in a group, but rather split-up and attended with other people that we knew. I was selling the last few issues of a fanzine before heading down to London the following week to print Anathema #1.

One afternoon, about two weeks after the Here & Now gig, I was at our house The Grange, when someone banged harshly on the front door. When I answered the door I saw several police officers and instinctively slammed the door shut. While they began to break down the front door I ran around the house alerting everyone that the cops were making a bust. I wasn't smoking marijuana but two or three people who lived there were. As the cops charged into the house some harder drugs, like speed, were tossed out of the windows.

There were about six officers, including an undercover cop who looked like a hippy. Without naming names, two people in our house got busted, essentially because there were about eight or nine cannabis plants growing in the kitchen. Those two people eventually had to go to court and pay a fine, as well as having their names printed in the local papers, causing some consternation for their parents, to say the least.

The undercover cop told me that we had all been under surveillance for a fortnight, ever since the Here & Now gig. He told me that they followed each member of the household for different reasons and they were surprised when they discovered that we all lived in the same place; hence the raid.

There was an officer in a suit, I can't remember his specific rank, but he entered the living room I shared with Mandy and discovered my 500 copies of Anathema #1, hot off the press from Interaction in London. He picked up a copy and waved it in my face, 'So you're the bastard that writes this shit.'

Things started getting a bit heavier as they started to apply the pressure on me. The cop in a suit and a female officer took me upstairs to the bedroom I shared with Mandy. The female office immediately noticed two yellow road lights that I'd picked up on the way home one night – I liked the way they flashed. She told me I could be arrested for stealing them. She also told me they'd found some loose bits of wiring, somewhere in a kitchen cupboard. The cop in a suit said that they could arrest me on suspicion of terrorism! The very idea was insane; here I was publishing fanzines that were anti-war and anti-violence, advocating non-violent demonstrations. The very last thing I would ever wish to do would be to construct a bomb to harm others – and if they knew me they would have known that I could barely wire a household plug. I told them that if they took me to court, I would sell more fanzines than ever before. They eventually backed-off and I didn't even get charged over the two road lights.

Quote from Geoff S. (Tick Tick) from recent communications-

'I've had quite a nostalgic day, listening to old tapes. You've really done me a favour Lee. I've been wanting to listen to them for years but I'm such a soft sentimentalist (I know it's weak and uncool) that I could never face them. I'm sat here drinking beer now and things are coming back to me about events over the years. I remember coming round your house near a bridge in Stockton. Oxbridge? And you had 2 of those flashing lights they used to put on traffic cones on your fireplace. I was with Steve W. and had, had half a tab of LSD that took no effect until we set off home.'

On a final note, as the cops eventually left, a few hours later, I watched the hippie undercover cop from my bedroom window. He had two cannabis plants sealed in plastic bags as evidence, one for each my housemates he was going to prosecute. The remaining plants he put into the boot of his car – was he going to have the dope plants destroyed? Or was he going to take them home where he could continue to cultivate them, before he smoked them and got high? It's an open-ended question that remains after every drug bust.

*

A few months later I did a stupid thing and gave the police another opportunity to have a go at me. I'd been loitering around Stockton High Street all day and then wandered into Tesco's. I didn't buy anything, but I did steal a pack of 3 Cadbury's Crème Eggs. In my mind, I jokingly call this little saga The Crème Egg Conspiracy.

As I left the store I was grabbed by two security guards. The police arrived. I was hauled off, charged, fingerprinted and then spent the night in the cells.

When I appeared at Middlesbrough Magistrates Court, alone because I didn't want to concern my parents, the police prosecutor produced a stack of my fanzines, all purchased by undercover cops at local gigs. The case took a weird turn and instead of the case being about me nicking 3 Crème Eggs it seemed that I was suddenly on trial for writing and producing anti-establishment magazines. I had no legal aid and no-one to represent me. I admit that I was scared.

The police prosecutor's words are firmly etched into my brain as he rapped his knuckles on the stack of my fanzines laid on the bench before him like they were some kind of evidence – evidence of what, I don't quite know, certainly nothing to do with a few lifted chocolate eggs. It was like he was saying 'Your Honour, what we have here before us is a youth who writes and expresses his thoughts, we cannot tolerate this kind of self-expression and as fellow Freemasons we should bang him up and throw away the fucking key!' Anyhow, this is what the police prosecutor actually said in the Crème Egg Conspiracy-

'Mr Gibson produces a magazine which criticises every aspect of society, while offering nothing valid in return.'

For a moment, I thought I was going to disappear for a long time into a black hole, or maybe get dropped far out in the North Sea wearing nothing but a pair of concrete boots, but finally I walked out of Court after receiving a simple £30 fine – ten quid an egg – fr*egg*ing *egg*spensive! But I learned my lesson well - I never shop-lifted again and got caught ;-).

What my writing, some of it so badly spelled I'm embarrassed to read it now, had to do with the case remains a mystery. I couldn't understand why the police regarded my writing as such a threat, unless it was simply the fact that I was asking questions about the nature of authority and I was upsetting someone else's status quo? Maybe I was standing on someone's toes? Maybe inspiring other people to ask awkward questions and to challenge the lies we were being fed? I don't know. But the warning I'd received earlier from Mandy and Vanessa's mum about the police wanting to see me go to prison was definitely beginning to rattle my brain. I began to wonder if maybe it was time to get out of Dodge City and dodge a bullet.

*

Shortly after that I hitched to Bradford to see a few bands. I used to like hitching there as it was only 60 miles or so and I could crash on the floor at Dave's bedsit in nearby Leeds after the gig. The band I intended to see was Southern Death Cult, who later became Death Cult, and then The Cult, who made it quite big. They were supported by The Mob, a band who came from Yeovil. I thought The Mob were the best band of the night and later staggered backstage to tell them so. That's when I first met Mark, Curtis and Josef.

The Mob were a cool bunch of guys and I especially liked the fact that their music was emotive, with good lyrics, and the music they played was outside of the typical fuzz-box, Crass rip-off, punk thrash that was becoming commonplace at the time. I didn't realize it then, but The Mob would continue to randomly criss-cross through my timeline when I eventually moved from North to South.

One evening I received a phone call from Gareth, otherwise known as Billy Oblivion, informing me that he'd received a call from a Tyne Tees TV show called 'Check It Out'; a youth-oriented television series that dealt with 'youth issues', produced twice weekly that ran from 1979-1982. It was one of the very few youth-related programmes on air in the North-East at the time. The programme was produced concurrently with a Tyne Tees music series called 'Alright Now' – the show in which John Lydon became angry at the interviewer's inane questions and walked out of the studio, viewable on You Tube. 'Alright Now' was a forerunner of TV show 'The Tube' that was presented by Jules Holland and Paula Yates.

Billy Oblivion said they wanted to do a feature about the Kiora youth-club that he was helping to run on the tough estate of Hardwick, where The The And had previously played. Mr Oblivion told me that he'd referred them to me as he thought I was doing more interesting stuff. (I attended the wedding when Billy later married Vanessa who first helped me print my fanzines – they have a daughter together, although their marriage later fell apart. His elder brother was one of the punks photographed on the front of the Clash single 'Clash City Rockers', unfortunately he later hung himself and Billy found him.)

Billy Oblivion was/is something of a local character in the Stockton region, tall, lean, witty, educated and well-read. He still does the occasional gig from what I've heard. He's the only guy I ever met who had a copy of Mein Kampf by Adolf Hitler on his bookshelf, but he was never a Nazi, he just liked testing people out. He even had a noose in his room, that kinda guy, flamboyant and funny, heavy make-up and seriously into his clothes, his image and his hats. I have to say that I was very surprised that Billy Oblivion actually deflected a chance to be on TV and bounced it my way. I think he was born for TV; he'd certainly be a hundred times more comfortable with it than I ever would be. In some ways, if I had to give you a snapshot image of Gareth, I would say that he reminds me of Richard E Grant in the film 'Withnail and I'.

When someone from 'Check it Out' called me and asked if I wanted to a section of their TV magazine I said OK, so long as whoever was going to be interviewing me travelled down from Newcastle to spend an afternoon with me, walking the streets of Stockton in order to get to know me a little bit prior to the interview. They agreed and the next day a guy flew down from Newcastle to meet up with me. That seemed funny in itself; a guy doing a 'youth issues' TV show, flying from Newcastle to Teesside to interview a 19 year old kid on the bloody dole.

When he arrived we walked around for a bit, stalking the High Street, cutting through the meat-market, idling alongside the River Tees, then heading to The Dovecot at lunchtime, my favourite bar, where we both got pretty drunk. I figured I might as well, I wasn't getting paid, but at least he was paying for all the drinks! To be fair, the guy who was going to interview me wasn't such a bad fella; I think he was sincere, in his own TV way.

A few days later the lighting and sound technicians, camera crew, interviewer and director turned up at The Grange, setting up their gear in my bedroom (at the same time cranking up our electricity bill), crowding it out. I was very nervous about being in front of the camera, so nervous, in fact, that I was shaking. It took them ages to get me chilled out. I was sitting on a metal trunk and kept tapping my nervous foot against it, pissing-off the soundman. I couldn't stop my nervous tap-tap-tapping and eventually they had to put a cushion between my foot and the metal trunk, then, at last I could talk and go tap-tap-tap at the same time and not piss the sound guy off. I was one twitchy dude – the crew hated me.

The feature was generally about my fanzines and so I explained the whole process of writing, designing, printing and selling them, hoping that it might inspire a few other teenagers to step sideways and do their own thing. That was my only goal regarding the TV thing.

When my mother found out that I was going to do this little thing for TV, she said to me, for some unknown reason, 'Don't mention Maz's death'. That threw me for a loop. Was his death some act of shame? Was dying in a factory, doing what had previously been my job, a crime of sorts? One we shouldn't whisper about? Do working class deaths count for nothing?

Why shouldn't I mention the loss of my friend who died in The Factory? His death has always been my trigger, the bubble in my spirit level when it comes to employers. Why should I let his death go? Why should his death hide in the shadows and be pushed aside and hushed-up like an object of shame? Why not bring it into the light, I thought, even if it was the flickering light of the idiot box – the magic box of TV that MES once referred to as the 'tragic lantern'? Did I mention his death during that interview? Of course I fucking did.

We then did a walkabout and shot stuff of me in Stockton, walking through the meat-market and down by the River Tees. The middle-aged, red-faced, whisky toting director, at one point, asked me to huddle down in the corner of a metal bridge that arched over a main road by the river. He wanted me to look helpless and beaten down, like someone homeless or hope-less, like some kind of sad and wasted junkie – I guess that was part of his 'vision' as a director. I had a bit of a row with him and totally refused to comply. I was already partly cynical about doing this thing and certainly wasn't going to be manipulated. I told him he had the wrong guy. I wasn't about being helpless; I was about standing upright and trying to change things, for the better. The interviewer, who I'd met previously, totally got what I was about, but this director, he didn't have a fucking clue. He knew absolutely nothing about the generation his programme was supposed to be dealing with. That moment really pissed me off, and I thought to myself, never again, these guys are worse than music journalists. I should have thrown that fucking whisky faced director over the bridge – or maybe I should have fed him to my glue-sniffin' mates?

Anyway, the feature got aired and that was my fifteen minutes of fame, all used up, over and done with. Good riddance to that. All said and done, it was not a very enjoyable experience. All it did was stress me out.

*

The following day I received a phone call from a journalist who worked for the Northern

Echo newspaper, asking to do an interview. At first I was a little uncertain, but then I figured 'Why not? The Falkland's war is on.' The journalist said they wanted a photo of me to go with their article. I've never been comfortable being photographed or filmed and so I said no, forget about it. The journalist was rather insistent and we eventually reached a compromise. I said they could have their photograph just so long as they agreed to publish one of my poems in the article. They honoured that part of our agreement, but I thought the finished article played things too soft and contained too many silly factual errors.

A date was set for the brief interview. I dropped some acid the night before and looked suitably knackered-out for their photo the next morning, holding up a copy of Anathema #1 in a Stockton street. It was for my own amusement that they interviewed me on an LSD come-down.

The article appeared in the May 13th edition, 1982. The front page showed a picture of a British soldier from Newcastle who was on active duty in the Falkland's monitoring a heavy machine gun onboard HMS Hermes. The bold headline proclaimed: HOWAY YOU LOT, WE'RE READY.

The bit on me appeared on page 10. Beneath the photo of me holding up my latest fanzine they wrote *'Verbal aggression turns to constructive criticism – Lee with Anathema'*. The bold text title of the article read - *'Angry Lee turns to peace and publishing'*. I mentioned bands like Crass during the interview but they are laughably referred to as a 'pop band'. They also refused to use the word 'fanzine', opting for 'magazine' and 'newspaper' instead. The article is full of inaccuracies, so typical of media fuckers. Doing the press thing seemed as pointless as doing the TV thing. Anyway, for the sake of the record, here's the transcript of the brief article written by Northern Echo journo John North (where is he now?) –

'Lee Gibson is an angry young man. He's an ex-punk, an ex-porter and an ex-tremely frustrated fellow. A victim, he says, of modern society which prepares youngsters for a life of work in a materialistic world, he is currently preaching a gospel of non-violence.

While many youngsters who leave school and find themselves on the dole just want to kick out at the nearest person or object, Lee has found a way of channelling his anger. No matter what time of day or night, when the inspiration hits him he simply pours it all out on paper. And his literary relief valve is helping other young people to cope with their disappointment in a society they say has slapped them in the face.

Lee, 19, of Oxbridge Lane, Stockton, writes, prints and sells his own street-level magazine. It could take him 3 months to prepare the 40 page document, and then many more weeks to sell the copies on street corners or at pop concerts. He makes nothing out of it, but it relieves his pent-up anger.

An amateur poet committed to world peace, to feminism and the fight against cruelty to animals, Lee finds a lot to write about, even if it does wake him up at 3 a.m. He reckons he is typical of youngsters in a society which trains them to work hard at school to get a good job and then gives them no work.

He did serve some time as an apprentice fitter but felt he was being exploited by the factory which could only give him boring work. Weeks after he threw up the job, his best pal took it and was later crushed to death at the factory.

When he did find a job he liked – as a porter at North Tees Hospital, Stockton – he was made redundant in spending cuts.

"I enjoyed the work of helping people so much I offered to work on a voluntary basis. They would not accept me because they prefer older people for that sort of thing."

Lee and his newspaper are to feature in a new Tyne-Tees Television programme for teenagers, Check It Out, which starts on June 3. He has just produced his sixth issue of Anathema and so far each one has been a sell-out.

"My first edition was really crammed full of verbal aggression against anything and anybody. Since then I've learned to channel it into constructive criticism."

Lee used to blame his parents for his ills, but decided it was the fault of society which teaches materialism and not the good of the individual.

"I was so frustrated I could feel the violence in me. Thankfully it never came out as physical violence as it does with many young people."

While following round a pop group he has seen outbursts of violence and written about them. He has written about the exploitation of women through newspaper nudes, and about cruelty to animals in places like abattoirs. He's on the dole, and buys his clothes at jumble sales, but his magazine gives him hope.

"I hope other young people who feel betrayed by the system will see that they can do something for themselves."

Lee summed up his feelings with this poem:

> A child in the walls of flesh,
> Within the womb
> Safe feeding on its mother's blood,
> A smack and a gasp
> Breathing anti-septic air
> Held tight
> Seeking its mother's breast
> Soon reading books
> Well read before
> Educated
> But he does not know what for
> Bullied, ridiculed and compromised
> Beaten into submission
> Acceptance of the lie
> Tricked with ethics
> Morals and standards
> Following the tired worn footsteps
> Of his father
> From the cradle to the grave
> With no laughter in-between.'

*

In 1982 I decided to organize a Crass gig in Middlesbrough to compensate for their last violent gig at Middlesbrough Rock Garden. I wanted to create a better scene. Crass were keen to return to the area and I maintained phone contact with Andy Palmer (Crass guitarist, aka B.A Nana) as I started to set things up. I have to say that Andy was a chilled out guy and he really helped me to get things organized. He knew that I'd never done anything of this sort before, on such a scale, and he really walked me through it. He never laid any pressure on me and when I needed to front money to book a place he sent it straight to me – all based on pure trust – I'm glad to say that I didn't let him down. It did feel strange receiving a cheque from Crass to pay to Middlesbrough town hall Crypt to book the gig, but everything about that gig played true; for me, that was what the whole anarchy-scene was about.

I was determined to set-up a Crass gig that was the very opposite of the bloody Rock Garden fiasco. I wanted it to be a safe place, not just for the band, but more-so for the people who wanted to see them play, and I wanted younger kids to be able to experience Crass as well, stepping beyond the bogus 21-age restrictions of the rock garden, without people getting head-butted in the face because they wanted to see a band play live or because they were cursed to come from the wrong impoverished estate.

I had to find a suitable venue that was controllable, but without bouncers. I had to find a decent sized PA system, and I had to find somewhere for Crass (eight of them), Dirt (four of them), and Annie Anxiety (just one of her) to stay after the gig. Set that little lot up, and then all I had to do was publicize the gig. The latter, I knew, would be the easiest part – word of mouth would quickly see to that – a lot of kids wanted to see Crass, and other bands, but many of them were too young to get into the Rock Garden with its 21 age limit.

For the venue, I needed somewhere that could hold up to 300 people and give access to kids from the age of 15 upwards. I decided to approach Middlesbrough Town Hall Crypt. I found out how much it would be to book the Crypt. I didn't have that kind of money so Crass (Andy Palmer), sent me the money in good faith. I booked the Crypt, along with a PA system. I didn't make a single penny out of that gig, nor did I want to. The gig was my mission, my simple goal. Fuck the violence; let's have a rocking gig where people can be free to switch on.

I then held a little group meeting with my friends who lived at The Gables, some of whom were not overtly keen on Crass, although Andy M. And Pete M. had already travelled all over to see them – they were carpenters so they could afford to travel, not hitch, but they were totally into Crass and Poison Girls. Anyhow, despite musical/political differences, everyone in the house agreed to let Crass, Dirt and Annie stay over for the night and invade our space. Once that was settled, we arranged to have plenty of hot food prepared for them for after the gig and everyone got involved in trying to make it a comfortable and welcoming stay for them. It was a strange time for us all. As for advertising, I designed simple photocopied A4 flyers that I photocopied at Stockton library and stuck them on a few walls, in Green (thanks to the hippy dude who first displayed my poem), and in the HMV, thanks to Blank Frank out of Blitzkrieg Bop. Word spread quickly. Tickets were only £1.25. Half price compared to any gig that was taking place at the Rock Garden at the time. This was deliberate. In my view, the Rock Garden was wrong all over the place – they allowed rampant violence and they over-charged. Stockton and Middlesbrough were in real need of an alternative, safer venue, although most people didn't know it. I thought I'd put on one gig as a light in the right direction. Call me Saint Lee ;-)

The gig took place on April 29th 1982 and sold out, thus all the overheads were covered and the bands got paid for their fuel costs and everything else it entailed getting them from

London to the Boro. We had no security, I just picked out a handful of pals who could look after themselves, pals who were secure enough in themselves that they didn't need to step-out and prove anything, guys who knew how to play it cool and calm things down should anything happen. The crucial thing about the gig is that I opted to have no bar, that way we reduced the chances of sporadic violence, and more importantly, younger kids could get in to see the bands play and pogo to their hearts content.

For me, the fact that there wasn't a single fight or act of violence throughout the entire gig made it a successful venture. All those phone calls to Andy Palmer on a pay phone and the basic energy it took to make it happen made it worthwhile. I've never organized many gigs, but usually when I've made the effort, they have rocked.

After the gig, when Crass, Dirt and Annie piled into The Grange there were people everywhere. We had food prepared for them and it was a fun and friendly night, if a little chaotic, especially in the morning as we only had one large bathroom.

The next morning, the band's drove off to their next gig, no doubt also organized by someone else like me – that's how Crass tours worked; it was the only way that they could happen.

*

Shortly afterwards my relationship with Mandy started to fall apart. I began drinking more than usual and one day, Dot, Lorraine's mum (who owned The Gables and the place next door that housed kids just released from detention centres), grabbed hold of me by both hands and told me it was time that I got out of there. I was quite stunned as I thought I was hiding my inner turmoil – but Dot saw right through me, like my emotional field was made of glass. She was very insistent – like something out of The Shining. I call her psychic – she saw my stress – she saw the solution – I ended up following her guidance.

A few days later our house phone rang (it was a pay phone by the front door). The call was for me. It was London Calling, to coin a Clash phrase. Actually, it was Dot's son, Martin L., whom I'd never met before. He asked me if I wanted to take a job in the hotel where he worked in Queensway, London, near Hyde Park. That phone call stunned me, and despite the fact that I'd never considered the idea of moving down South, on a whim, I said 'Yeah, OK.' And so, due to the hidden hand of Dot's influence, I moved to Das Kapital – The Big Shitty – Rat City - London.

Part Two:
Fanzine Interviews

With

MARK E SMITH (Middlesbrough Rock Garden)
POISON GIRLS (Mail-cassette recording)
CRASS (Dial House, Epping)
ANDY T. (Rochdale)
POISON GIRLS (Leytonstone, East London)

The following interviews (time capsules) are from various issues of my fanzines. As I don't possess a single copy of any of the 13 'zines I produced, essentially due to moving around so much and being homeless and squatting, I've had to find them on line and download them. Surprisingly, I managed to find about five of them, but not in their entirety – from what I've read, people cut bits out of my fanzines and stuck them on their walls, back in the day, hence, the following interviews are extracts of what has managed to survive across the years.

The way I look at it, better something than nothing...and it's weird how so much of what is discussed here is still relevant...

I've inserted lyrics from some of the songs mentioned during the interviews in order to break it up a bit, and also to illustrate the attitudes, talents and vibes of the very different, talented and highly individual people I spoke to, hopefully bringing their angles into the light once more – or at least bringing their natural light into new angles.

I was just a teenage kid at the time...forgive me for my sins.

INTERVIEW WITH MARK E SMITH (THE FALL)
MIDDLESBROUGH ROCK GARDEN
15th NOVEMEBER 1980
PUBLISHED IN 'PROTESTING CHILDREN MINUS THE BONDAGE' FANZINE #2 AND 'ANATHEMA' #1

As arranged by previous correspondence this interview took place after the gig. I was assisted by Gary Widdowfield, guitarist in local band Tick Tick, who supported The Fall that night. (As I've been told, I recorded the Tick Tick set that night but somehow managed to smother my favourite song by them by accident; 'Ha-ha-hand, Ho-ho-over – Fist!' For that sin I do apologise.)

Me and Gary were both a bit drunk and we launched into Mark E Smith at the same time. Mark was wired – speeding - and it didn't take long for him to step up and step forward and tell us what he thought – I think we were all wrecked but I also think some real truths are exposed in our rambling conversation. I have to say, Mark was courteous, funny, engaging, and sincere. He looked us in the eye and he would not back down – he was a great fella to chat with. He spoke from the heart, and his bullshit detector was turned on to the max -

Gary: There are people who discuss major issues in their songs, then there's you, The Fall, you do stuff like 'Fiery Jack'. Why do you choose that style?
Lee: To me, I think of Fall songs, there's the type, like you said, 'Fiery Jack', others mainly about dope, like 'Rowche Rumble', and then there's 'Popstock' and 'Printhead'. You're either about dope or anti-rock'n'roll, the rest, I can't really relate to.
Mark: Er…yeah…well, I don't know really, I don't know what you're getting at. I just wanna write stuff, stuff that will really stand up. The stuff I write should be like, I think it should be heart stuff. It should be stuff that lasts as writing, not as reading or you say it like a poetry book, but stuff that is happening to me and is happening all over.

YOUR HEART OUT
Just take for instance
a time of great depression
Fade out of reason
bad time's in season
Don't shut your heart out
Don't cry your eyes out
Don't cry for me, Mexico

Or Savage Pencil

I'm nearly healthy
And they try to take my eyes out
Friends try to work my soul out
But I don't sing, I just shout
Heavy clout, heart out
Now here's a joke
to cheer you up:
Old times no surgeon
Just magicians and dungeons
There they take your heart out
with a sharp knife
It wasn't fake
They had no aesthetic.
That joke's pathetic.
Just look at me
Too much speed
But very plain
You're lucky, friend.
You've got one to take out
You know what I'm talking about!
I don't sing I just shout
All on one note.
Sing, sing, sing, sing
Look at me, I just ding

Mark: You know, like a lot of our stuff is pathetic, man, like 'Witch Trials' stuff. We did that in '78, most of the fucking bands are churning that out now, the depressive stuff like 'Frightened' and the poppy stuff with the keyboards. I was doing that years ago, and 'Dragnet' is the same, all these bands coming up two years after we've done it, not that that makes any difference. If I write a thing that sounds similar to a thing I've written earlier I rip it up. I'm always looking for new subjects. The only thing to do is strive in your music and in your lyrics, strive, not like fuckin' fancy work, but strive and keep it turning over so you're always turning up new things. I met a load of guys from Perth last night and they were really into the 'Witch Trials' period. They got a mini-bus to come see us in Edinburgh and I had a really good rap with them, like they were saying that 'Totales' album really fuckin' puzzles us, and that's it, and 'Dragnet', that's really bad production, and I said yeah, it's making you tick over and that's all you can do, I mean, that's the point of it. If people like you, it doesn't mean anything. People like loads of bands and it goes on, but people go, like…this really freaks me out, I don't understand why they've done this…it's making people tick over and that's its worth. It's proved its point already.

FRIGHTENED

Someone's always on my tracks
In a dark room you see more than you think
I'm out of my place, got to get back
I sweated a lot, you could feel the violence
I've got shears pointed straight at my chest
And time moves slow when you count it
I'm better than them, and I think I'm the best
But I'll appear at midnight when the films close
Cause I'm in a trance
and I sweat
I don't want to dance
I want to go home.
I couldn't live in those peephole places
They might get to know my actions
I'd run away from toilets and faeces
I'd run away to a non-date on the street
Cause I'm in a trance
and I sweat
I don't want to dance
I want to go home.
I feel trapped by mutual affection
And I don't know how to use freedom
I spend hours looking sideways
to the time when I was sixteen
Cause I'm in a trance.
I'm frightened.
Amphetamine frightenedI go to the top of the street
I go to the bottom of the street
I look to the sky, my lips are dry....

Lee: Another thing I wanted to know; when you release a single, I don't know if it's intentional or not, but you wouldn't take a single from an album, like the UK Subs do and bands like that. Then all of a sudden you release a live album…fair enough, it's live, so it's different, but why didn't you put all new tracks on it?

Mark: As you say, I don't want to become predictable. On 'Totales Turns' loads of people sort of said…fuckin' hell, The Fall, the guys who don't put singles on albums are bringing out…but I mean, 'Totales Turns' was an album of atmosphere. It took us an hour to compile. I didn't pick out all the stuff that sounded good. I picked the stuff that sounded interesting. 'No Xmas' on that album is about the worst 'No Xmas' we've ever done, but I thought it was interesting, that's the point of it, bringing out stuff that's interesting. You've got the fuckin' power to release records and that's when you should start fuckin' doing things like that, not going, oh yeah, this is a lovely version of 'Xmas', even better than the recorded one, put that on. 'Totales' was a document. Live albums stink and that was the point of 'Totales Turns'. If you want a live album, here's a fuckin' live album. That struck me with the P.I.L. thing…I've only heard one side of it, but it sounds to me as though the bass has been done in the studio, overdubbed, you know? It's very neat, but 'Totales' was just like bleauuurgh! The first side of 'Totales' was the worst gig we've ever done, even worse than tonight.

Lee: Did you actually play working men's clubs?

Mark: Yeah, that's the attitude behind it. As I was saying for 'Totales', I had loads of tapes and I even had arguments with the band about that, like from Middlesbrough Rock Garden last year we had some great versions of 'Fiery Jack' and 'No Xmas' on cassette and the band wanted to put them on and I said no, it's not worth it, you've already released 'No Xmas' and it was OK, so bring out a version that's urgh.

NO XMAS FOR JOHN QUAYS

The x in x-mas is a substitute crucifix for Christ
No Christmas for John Quays
The powders reach
And the powders teach
And when you find they can't reach
There is no Christmas for junky
He thinks he is
More interesting
Than the world
But buying cigs
Puts him in a whirl
A packet of three-five fives
555
A packet of those over there
And 20 special offer cigars
Found talking to the cigarette machine
Into nicotinic acid
Good king Wenceslaus, he looked out
Silly bugger, he fell out
He spits in the sky
It falls in his eye
Then he gets to sit in
Talking to his kitten
And talking about Frankie Lymon
Tell me why is it so?
Tell me why is it so?
Out of his face with The Idle Race
Out of the room with his tune
Although the skins are thin

He knows its up to him
To go out or stay in
I'll stay in
I'll stay in
You
Me

Lee: One thing I've noticed in the media and stuff like that is most Fall reviews of gigs and records seem dead favourable. You seem to have a few friends in the press. They put half a page on what they think you are, and the last couple of single reviews have said stuff like…This for The Fall is I hope a hit.
Gary: Well, I don't know, 'Elastic Man' in Sounds.
Mark: Oh, yeah, we've had a few bad reviews.
Lee: But ninety-nine percent of them seem to be in favour of you.
Mark: I know what you mean, but I think that's because they're frightened of us; the press.
Gary: I think there's a lot of people who hate you.
Mark: They do. Sounds, they're really down on us. McCullough's started disliking us and there's nobody in Sounds who fuckin' likes us. It's really funny. It doesn't matter to me, but the press, I'm sure of it, I'm sure a lot of it's 'cos they're frightened of us. I mean, they can't fall us for anything (laughs). No way are we gonna get it together as stars, that's the way we are, it's true. Even if we were millionaires I don't think we'd come over like that. So you don't get into the old British thing of build 'em up to knock 'em down. They can't fuckin' do that. They can't say, oh yeah, The Fall said this three years ago and now they're on a big label. We haven't gone on a big label.
Gary: It's not that sort of material, really.
Mark: What we're trying to do now is get out of the Rough Trade angle, but we all know about Rough Trade, we all knew before they did. A lot of press are frightened of us and I think it's really good. If you ever notice our bad reviews you'll see they're really confused, we get a lot of bad stuff like that lately.
Lee: I think the same applies to Crass.
Mark: Yeah, Crass are really like that.
Lee: What do you think of Crass?
Mark: I don't agree with the political things, but I think the music is great. I really love the cheap way they use the drums and that. I read an interview with Gary Bushel, did you see that in Sounds?
Lee: Yeah, ripped-off from fanzines.
Mark: That was really good. We used to play with Crass years ago. We got on with them really well but they got into this anti-bomb stuff. You get fuckin' guys throwing glasses at us and they've got Crass on their fuckin' backs, so you sort of go,' Crass, eurghh', but you meet them and they're great. I mean, I won't live on a commune or anything like that. I'm dead anti-socialist, me, but I think it's great the way they've done it without any fuckin' help, no record company help. It's an amazing phenomenon really.
Gary: It is, 'cos kids, it might be due to a fashion, you know, but it's worked, that's the point.

Mark: Yeah. If you go round where I live, you see 'Crass', you know, I mean it's not Crass who've done it, it's the kids who are into it and it's good. And their stuff, they're really honest when they record a live album. I mean, I think the lyrics are really funny sometimes. It's like Black Sabbath, when I listen to Black Sabbath, I like listening to Black Sabbath now and again, they're so honest in a way, they are laying their heart on the line (laughs), Crass are like that, you know?

Lee: One thing I noticed, that disappointed me when Crass played here, was you could see these kids with Crass armbands on, y'know? Paying more for a designer Crass armband than they did to get in here, and they are getting exploited by the cash merchants. Crass can see these kids, but they don't do anything about it. If that was me and they had things on with our band's name on it I would say what the fuckin' hell are you wearing that for? Talk to me and get involved, not just get ripped-off by someone, but Crass didn't say anything and I was pissed-off with that. How would you feel if they started selling Fall silk scarves and things?

Mark: Yeah, we try and get away from things like that, but there's not much you can do about that. You can see, especially with Crass, that's one of the faults if you go with an independent label and you disregard the press, so, I mean, Crass aren't going to have guys working for them, they're not gonna pay guys just to do their t-shirts and badges. Like, Adam Ant is really getting into all that stuff now, controlling it. If Crass saw, like we did, and don't associate with all that shit, then you get some sharp guy, you can go to them guys and say, like we have, say 'You're making Fall t-shirts and Fall badges, fucking stop it', right, but they say 'OK, we'll stop it', and they do, but people are buying them.

Gary: Can you control it or what, though?

Mark: It's like everything else. It's like you can't really knock fuckin' Top of the Pops, 'cos people are into it. The top twenty wouldn't exist if people stopped buying singles. This is where I disagree with Crass and The Pop Group, and people like that, you can't knock everything 'cos the people are into it. It's no use saying the bands are full of shit, this is what puts me off bands, bands are always going 'Its the record companies and it's the business' and all this fuckin' shit, 'cos they couldn't operate if the bands didn't co-operate, could they? I mean, could they?

PRINTHEAD

Hey badges tinkle
T-shirts mingle
Hey you horror-face!
I'm a printhead
I go to pieces
I'm a printhead
I go to pieces yeah
End of catch-line
End of hook-line
We had a two page
It's what we needed
I'm an ill head

My face increases
How my head increases
Real problems, biz
So how is it, yeah
That I've reached here
I thought this game
Would do me good
How could printed vinyl bring you out to here?
We laughed with them
When it was take-the-piss time
I'm no egghead
But I'm an ex-worker man
W.C.-hero friend - and not water closet!
There's a barrier between writer and singer
Uh-huh he's a good man
Although a lazy one
The singer is a neurotic drinker
The band little more than a big crashing beat.
Instruments collide and we all get drunk
The last two lines
Were a quote, yeah
When we read them
We went to pieces
We went to pieces, yeah
We went to pieces, yeah
Regularly
One day a week
I'm a printhead, yeah
Twenty pence a week
Dirty fingers
Printhead X 3
With print you substitute an ear
For an extra useless eye

Lee: I believe in bands trying to set up their own labels.

Mark: You have to have a lot of capital, I mean, we've never done it, we've fuckin' been poor. Rich bands, it's always rich punks who set up independent labels you find.

Lee: We've been thinking of a flexi-disc, three songs on one side.

Mark: It's a fuckin' hard thing to do. I've always been dead cynical about the independent scene. I always was from knowing The Buzzcocks. That new album was financed by Pete Shelley's dad. To claim that was like proletarian to the fuckin' movement is crap, all independent bands means is they've got loads of brass. You notice all the working class bands sign up to the big labels, you can't blame them. UK Subs and Echo and the

Bunnymen. They've got to do it or they starve, which is what we went through, but we're in a position now where we sell enough through independents to eat off. But it took like a year of hardships. I'm not going to whine about it, but it did. You gotta stick by and not take money that you haven't earned, which is what the record companies do. They give the bands loads of money and they're continually in debt, like, when you're in debt to someone you do as you're told or you're taken to fuckin' court.

Lee: And you get manipulated.

Mark: Right, yeah, all those bands who get £100,000 advances, Teardrop Explodes, U2, and that, I think they're good but they're destroyed by going round the country and playing to a hundred people who really wanna see them, and the more they tour, they have all the roadies and the PA crew, the more they're getting into debt, and the more they've gotta make a good single, the more they've gotta make a smooth album. It just escalates; you can see how it happens.

Lee: Why don't you put the lyrics in with your albums?

Mark: I think it takes a bit of the fun out of it.

Gary: That's right. I've listened to somebody and I've seen an LP with the lyrics and it's been pretty disappointing. When you listen to a record, you look at them anyway and you think 'Oh yes, so and so, so and so', you lose it.

Mark: Yeah, you're not listening really, are you? There's loads of kids write 'I like that verse', and they write this verse out and it's totally different to what you wrote and you think 'Fucking hell, that's great!'. I mean, it's really good, the things that they're coming out with, people are ticking over.

Gary: You should write back.

Mark: Yeah, write back and say your lyrics are great (laughs).

DICE MAN

I am the dice man
And I take a chance, huh
Do you take a chance, huh?
Where you two going?
Where you two going?
Is this a branch on the tree of show business?
Do all these musicians
Have a social conscience?
Well, only in their front rooms
But I am the dice man
And I take a chance man
Do you take a chance, huh?
They stay with the masses
Don't take any chances
End up emptying ashtrays
But I push, push, push, push
Throw the bones and the poison dice

No time for small moralists
Cos I am the dice man
And I take a chance, huh
Do you take a chance, fan?
They say music should be fun
Like reading a story of love
But I wanna read a horror story
Where are you people going?
Where are you people going?
Is this a branch on the tree of show business?
But I am the dice man
A balls-on-the-line man
Do you take a chance, baby?

Gary: When you were on Step Forward, you did that 'two steps back', was that some kind of a jive at them or not? Step Forward (Records) and two steps back.
Mark: No.
Lee: Have you been offered any big money deals by CBS or anyone like that?
Mark: Virgin were after us at around 'Witch Trials' time.
Gary: It's quite amazed me how The Fall have got on commercially, really, 'cos at the start I thought you were pretty vague, nothing really. It's just developed.
Lee: Do you think you'd enjoy it as much if you caught on, like, say Crass?
Mark: There's a bit of a buzz about us again, there always is.
Gary: The Fall are quite like Crass at the moment. You had a big audience here tonight for one thing.
Mark: At Leeds the other night people were queuing outside, and for Leeds, we fuckin' hate the place, we've hardly played there. The guy was saying they had twice as many people as they've ever had, fuckin' weird. It don't bother me, I think there was more people here tonight than last year. It's funny how people are influenced, there again, it's the people's fault, it's funny how they are influenced by a little snippet in T-zers or an album review. It will make them go to a gig. We played Edinburgh last night to 600 people, double we've ever played in Edinburgh and we've played there a lot. They just sat staring and then went fuckin' crazy
when we went off; it was suspicious, more chance taking than tonight was.
Gary: How do you decide these concerts to play? Why come here again? Last year, I didn't think it was that favourable.
Mark: We still need to do gigs to eat as well, you know? We do need the bread. This is where I fall out with the left-field bands. I'm not into that, like PIL and The Pop Group, they always play London and they play fucking Birmingham and they never go to asshole places where people just get into it.
Gary: It's a joke when you go to these places and it's half a laugh, do you have half a laugh?
Mark: Well, it was pretty intense tonight. It was fuckin' really heavy, especially going round the pubs tonight and seeing all the kids there, seeing what they were into.

Lee: I enjoyed the gig, but not the crowd.
Mark: It was the whole atmosphere, the whole town was like that, and I mean I'm not going to fuck-off from it. Like the Liverpool bands, I'm not trying to knock Liverpool, but they just piss off down fuckin' south. It's dead easy playing the south.
Lee: Yeah, like we're both in local bands and we do gigs around the area and you find you're playing to the same old faces, but those people really care about what you're doing.
Mark: Yeah, it's right, that. That's how we started out. We just played Bury and Blackburn and Chorley, and we still do. It's worthwhile doing stuff like that. You go into some towns that are a bit out of touch and they appreciate anything so they're dead receptive. I mean, like tonight, that's why it was so different to a year ago. Now they've been taught about ska and skinheads, like you say, they've been avenued. Like a year ago they were just into the music and they're dead receptive, I always did dig that, it's great. I mean, we played Chorley, which is a real mill town, the people are all into Bread and things like that and everybody looks the same in the family and it's fuckin' amazing, like we were going 'Ahh, a fuckin' witch town'. We thought they were all going to be into Crass and try and kill us and things like that, but they were great, there was old fellas there just into rock music, you shouldn't leave people out like that, it's easy for people like PIL to say 'Fuck it'.
Lee: We did a few benefit gigs and one for Oxfam. I like the idea of giving the money away sooner than get it myself.
Mark: Oh, I think that's a load of crap, really.
Lee: Also, if we got a record out, I'd be happy breaking even.
Mark: Well, why not earn money out of what you do, what you put into things, why not earn money? This is where the record companies really screw bands, 'cos bands say 'I'm just into the fuckin' music', it's crap.
Lee: Well, that's one thing I like about Crass, they seem to have brought record prices really down.
Mark: That's a good thing, like, you gave the money to Oxfam, it's not going to the starving kids. Like the anti-nuclear thing, you do a gig and earn £200, that goes towards secretaries booking more bands, and anti-nuclear badges, it's a waste of money. Musicians are really hungry. I think that's why music's in a bad state. There's bands who would give their left arm to go on stage and the club owners know that all the way along. People say why don't we play Glasgow, 'cos the Glasgow club owners are criminals who are used to getting half-famous bands down for say £60, get loads of kids in for two quid a head, making loads at the bar, 'Fuckin' hell, yeah! I'm really into rock music!' I won't go out of my house unless I'm going to break even. I'm not going to risk getting bottled and all that shit, just to break even. I'll do it if it's like a youth club in Chorley, but I'm not going to do it for some club cunt so he can make a load of fuckin' money on the bar, which is why we went on at half-eleven tonight. They treated us like shit. Stuck us in a little room. I'm wise, I'd rather the populous reject me than be a fuckin' party to it, d'you get me drift?
Gary: Welllllll…
Mark: You've got to think about these things after a while. The Pop Group would play here for £50 if the guy rang them up. They think they're causing a revolution. Crass fuckin' played here, man, what kind of a revolution is that? I went to see Crass in Manchester and there was

a load of skinheads and national Front there, getting in for 40p. You go down to the lowest common denominator and you get the lowest common denominator. There's the PIL attitude, which is like charge a load and rip the bastards off they're all stupid, which I don't agree with. There's the Crass attitude of which is like every dick in the street is like a great person, which is a load of crap as well.

Lee: When you first started off in The Fall, did you have any aims? Did you get into a band thinking I wanna do this or I wanna do that? Or did you get into a band thinking I wanna be on stage, or was it a mixture of both?

Mark: It was both really. I was writing. I was a really frustrated person, a bit of a trouble maker, believe it or not.

Gary: The things you go for now are different though, aren't they?

Mark: Yeah, they are. I mean him saying, I started off like that, thinking like that, why doesn't everyone play for nothing, but I've always been pretty cynical all through my life. I think you've gotta be your own judge, your own fuckin' man, and that's the only answer you've got. What other people think is irrelevant.

Gary: It's purely chance how you get there though, isn't it?

Mark: Yeah, it's all fuckin' luck.

PART ONE OF AN INTERVIEW WITH POISON GIRLS BY POST/CASSETTE OCTOBER 1980 PUBLISHED IN 'PROTESTING CHILDREN MINUS THE BONDAGE' FANZINE #2

(This interview was done after a violent Poison Girls/Crass gig at Middlesbrough Rock Garden – the band members present for the interview, done in my absence, were Vi Subversa (vocals/guitar), Richard Famous (vocals/guitar), and Lance D'Boyle (drums, backing vocals and creator of the Poison Girls magazine 'Impossible Dream'.), and Nil (a long term friend and collaborator with the band).

Lee: Comparing your lyrics with 'Closed Shop' through to your album 'Chappaquiddick Bridge', they seem a lot better now. What inspires you to write a song?

Lance: For me it's not so much a matter of inspiration but of finding a way to say something. I write a song if I find a way to say something which is difficult to write about or think about clearly.

Vi: Since I've got a place to write songs for, it's like finding a voice, and for me it's to do partly, and quite importantly, to do with finding a way to use that voice. To me, it's like daring to say things that I haven't been able to say before, and what they're about depends…'The Bremen Song' was written because that thing was lurking very deep for a long time and something triggered it off, a TV documentary meant that it would be a thing called a holocaust and people were aware suddenly and I could work with that, and 'Jump, Mama Jump' was to do with the real instance, about getting my own kids to school on time, well, not getting them to school on time, but the energy for it. I don't know about inspiration, but the energy for it comes from feeling that I've got a chance, a medium, a vehicle to use and just finding a way to dare to use it.

Richard: I think our songs have always been real, even when we first started. It was impossible for us to write 'She loves you, yeah, yeah, yeah.

Vi: Yeah, but then, I mean, I want to be able to write, you know, 'She loves you, yeah', and those sort of lyrics are right for eighteen year olds to write about, but they're not right. It feels like it requires a bit of cheek for somebody like me to write a song like that, but one of these days I will, and…er…is any of this going to be censored?

STATEMENT
I denounce the system that murders my children

A PUNK ROCK FLASHBACK

I denounce the system that denies my existence
I curse the system that makes machines of my children
I reject the system that makes men of machines
I reject the system that turns bodies of my own sweet flesh
Into monsters of iron and steel and war
And turns the hands of my children into robot claws
I reject the system that turns the hearts of my children against this earth
I curse the system that turns the genitals of my children
Into factories of fire and destruction and rapes our flesh
and tears our womb, this earth our home

There are no words, for us no words

When the fireball rapes the flesh of the earth
When the fireball tears the womb of the world
When the bullet rips apart the son and the lover
When the bullet rips apart the son and the lover
Lays to waste the womb-work and the labour
Where are they that will cherish my flesh
Where are they that will cherish my children
The men that will stand against the death-dealers
The children who can say no to the life-stealers
Where are they that will curse the death -dealers
I denounce the system

There are no words for us no words

Rooted in pain they sell their own flesh
Rooted in pain they do anything for money
They deal in death with minds that feed on hate
In fear of life they kill without pity
In fear of love they wound and they rape
In fear of love they rape without pity
Where are they that will cherish my flesh
Where are they that will cherish my children
The men that will stand against the death-dealers
I denounce the system

There are no words for us no words

Only a curse leaps from my throat
Only a curse leaps like blood from my throat
To curse the warlords that lay to waste our labour

That lay to waste the womb-work and the labour
That lay to waste the womb-work and the labour
That lays to waste
That lays to waste
waste... waste...
waste... waste...
waste

Lee: On 'Hex' you mainly sing about domestic life. Have you ever lived like that, or is it all based on observation?

Vi: Well, that was specifically directed to me and I've got two dreadful children, and yes, it's all really real. 'Jump, Mama Jump' was real. Actually, I suppose you're talking about 'Under the Doctor' 'cos that is the one that most people seem fascinated about. Did I really have a nervous breakdown? Did I really get ECT (electro-convulsive-therapy)? I did have a nervous breakdown one time, but I've never had ECT, but I could have done, and it's always there, isn't it? It's a sort of option. You go along and you get dealt with and it would be so nice and it's like getting a pram and being wheeled around again and getting someone to change your nappies for you, and no, I've never actually given up to that extent, but I know what the pressures are towards it and I reckon everybody does!

Richard: The thing I noticed about that question about 'Crisis' was 'did' you ever live like that? As though it's a thing of the past and I don't think you're the only one who thinks like that. We all live like that and we still do live in that environment that's described in that song.

Vi: Yeah, we don't want to eliminate the subjects involved that we write about biologically.

Richard: It's a victory, a sort of victory in living like that and somehow not to live like that.

Vi: Yes, well, except for the way that we live now, for me, is very definitely a part of reacting to the established norms of how you live and that it was very difficult, just myself and two small children in isolation, which I did do for a while, and now we're all living together. Those of us that do now stems directly from me wanting to break out of that isolation with small children. All that means is that we all share the crisis but it's not half as fucking heavy as to try and do it on your own.

Richard: I think there's an assumption that the quality of what we're talking about in 'Hex' is just to do with our home and it definitely isn't. It's happening on the streets. It's happening in the supermarket. Well, you know, we go to supermarkets like everyone else and you're there all lined up with rows and rows and rows of sweets, cakes and junk food and really anti-septic environments, and that's as much a part of the domestic stuff as the sort of crisis you have to get through to maintain those sorts of places.

Vi: What do you mean by crises you have to get through?

Richard: Well, I mean all the EEC's, or the Common Market stuff, and the whole political situation at the moment is in such a state because you can't actually sustain the sort of lifestyle you're being forced to live.

Vi: That's very much what the song 'Crisis' is about. It's an attempt to find poetic, if you like, images, linking sounds and violence from the streets outside with our terror inside the house, trying to make that kind of link, that the isolation and the inspiration of the domestic situation is precisely because of the crisis that's manufactured outside and vice versa, and we're controlled in isolation in domestic units for the basis to be marketed to and it's a situation that is in itself in a state of stress, the marketing situation is in stress and so the stress spreads right through the whole structure of society so that the individual person, the marketing molecule, you-me, you know, inside our little wood worm orifice is in stress itself, the whole timber's in stress.

CRISIS

Is it normal is it normal - Is it just another day
Have they emptied out the rubbish - Have the kids gone out to play
Are you waiting while the bath fills up - Watching while they read the papers
Read the headlines over breakfast - Breadlines deadlines has the milk come
It's time to have a crisis - Is it safe to go out shopping
Crisis crisis panic buying - Water dripping on the carpet
Is it normal is it normal - Is it just another day?
Are you waiting while the bath fills up - Watching while they read the papers
Have the shops ran out of rubbish - Is it time to have a crisis
Spill the beans - And take your clothes off
Can you stand it if I touch you - Watching while they read the papers
Water dripping on the carpet - Can I say no will he hit me
Plaster falling off the ceiling - Can you stand it if I touch you
Break the ice burn the house down - Is it normal is it normal
Is it safe to go out shopping - Leave the kids outside the
Toilet water dripping on the carpet - Leave the kids outside the local
Strangers tapping at the window - Is it time to have a crisis
Watching while they read the papers - Peel the onions ask no questions
Hit the baby stop it screaming - Can you stand it if I touch you
Break the ice and burn the house down
Normal Normal Crisis Crisis
Normal Normal Rape Crisis
Normal Crisis Normal Crisis
Crisis Murder Normal Normal
Is it normal is this normal - Is it just another day?

Lee: From what I gather, Poison Girls, along with Crass, seem to identify themselves with punk. To me, punk became corrupted ages ago. Why do you associate yourselves with such an exploited tag?

Richard: I don't think we've ever labelled ourselves with a punk tag, so that's not true. I mean, other people have said that we are a punk band.

Vi: yeah…it's not as easy as that to dismiss it as that for me. I mean, I agree that punk has, as a kind of movement, been corrupted and commercialized, but the spirit or the essence or whatever of punk is one that I do embrace and always have done, even before the word was coined, and it was easy for us to identify with it and to come in with the tide that punk came in on, we couldn't come in any other way and I think it would be unreal to reject it out of hand just as a tag. It's not just a tag. The corruption you're talking about in the question is what sees it as a tag. The actual impulse behind the punk spirit is permanent, dare I say, immortal.

Nil: What is the impulse behind the punk movement?

Vi: Well, you look at the dictionary definition of rubbish, prostitute, rotting wood, and that's it, isn't it? That which is not conforming to respectable morals of civilization, that which farts in the drawing room, that which recognizes that we're all animals really and not part of the machine. I don't think we're ever gonna be totally degraded, impulse, in itself, can't be degraded.

Richard: There's two things, isn't there? There's punk as a fashion, and punk started off as a fashion and has got less and less of an elite fashion, but there was something real that happened in that time, '77 or whenever it was, which we recognize by being a part of at that time. By maintaining our independence, I think that's the only way we can avoid actually going back into a situation like there was before.

Vi: I think the word comfort is quite relevant, and what you're talking about, pre-punk fashion, or whatever, was when it got so bloody comfortable and so everyone got off on itself, it's so masturbatory, or whatever, that it became decadent, or in itself decadent and the energy went out of it, and nobody was bothering to say anything and it was comfortable. The punk thing was an awakening, and that's to do with not settling for comfortable values. I don't see how anyone can settle for comfortable values anymore. What comfortable values can there be when the likelihood of a nuclear blow-up is 5% greater every week? How can we settle for comfortable values? The only way to do that is say, 'Well, let's all do what we like best until we die'. Even that ain't easy, what with the price of things today. (laughs)

Lance: The way I relate to it is in terms of my imagination, or witnessing the way everyone's imagination works. Imagination is a weapon which you can use to liberate yourself and be able to do what you want to do and be who you want to be. It seems to go in cycles – the start of the hippie movement, the start of the psychedelic movement, the start of rock'n'roll and The Beatles were all periods when imaginations were awakened. People started to do things that were different, talking about different ways of living and experimenting with them and growing up different to the way their parents did. Then it seems to expand and grow into something, and then it turns into a cliché and it dies. People start to make money out of it. People start to use the style of it, while not even understanding the content of it, without relating to why or where it came from.

STATE CONTROL & ROCK'N'ROLL

State control and rock and roll are run by clever men
What they sell is selling very well and the price is up again
State control and rock and roll are run by clever men
What you know is what they show so it all goes round again

State control and rock and roll are run by clever men

Politics are ultra chic and wars are in again
State control and rock and roll are run by clever men
Revolution's this year's thing we're on the streets again - and again

State control and rock and roll are run by clever men
It's all good for business they're in the charts again - and again
State control and rock and roll are run by clever men
They build you up and they break you down
Then you're on the dole again and again

You know it's true but what can you do
Look for a gap and get out of the trap
It's a vicious circle try and break loose
Break out of the trap
Get out of the noose
You know it's true but what can you do
Cos what you're feeling
Is a human being
Not this year's thing or last year's thing
This year's thing or next year's thing...
State control and rock and roll
Are run by clever men
It's all good for business!

State control and rock and roll
Are run by clever men
And anarchy is this year's thing...

PART TWO (incomplete) OF AN INTERVIEW WITH POISON GIRLS BY POST/CASSETTE OCTOBER 1980 PUBLISHED IN 'ANATHEMA' FANZINE #1

ee: When you released 'Persons Unknown', the money was said to be going towards an anarchist centre. What's happening? Also, when I wrote to Iris Mills, she said she didn't see it as a place for bands. How do you feel on this, and how do you envision the centre?
Richard: Factually, the record raised over £5,000 for the anarchist centre. I think they're still looking for premises.
Vi: I think the premises bit is crucial. It's to do with what happens to the profits made from records. We could have split the money equally with Crass, though we wouldn't have sold as many, 'cos I think, again, the spirit, the imagination for a lot of people was fired, for that

need to have a place of our own. Who 'we' are, I don't know. I don't know if anarchist is the right word. It's just that need for a place. Lots of people have got property, all the big corporations own most of the property, and there aren't many places where people can identify with those values and actually go and meet people like that and talk about the world we live in, and talk about our real needs. The money will provide for a place, a few hundred square feet or whatever of property, to actually get it back off the people who can tell us to fuck off, clear off and shut up. That's what is wanted and it's difficult to find these premises. As regards the bands, it would be very good if bands or anyone could get up and do their thing and make a noise. That's what is really hard to do. We've all got to clear out and shut up. I was thinking about all the people I know, like Action Space for example, and other organizations that provided venues which are being threatened by having government resources withdrawn, because what the government gives, the government takes away whenever they want to, from persons or organizations. I think more and more people are going to identify with that need to procure a place for staying alive in, but it's taking some pretty corrupt forms at the moment. There are people who want to have underground bloody shelters where they can have living tombs against the nuclear bomb. Basically, what we all want is a place to stay alive in, and to grow in, and that for me is what it symbolizes. I hope, even if one room or office can be found out of that money, people can have an address to write to or a place to go and meet other people and talk about those problems.

Lance: It represents to me, maybe somewhat symbolically, another line of development, because what we're trying to do in the band is talk about what's going on and we're singing about what's going on. We're singing about what we don't like and it's mainly critical, and it's mainly communicating feelings and giving voice to people's resentments and disappointments and maybe hopes. But I think there's really another stage, which is what do we do next? Do we sort of voice our various complaints and not do anything else? The Anarchist Centre represents to me something positive, something to do. All the people who identify with what it says and see the Centre as a positive step, we can take in the creation of a supportive environment where maybe something can get done, and building that up along those sort of specific aims for the Centre. For myself, I'm not too bothered if bands can play there or not.

Vi: For me, it focuses on the need for taking back our space, our property from the people who do tell us to keep out, keep off, or pay too much money to get in. I think more people will identify with that need. I want to change one thing I said in a previous question, what I said about having dreadful children; I want to change that to lively children (laughs).

(Note - Wapping Autonomy Centre, also known as The Anarchist Centre, was set up in a rented warehouse space in the Wapping area of London Docklands from late 1981 to 1982. Bands that played there included Poison Girls, Crass, The Mob, Anthrax, Zounds, Blood and Roses, Flux of Pink Indians, Dirt, Conflict, The Apostles, and Hagar the Womb. Unfortunately, the centre's open door policy also attracted a large number of drug users, petty criminals and unwanted police attention. These factors, combined with problems finding the monthly rent, ultimately led to its closure.)

ANOTHER HERO

There's no escape from barren weather
The cold war and the upturned collar
Our agents are all under cove
There are no treaties to deliver
The red man trapped in his enclosure
The black man aiming from his shoulder
The white man dying of exposure
And children everywhere grow older
The Hollywood avengers
Are drunk and disqualified
Missionaries on morphine
Lie giggling and paralyzed
On and on the bullet glides
To find its mark between the eyes
It finds its mark
Another hero bites the dust
There are no wise guys to save us
Against the merciless crusaders
There's nowhere safe to hide from raiders
Who capture hostages for traders
The red man trapped in his enclosure
The black man aiming from his shoulder
The white man dying of exposure
While women everywhere grow bolder
Kissinger and Nixon
Are hiding in the abattoirs
Maggie Thatcher's patching up
Her makeup in the broken glass
The bloody iron shows
As she drives past in her armoured car
As she drives past
Another hero bites the dust
The hit men in their chosen places

Fix their sites and hide their faces
Slip through the crowd in narrow spaces
Slip through the night and leave no traces
The red man trapped in his enclosure
The black man aiming from his shoulder
The white man dying of exposure
As dead men everywhere grow colder
The cowboys and the Kennedys

Are grabbing what there is to sell
The president's advisers
Advise us all to go to hell
And those who deal in weapons
Are rumoured to be doing well.
The rumour goes
Another hero bites the dust
There are no heroes fit to rule
They're all half saint, half bloody fool

Lee: Define your meaning of anarchy. The reason I ask this is that it might clear away a bit of confusion, thanks to the media distorting everything.

Vi: Yeah, good one.

Richard: I think our version of anarchy, or our understanding of anarchy, is to do with personal freedom and being able to individually work in a way which we create our own rules and our own standards, which are then negotiable between ourselves.

Vi: To me it means breaking down structures that are built up in order to defend lies. I'm very tired of conforming to the lies that most of the structures that we live in defend. One of those is to do with rights of access, depending on who you are in terms of age, sex, or what you're allowed to do, and for me they are lies, because I've lived long enough, I'm not satisfied being told what one can do in terms of what sex I am or how old I am. There are too many lies, and because they're defended by structures, whether they're brick walls or mental brick walls, the impulse to break those down and de-struct, de-structure, the defence mechanism that defends lies.

Nil: For me it's to do with not being content to allow someone else to do my thinking for me, whether that somebody is a politician or the un-named general public. The unspoken social restrictions which define what we are, define what we ought to think.

Vi: I think what we're involved in is how we ought to be able to define our lives and the way spend our energy and our resources more in terms of our real needs, whether we are people who don't want to go to school anymore, and you don't want to choose between this school and that school, or this way and that way, the need to be able to jump, to make a jump out of the existing choices which are usually between two or more evils, two or more things that we actually don't want and to postulate the possibilities, maybe the impossible dream, that we could actually determine a third choice or a thirteenth choice, which is the one we actually want and to be able to focus together on what those choices might mean, what we actually want to do. Like on a very basic level, not choosing between this government and that government, but postulate the possibility that there might be another choice because this government or that government all seem to lead to the same thing, which is death and disaster. So maybe there's another way out? Maybe we can leap or jump? And that's what I meant about anarchy for me meaning the destruction of defence systems that we use to protect the given way of thinking. That means we're taking on all the people who have vested interests in the given way of thinking, and that includes the music business, because the music business has very, very heavy invested interests in us continuing to choose between this crap band and that crap band, and saying which is the top of a thousand crap bands expressing a thousand different versions of crap values…"I'm your baby, yeah, yeah, yeah, all you've got to do is fuck me and I won't have any more problems'…and to just postulate that there might be another way of relating to somebody and to express that in the music business is actually attacking a lot of peoples vested interest, that's the sort of comic strip example of what I'm trying to talk about, which is that we don't actually have to dress in the sort of clothes, any of them, that are offered us, or occupy the kind of buildings that they're offering us to live in, if any, or accept any of the barren alternatives. I'm not saying for myself or for the band that we can't see any beauty or joy in the world that we're living in, buy by and large, our imaginations are trapped and tied down and nailed down and crucified, and to dare to imagine things that are a bit different, god help you.

Lance: I think it's the case that the word anarchy is being corrupted as much as the word punk has, which makes it difficult to say you're an anarchist and to communicate anything about what you really mean.

Vi: I think the responsibility of using the word is quite huge because we can either go along with the general corruption of the word and by our behaviour, rob it of its meaning, or we can actually try to bring some life into it, which is why I want to continue as a band because I think what we are and what we're doing actually does break down some of those systematic defences. You know? What ought to be. I hope that kind of presentation of our band continues to be, or improves on being a challenge to what people expect to see on a stage. The temptations are enormous as we go on, when it's offered more and more as a possibility that we can become more and more, as you would expect, become more glamorized and more comfortable. I always want to maintain that edge though, between what the business, or the expectations, or the minds of the music world will do to us and what we actually continue to be, which is to continue to survive as a live band, performing in the flesh. All these words are fucking de-valued. I mean, life. What do we mean by it? Not just anarchy or punk or life or love, it's hard to talk about, isn't it? I know what I mean by life and it contains some of the words we used this evening, like risk and excitement and imagination.

Lance: That's why we write songs.

(Note) – The rest of the Poison's interview is missing from the only copy of the fanzine that I managed to download, I've enclosed the following lyrics to compensate.

PERSONS UNKNOWN

This is a message - To persons unknown
Persons in hiding - Persons unknown
Survival in silence - Isn't good enough no more
Keeping your mouth shut head in the sand
Terrorists and saboteurs - Each and every one of us
Hiding in shadows persons unknown
Hey there Mr. Average -You don't exist you never did
Hiding in shadows persons unknown
Habits of hiding - Soon will be the death of us
Dying in secret from poisons unknown

This is a message to persons unknown
Strangers and passers-by - Persons unknown
Turning a blind eye - Hope to go unrecognized
Keeping your secrets persons unknown
Housewives and prostitutes - Plumbers in boiler suits
Truants in coffee bars - Who think you're alone
Big men on building sites - Sick men in dressing gowns
Agents in motor cars - Who never go home
Women in factories - One parent families
Women in purdah - Persons unknown
Wild girls and criminals - Rotting in prison cells
Patients in corridors - Persons unknown
Statistics on balance sheets - Numbered and rubberstamped
Blind and invisible - You're lost in your homes
Liggers and layabouts - Lovers on roundabouts
Wake up in the morning – with persons unknown
Accountants in nylon shirts - Feminists in floral skirts
Nurses for when it hurts - Persons unknown
Astronauts and celibates - Deejays and hypocrites
Liars and lunatics - Persons unknown
Hopefuls on football pools - Teachers in empty schools
Kids into heroin - Not yet full grown
Typists and usherettes - Black men who can't forget
The lonely who long for - Persons unknown
Closet idealists – Bald headed realists
Rastas and bikers - The voice on the phone
Pimps and economists - Royalty and communists
Rioters and pacifists - Persons unknown
Visionaries with coloured hair - Leather boys who just don't care
Garter girls with time to spare - Persons unknown
Judges with prejudice - Dissidents and anarchists
Policemen deal dirty tricks - To persons unknown
Strikers and pickets - Collectors of tickets
Radical architects - The queen on her throne
Soldiers in uniform - Sailors and stevedores
Beggars and bankers - Perjurers and men of law
Football crowd hooligans - Bunking off school again
Workers down tools again - United's at home
Smokers with heart disease - Cleaners of lavatories
The old with their memories - Persons unknown
Flesh and blood are who we are
Flesh and blood are what we are
Our cover is blown...

CRASS INTERVIEW – MAY 1981 - DIAL HOUSE, EPPING. PUBLISHED IN 'ANATHEMA' #1

I hitched 250 miles to meet up with Crass at their communal house and stayed with them for a few days. Band members present during the interview were Penny Rimbaud (Drums), Andy Palmer (guitar).Eve Libertine (vocals), Pete Wright (bass), and Steve Ignorant (vocals).

Lee: What's 321984, it's a countdown to something, but what?
Andy: 321984…1984.
Lee: What's going to happen then?
Penny: We're going to stop playing. When we first did it, it was 711984. It was just a way of saying to people 'watch out'. Just creating a definable time.
Andy: The image of 1984 is related to the book.
Lee: Will you stop playing, or not? I think you should just carry on until you can't do anything else.
Andy: What? Now? (laughs)
Penny: Virtually most of our time now is devoted to one aspect of the band or another, and there are a lot of other things that we could be doing and a lot of things we want to be doing but aren't able to, and there will come a time when what we're trying to do with the band will become stale, because we won't have enough time to sit down and do a bit of writing, and the inevitable consequence of that is when we do come to sit down and write a song, it will have less strength behind it, and there isn't gonna be enough time to really think.
Lee: That's the good thing about not being on someone else's record label, because if they push you to do an album for Christmas, you can't do it….You released the book 'Reality Asylum' in 500 copies. Are you going to release it again?
Penny: Yeah, I want to.
Lee: Is it in a similar style to what you write in 'International Anthem'?
Penny: No, not really. Some of 'Asylum' was taken from it. It's more like a long 'Asylum'.
Lee: More direct?
Penny: Yes, not sort of story.
Lee: What's happening with 'International Anthem'?
Andy: Well, that's another thing that we haven't had time to do.
Penny: I think the cover for 'Nagasaki Nightmare' took maybe two months, which is having discussions with Mike, who did the writing, what should and shouldn't be there and getting the illustrational work together, it took two months to do it, pretty solid work.

Eve: Someone sent us a thing they'd done on 'Nagasaki', they'd taken all the information and the pictures off the cover and zeroxed it and stapled it together and it was a really thick book, like your magazine. It's amazing to see it like that, just typed.

Penny: Most of the covers take us anything up to two months do, so you can imagine trying to fit in other stuff on top of that, like recording stuff, and other people's stuff as well.

Lee: You seem to spend more time recording now. '5000' seemed pretty rushed, compared to now.

Penny: Well, that's twofold…first thing, we can afford to take a bit more time, and secondly, when you listen to 'Feeding the 5,000' there's an awful lot on it that you can't hear. We want to develop the ideas on that, and ability, like a lot of it has been mixed terribly, it was the best we could do at the time, with the time we had to do it and the experience we had, but as we've learnt more about how to use a studio, we don't go by what we would have done then.

Andy: You become more demanding of the things you're actually putting out.

Penny: You listen to the difference between 'Asylum' on 'Feeding' and the 'Asylum' as a single, we would have done the 'Asylum' on 'Feeding' the same as the single if we'd had the ideas. It was the first time we'd worked in a studio. We didn't know what to do. We didn't know what the possibilities were.

Andy: I think as time goes on you get better and better at doing it; you know what to do to bring certain things out.

Lee: Some people say Crass records are badly produced.

Penny: It'd be interesting to know precisely what they think they mean, what standard they're judging it by. I mean, you can make anything sound like Abba if you put a few facile, stupid, musical components over it, and make it sound like The Angelic Upstarts by putting the bass drum up, that's all it takes. If nothing else, our stuff has got a certain consideration to it, in terms of production. What we do is under produce. It's so easy to make something sound like Judas Priest, it's all technique. When I did that thing with Captain Sensible – he knows all the tricks. There's formal things for doing a voice, for example, you've got a one-eighth of a second delay on the voice so it's gonna sound like Elvis Presley, all these things are a complete studio routine and we don't use any of them 'cos they're all just studio techniques.

Lee: Have any of you had any past music experience, either music-wise or record-wise, before?

Penny: Not really.

Lee: 'Cos you seem to have it pretty well sussed out and I think you'd need some experience behind you.

Penny: John (Loder), who does our recording, when I first met him he didn't have any equipment at all, except this car stereo. He used to muck around with noises, put it in his car and listen to it. We've grown up together, so that's an influence there, John's learnt as well.

Andy: We didn't have it all sussed out, either.

Lee: You've done quite a few benefits for CND, what have they achieved?

Pete: CND receives more coverage now than it did six months ago, or a year ago, people are better informed about the bomb, and really, it can't do more than that.

Penny: The marches and things are a celebration, a day off. Marches are designed to make people feel there are other people like themselves. I don't think anything is going to change through a march, but the people themselves do change, and I do think it affects public opinion. But people who live in areas like this who choose to follow the ideas CND put out, for the average middle class citizen to put a 'Fight War Not Wars' sticker on their car is quite strange. To us, it means nothing, but living in Rose Glen in little nouveau homes, they're probably communists to everyone else, red bastards to everyone else, that's the way they're responded to. On that level it does have a threat. On our level we want to see a more radical change. It does filter through. CND offer a central agency for information, like, the Daily Mirror did that article on the bomb, I'm sure all that was straight from CND, y'know, get on the phone and say can you send some stuff down, it is a central agency.

Lee: When you do CND benefit gigs, where does the money go to?

Eve: Wherever we're playing, it goes to the local branch.

Andy: Say we do a benefit for Bradford CND, then a lot of the money will go towards getting them a printing press or facilities to make it easier for them to produce leaflets and stuff.

Penny: I think all we can do, we obviously have an effect in the area that we do, the real effect we can have as a group is for example the Anarchist Centre, which they now have a place set up. It will have a really long-standing effect, far greater than our lyrics. We can individually influence certain numbers of people who next week will be following Killing Joke 'cos we put a bloody woman singing on our record, and that does happen. The long term effect of what we do is something like 'Bloody Revolutions', whether anyone liked it or not, regardless, 'cos it has financed and bought property in London and it is going to be promoting ideas to middle of the road people that will in time have an effect on the culture that we live in.

Lee: Plus it might help people who feel isolated.

Penny: On a radical level, I really don't visualize much change, apart from the middle of the road level, which we can't do as a band, but we can do it by supporting people who are working on those levels and create more change.

Lee: I think the revolution starts with yourself, doesn't it? It's like little things, like eating meat or not eating meat. It's a stance against it all, that's where it starts.

Penny: I think that's where it finishes, myself. I don't think you can go beyond that, the personal stance, and as an example to other people, following those examples of it in their own section of it, I don't think the revolution ever goes beyond that.

Lee: A lot of people have the attitude 'I'll stop eating meat if everyone else does', instead of doing it themselves, they wait for everyone else.

Andy: That goes on with pie in the sky ideas of revolution, change the world tomorrow. Because what happens is that attitudes follow on, you should be the first to do it, by myself, for myself.

Pete: People will eat meat tomorrow because today they ate meat and yesterday they ate meat.

Lee: In Scotland, at Perth, you met up with fascist violence. How do you think it can be dealt with and confronted?

A PUNK ROCK FLASHBACK

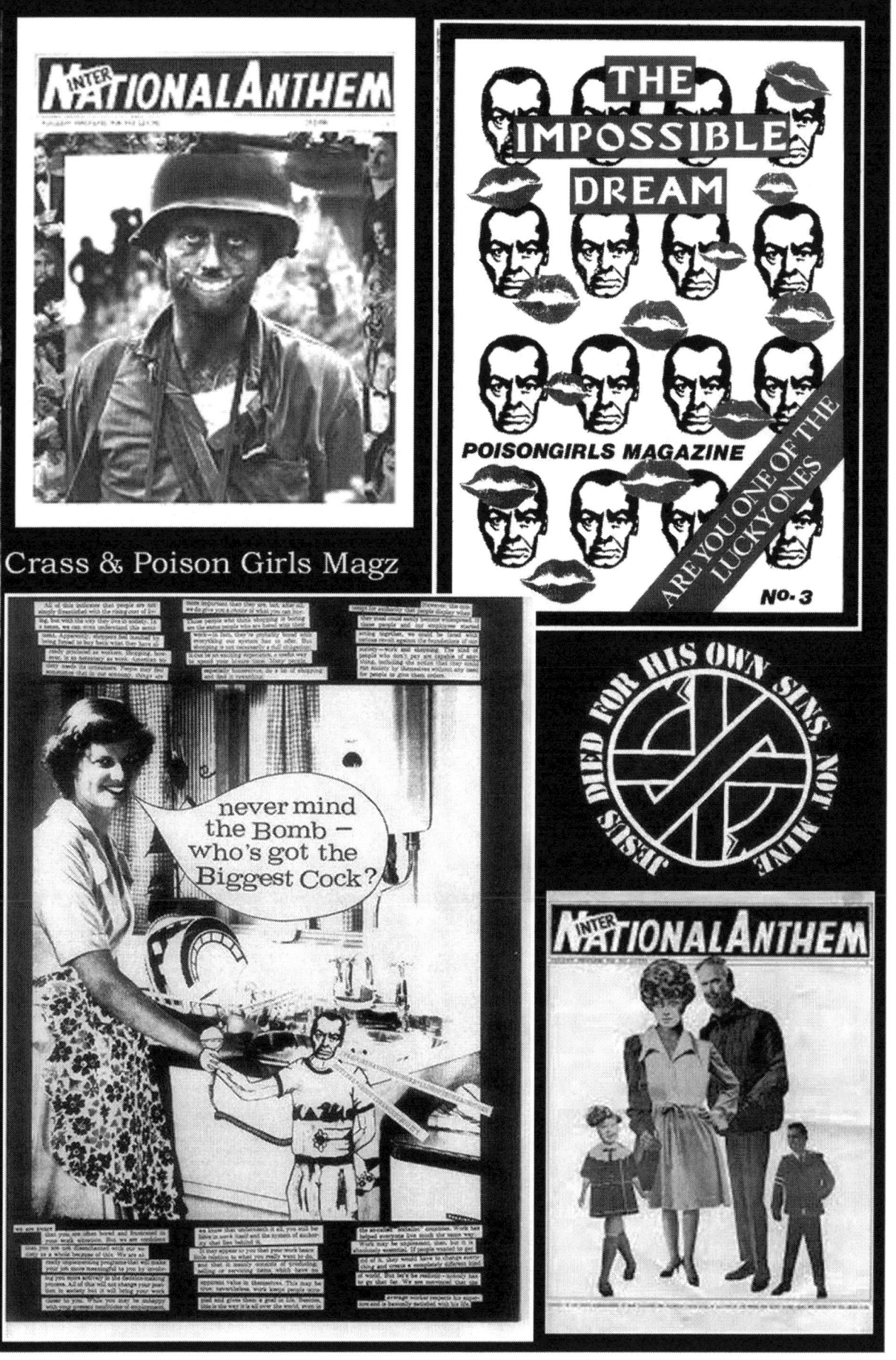

Crass & Poison Girls Magz

Penny: They're not fascists by philosophy, they were fascists by doctrine that evening and the next night they won't be. The people who turned up at Perth, the leader of them seemed pretty well read-up, he seemed to know all the jargon. Next evening he'll be something else, but because Perth was suddenly invaded by all these people who he didn't know, he was frightened by that, so he responded by using all that jargon. They're not fascists, 'cos that's a philosophy, it's quite a serious one as well. It's absurd to say skinheads are fascists because they wear swastikas. When people are confronted with reality they back down, as long as they are not confronted with reality the situation will run how they want it to. If people at that gig actually managed to stop them, they will stop, if you actually confront them with what they're doing, which is often impossible 'cos they're so psyched up, if you can say 'Oh, excuse me, what exactly do you think you're doing?', invariably they will stop, they don't know about they're doing or why they're doing it, they don't actually care about it, it just happens to be the trap they've been caught in. Genuinely, I don't believe there's any substance to it at all. There is a genuine unpleasantness, a threat to people with specific comfort, but if people were less afraid, at Perth, which you were at, if people had not been so intimidated by those people it could have been a lot better. Also, if people hadn't of responded in such a violent fashion – that guy who was supposed to be doing security, I think to some extent asked for it, jumping up and down like Popeye, he was asking for it.
Steve: Popped eyes…Popeye…ha-ha-ha…sorry.
Penny: He looked like Popeye, didn't he? Jumping up and down, it was stupid and provocative.
Lee: How do you stop people if they're kicking hell out of someone?
Pete: A lot of people were actually constructively suppressing the groups of people, blocking off people and actually doing their bit to control the situation.
Andy: I think it snowballs. Your immediate reaction is, we've got trouble from fascists, how do we stop it? That's what happened when the Anti-Nazi League got together. They immediately assumed that because people were wearing swastikas that they were Nazi's. So they got the ANL together, they brought out badges, Pogo on a Nazi, etc, and you get people calling themselves Nazi's because they've been labelled by some self-righteous wanker who started up this campaign called the ANL. It snowballs, so really, treat people without labels. Do whatever you feel you can do with the situation you are confronted with.
Lee: At Perth, as soon as we got the leader out of the way the violence stopped, follow the leader again.
Penny: Yeah, it's always like that.
Lee: Why have Poison Girls decided to leave Crass Records?
Andy: I think they thought it would be good for them to go out and do gigs and bring records out independently from us to see, to try and find out for themselves what their specific audience is.
Lee: Doesn't it get boring doing 'Banned from the Roxy' and 'Owe us a Living'? 'Cos I've seen you quite a few times and you start and finish with the same songs.
Pete: It does get boring playing them, but it's not boring for the people who come to see us. We do play a few new songs that people haven't heard before, but that's not what it's about, 'Roxy' and 'Owe us a Living' are still valid statements.

Andy: Even more valid now that punk is dead, ha-ha. People come along to see us doing stuff that they've heard on record to see if we can actually do it. A lot of people come to see if we can do what we say we can. We play those songs because people go to hear them. If there's a gap in between gigs we change the set. It doesn't get boring doing 'Roxy', it's really good, people don't want to go to a gig and be deadly serious.

DO THEY OWE US A LIVING?

Fuck the politically minded
Here's something I want to say
About the state of nation
The way they treat us today
At school they give you shit
Drop you in the pit
You try and try and try to get out
But you can't
Because they've fucked you about
Then you're a prime example
Of how they must not be
This is just a sample
Of what they've done to you and me

Do they owe us a living?
Of course they do!
Of course they do!
Do they owe us a living?
Of course they do!
Of course they do!
Do they owe us a living?
OF COURSE THEY FUCKING DO!

They don't want me anymore
Cause I threw it on the floor
They used to call me sweet thing
But I'm nobody's plaything
And now that I am different
They'd love to bust my head
They'd love to see me cop-out
They'd love to see me dead

Do they owe us a living?
Of course they do!
Of course they do!
Do they owe us a living?

Of course they do!
Of course they do!
Do they owe us a living?
OF COURSE THEY FUCKING DO!

The living that is owed to me
I'm never going to get
They've buggered this old world
Up to their necks in debt
They'd give you a lobotomy
For something you ain't done
They'll make you an epitomy
Of everything that's wrong

Do they owe us a living?
Of course they do!
Of course they do!
Do they owe us a living?
Of course they do!
Of course they do!
Do they owe us a living?
OF COURSE THEY FUCKING DO!

Don't take any notice
What the public think
They're so hyped up with T.V.
They just don't want to think
They'll use you as a target
For demands and for advice
And if you don't want to wear it
They'll say you're full of vice

Do they owe us a living?
Of course they do!
Of course they do!
Do they owe us a living?
Of course they do!
Of course they do!
Do they owe us a living?
OF COURSE THEY FUCKING DO!

Lee: What's the new album going to be like? 'Cos '5,000' and 'Stations' were both punk type music, but 'Penis Envy', that's really good 'cos I think your music has progressed a lot. Is the new album going to progress as well, or are you going to go back?

Andy: Oh, no, not back.

Lee: I think the lyrics on 'Penis Envy' seem a lot more thought out.

Andy: In what way?

Lee: The areas they attack, some of it's quite new to attack.

Andy: Why, if they're new areas to attack, should they be more thoughtful?

Lee: Well, the early stuff was aggressive – I could imagine you being pissed-off with something and writing it down.

Pete: They are more personal. The early stuff was dealing with systems, not women. They're far more personal.

Penny: The material was obviously chosen to put on 'Penis Envy', it had a certain quality. We have a book for people to put songs in, some have been there for years, so some of the material on that is very old and we'd never felt it was usable before. 'Berkertex Bribe' was a really old song. Actually, Steve used to sing it about three years ago, then it went into disuse because we didn't know how to do it really. It's much harder to write songs now, 'cos when you write them you know that 50,000 people are going to sit down and read them and think about them and listen to them, it's a very different feeling actually knowing that sort of number of people are involved in what you are writing, where 'Feeding the 5,000' there were only a few, which doesn't mean you are less careful, it's just that the actual considerations are different.

Lee: Does it surprise you that you're as popular as you are? Did you think you would get this far?

Penny: We knew it was good because we meant what we were doing, but what was surprising was the response. On one hand it's a surprise, on the other it isn't. The surprise is that so many people care.

Lee: How do you feel on Northern Ireland? 'Cos a lot of fanzines seem to ignore the subject and lots of bands avoid talking about it.

Penny: That's what the next 'International Anthem' is dedicated to, probably what the next single will be devoted to, and I think we've made fairly consistent comments and statements on Northern Ireland. I would of thought how we feel about it is expressed in everything we do. We feel a compassion for everyone involved, and I feel as much compassion for the squaddy who finds himself in that situation as I do the IRA who find themselves in that situation, and I deplore the actions of both of them. Both of those people, through the use of power, are trying to create a new order. Until the people realize that the only order is their own order, there will be no change. As long as people accept oppression in one form or another, then people are going to get hurt.

Andy: That's the problem really, what's going on over there is the result of all sorts of arbitrary fuck-ups. It goes back such a long way in history, it's difficult to understand exactly what happened and why there is a situation of violence. It all seems to be tied up with people's dependence on religion.

Penny: I actually feel that the situation is very understandable and quite easily understood - how it all came about. The situation didn't arise because people read the bible any more than the situation in Nazi Germany-
Andy: What are you saying, exactly?
Penny: I think humanitarian interests are terribly bourgeois in the light of what they're doing, peace movements, the humanitarian cause always gets taken over with middle class values. As I was saying, on the same level the concentration camps evolved because of people being Jewish, which is the same as Hiroshima evolved because of people being Japanese, is it any justification that because people were Japanese that they should become involved in Hiroshima?
Andy: People who were Jewish, that was imposed upon them.
Penny: Roman Catholicism, simply because a Roman Catholic is white and a Protestant is white, nobody see's it as a racial issue. In the same way that thousands of Jews who were no way whatsoever identifying with the Jewish Sabbath, but in Nazi Germany they investigated anyone two generations back and anyone with the slightest Jewish blood was analysed and destructed as being Jew by the system. Traditionally, a large number of Jews are Marxist, involved with Communist thought, they were still Jews the same way Roman Catholics were when Britain invaded Ireland. Totally irrelevant if people were followers of the church, the very fact that they inhabited a certain area defined them as being Catholics. The fact that they objected to the papal way of life, non-the-less they were still Catholics and non-the-less they still are. The fact that the majority of people in Northern Ireland who are defined as Catholics, large numbers of them have no identification with Catholicism, but they are oppressed as Catholics.
Andy: Who are they oppressed by?
Penny: They're oppressed by Protestant Barrister rule.
Andy: So long as people go on seeing people as Catholics and as Protestants the troubles will go on.
Penny: Yes, of course they will. I was criticizing you when you said you couldn't understand how it all came about, how one now deals with it...we're all ruled by our own culture, aren't we? We are ruled by various definitions that language gave us. We are unavoidably British, whether or not we identify with that. We could say we were part of the English speaking nations but people would still be able to tell that we were English because of the accent we use, and even further than that, each one of us has a different accent. I can tell a large amount about each person's supposed background because of that. In the 'Class War', one knows who will derive, be put up against a wall and have rocks thrown at them, you can do that instantly, regardless of what one thinks and believes. Gary Bushel (Sounds music journo) can say things about us in the way that he does because some of those things are indisputable and meaningless because our personalities don't happen to coincide with the definitions he's used. None-the-less, one can't dispute the social syntax that he's using, like, there's no point in someone at the gates of Auschwitz saying 'I'm sorry, but I don't actually support the Jewish cause.' If they happen to get the wrong name and the wrong parent, it doesn't matter a bullock what they support, 'cos they cop the same load, and ultimately it's the same in violent situations.

Lee: A lot of people have adopted the one attitude that the British are over there doing a good job and keeping the peace and the IRA are just vicious murderers who haven't got any cause at all.

Penny: I think the IRA are vicious murderers and they've got an enormous cause. Everyone's got a cause. You could argue that the British have got a cause, it's all meaningless, like the boy who put his finger in the dyke, at some point or other you've got to get your finger out. All of it is irrelevant. The IRA are as irrelevant as the British presence over there. It makes no difference, it's the same as Vietnam, you can have the most sophisticated nation sitting on top of the most rural community and ultimately the community will have its way. The people do have their way, it may take thousands of years, but in the end they will have their way. You can't stop the people; maybe they just want to go back to another form of oppression, like in Poland, for example. The strikes against Russia were very largely the result of the Pope, if it hadn't been for the Catholic Church I don't suppose the strength of that strike would have been maintained, it's because of that total dedication to the Pope that they managed to see it through. You can say what a load of shit, invariably that's true, what a load of shit, but on the other hand it's very inspiring.

Lee: So, in a nutshell, just what do you think the solution is? Just let the people sort their own troubles out?

Penny: Actively, through example, demonstrate the solution. If everyone did this, if everyone did that, how else can you do it? When, and if, we tour Ireland, we will tour in south and north Ireland, and we'll play in Protestant and Catholic areas and hopefully through our presence there, through the way in which we relate to each other we will inspire other people towards seeing some sort of an alternative to the ones that are operating there at the moment. There's no other way except through example.

Andy: It's not enough just to come up with, you know, just sitting there in your front room saying if they did this and they did that, you can't give a solution unless you actually go in there with an open mind and just be there and live there and see exactly what's going on, and maybe come up with a solution, otherwise I don't think you're qualified to say what should go on.

Penny: If one polarizes the enemy, if we went to Northern Ireland and already concluded that every British soldier was a pig and a fucker, in groups like that, then there's no chance of vanquishing it. If we automatically react to being searched in the streets with aggression then we'll have aggression pushed on us. If we respond purely to it, then to some extent that's how we'll be treated. I do believe that. I genuinely believe that people will respond to the manner in which you treat them. You can't pretend, like that silly idea if you talk to plants they'll grow better. Flowers know whether you're there or not there. You can't pretend to love something if you don't love it and if things were part of everything, you can't divide from it and say 'Oh, you're nice', to make it grow better 'cos it knows what you really feel, it is, as you are. It's the same with people, sort of a stupid charade that people surround themselves with and I genuinely believe that charade is breakable. If you can be bothered to do it and if you've got the strength to do it, and you're feeling well enough to do it, you can break through. Maybe it will take twenty years to get through to some people, but if you feel it's worth it, then do it. What we try to do at a gig is touch as many people as possible, not physically, but through our presence and hope some of it will rub off, that's the solution, living your own life and as an example to others.

Lee: That's all Crass can do as a band really, isn't it? Touch people, like you said, and hope that they start to do their own thing.

Penny: That's right, that's the only value of it. There's no sort of personal gain from it as such, you know, gigging and that, what else do we get out of it?

Andy: A chip butty and tea!

Penny: That's the sort of thing that makes it worthwhile. This house, for example, was set up in the hope that it would inspire other similar situations. It's a sad reflection really, probably hundreds of people have been through this house and there aren't really any other situations or examples like this. If all those people had gone out of here, they've all benefited from that freedom and time and space, if they'd done something, there'd probably be another fifty houses dotted around the country that operated on this level, but I don't know of any.

Lee: Do you find it hard, living collectively, or not?

Penny: No, not particularly. Everything else that goes on is so designed to singularize and minimalize vision, like those two guys in our garden, in the orchard, totally violating something that exists, not because they want something, but the attitude with which they want it. Suddenly, two strangers are walking around our garden, saying they're going to take part of it. They could have been two people who would like to share and said 'Well, look, you've got that space and this is what we would like to do. How does that seem with you? How can we share that?', but it's not like that, they're aggressive and that's how it is with those sort of people because they don't understand what it is to share anything, they don't know what giving is, they only take.

(Note – due to side one of the tape cassette running out and it taking a few minutes before anyone noticed, this is where the rest of the interview continues…I'm sure you'll catch up with the drift.)

Penny: …….Everything that we own and possess, which is life, which is total, is then stolen from us, stolen from us by birth. Before that, we possess all that, but through birth it's stolen from us, through insensitivity. All our perceptions start being narrowed down, divided, the unity is destroyed, the unity that is us as totally knowing beings, unity to which we return, that we had before birth. It's stolen from us because people want to use power. They're not interested in us, if they're interested in us they'd leave us alone, or if they were more interested in us they wouldn't even have inflicted life on us that divides us from life, as a human that is divided from the thing we all the time pursue; life. We are probably the only being on the planet that exists with that alienation and all our lives we seek to find, to destroy that alienation, because everything's stolen from us and then we're given it back like some sort of fucking privilege. We're given a little plot of land, we're given a little identity, we're given them as though we ought to be fucking grateful for them, and it's all been fucking stolen from us in the first place. We can't travel to London without being taxed on the road or paying on a train, we can't sit on a piece of grass without being told it's someone's, it's ours, and I'm not being simplistic. It really is ours and if we know it's ours then we'll cease to care a fuck about the stupid, petty restrictions that people have created

in the world and realize the world is ours and we don't care about the ugly, grey people who stand in our way. I know there's someone out there who will try, and there's someone all over the world that will try, but I don't give a fuck about those people. They don't exist, they don't exist in the world, they live in a stupid pit. I'll go into that cage, and part of being in the band is being prepared to stand in that cage and try and say to people, 'For fuck's sake, get out of it'. That's where it is, they don't exist, they don't live, they don't know what it is to love 'cos they don't know what life is, 'cos they're prepared to believe in all that stolen property.

Lee: That's the thing with anarchy…you're brought up to believe you need a government and you need a policeman to keep order and to protect you, things like that, like people aren't responsible enough to live in peace, they have to have someone there to do it for them. As I said earlier, I was reading that book by Errico Malatesta, (His Life and Ideas), and he was saying that if, from birth, you had your legs bound and you were told that if you removed the chains that you would die, then you would believe it. It's the same as the government, if you're told all your life that you need a government, then you'll accept it and believe it, and that's what school does, it prepares you for the system.

Penny: School is a total violation, as is the whole concept of a family and the whole of parenthood, it's a total violation of what parenthood could be. Giving birth is an absolute violation of life, it's got nothing to do with the birth, the average baby is an utter violation of life, there's no birth involved. It's the fucking of totality, the booting and bruising of it into some malleable pathetic little object with a pathetic little name, a pathetic little identity, with a pathetic little future, and that's where it stays. It stays in that pathetic crumpled-up form until it dies, and that's all we can do in life, to realize that we've got that, if only we could remove all the veils from it. It's up to us to do it. There's absolutely no-one who will do it for us. There's nothing else you can do. All of this is pure fabrication, it doesn't mean anything, ultimately, growing beautiful flowers or tanks with fish in means fuck all, it's all a fabrication, that's a more beautiful representation, to me, anyway, than all of that grey shit we live in. Ultimately, this is another ball of shit and that's just as much shit in anyone's else's eyes, it's my expression and the expression of other people who share that expression, it's shit none-the-less. It means nothing. It's all limitation, another sort of prison, really. We live in this beautiful garden because it's an oasis, it's own utopia, it exists as far as today, and it doesn't even exist that far because people walk in violating it. As far as possible this is an oasis where we can escape all that. This is a violation in itself, the fact that it is a prison in itself. I don't like going anywhere. I don't like the people I meet. This is the only place I feel real, but it's a prison because of that, it's the same as the little boy with bound feet. I should be able to put a match to this place and walk away from it, but where could I walk to? There are so few untouched places. What we've tried to do is make this place untouched, we haven't done things to it that other people have done. We don't spray the garden. It's a real joy to see dragonfly in the garden because we know that they're safe here, that's real, to some extent it's the same with people; they know they're safe here, less safe as concepts. There was a time when concepts didn't come here. London didn't exist here and all of that didn't exist either because we didn't recognize it, because we never went out, but we allowed it in. It's just a reclamation job, really, it's all that we can do, as what we try to do in the band is to operate on that level. We can't be telling people how they should be reclaiming what they've had stolen from them, but we can at least point out that they have had something stolen from them.

Lee: It's finding your own method, really, isn't it?

Penny: Well, everyone has their own don't they?

Lee: A lot of families, like my mom and dad, for example, got their little council house and they're content with that, at least they think they are. They don't give a fuck about what's going on, the bomb and all of that. You said about creeping in, most people don't let it creep in. I think everyone should take some responsibility for what's going on around them, like, people are getting slaughtered in El Salvador, you should feel something, in a way, to want to do something about it.

Penny: I don't actually feel guilty, but one is responsible, there's absolutely no doubt about it at all. We're totally responsible for every single thing that happens. I don't think one should feel guilty about it, I don't feel guilty about anything at all. I do feel responsible for everything, which is a very different sort of thing. Guilt is the negative side of responsibility, and I think one can be acting totally responsibly by say, well, my way of demonstrating an alternative to that violation is to go and sit on a peak somewhere and never move for the rest of my life.

I read this article by an Italian journalist at about the time Saigon was about fall. She was with some Buddhist monks and she couldn't decide whether to stay with the monks who were quite clearly demonstrating about world peace, or whether she should she should go to Saigon and equally become involved in a statement for world peace, two extremes. In the end she decided to go where the action was. But where is the real action? The real action is just as much in Saigon as in the solitude of those monks. I don't think one has to be running around doing things to be actively doing something.

When I was describing how it was before in this house, we allowed things in because we thought we might be able to have a wider influence. We had learned and succeeded in making one positive demonstration about survival, and you can't lose that ability. It took maybe ten years to learn but it can be very quickly handed over, to do stuff like feeding yourself. It takes a long time, but it takes only a day to teach someone, and it was inevitable that out of this place that something more socially based should develop, which it did do, but I don't see that what we were trying to do ten years ago was negative or an evasion of responsibility. I think it is a very responsible thing to be doing. The fact that we didn't recognize the bomb as being of any relevance what-so-ever doesn't detract from what we we're saying about CND earlier, it makes no difference at all if thousands of people walk up and down Piccadilly, what matters is what each individual does when they go home and how they live their lives.

Lee: The bomb threatens your life though, doesn't it?

Penny: Well, that doesn't fucking matter. I was just thinking that if the only reason people care about the bomb is their own pathetic little lives…I don't care a fuck about my life, as such I've had a really nice one up to now, that's not the reason I care about the bomb. I care about the bomb because if I look up into the sky, it's beautiful, and I don't give a fuck about people if all we can do in all our thousands of years upon this planet is destroy ourselves, then that's tough shit, I don't care about it. All I care about really is the beautiful, silent existence that we will destroy by that, and that doesn't really matter either, really. I don't care about silly men trying to kill each other or if there's innocent people who never did anything about it, I don't care about that either, and ultimately, if I believe it's going to happen to me, I don't care about that. Either way, you're trapped. All I care about is the innocent, silent beauty that we could of had being taken away forever and we're left with a grey pool, until trees blossom and the snow melts and some other greasy slimy shit climbs out of the pool and starts it all over again.

It's made me sad, to an extent, particularly the young people who come here, their fear is not only total fear, it's personal fear. It's the same fear that makes people dig silly holes in the garden to hide in, it's just personal stuff. There's nothing worth dying for and on the same level there's nothing worth living for, if there is, people don't deserve to be alive, there's too much in life for people to start dividing it all up. It's all glorious and it's all a pile of shit. You can't divide it up. If you do, you don't deserve to be alive. It's just grey people.

Lee: Everybody's brought up by the system to serve the system, why do you think some people question it and try to step outside it?

Pete: You can't step outside the system 'cos there's nowhere to go.

Penny: There's always the thing of how do you see beyond it. I think it's very precious working with certain forms of behaviour and certain methods by which people can perceive beyond the definitions that they've been given. The obvious case is that there are certain drugs which do have different perceptions, which I don't agree with, I don't agree with that method, but it is a method of transcending the certain ground of perception. Our whole method of seeing is a condition which is different between each culture. There are some cultures that don't actually see with their eyes, they see with their ears. In the jungle the natives tend to see with their ears, the dimensions of when they see something is very different to how we see something, like the Chinese see on the horizontal plane, we see left to right because we read left to right, so everything's created in this left/right bias, progression is seen in left/right movements. Walking along it is hard to imagine walking from left to right when you're walking forward. The mind's eye, which is blind, is moving from left to right. They're dimensions and they're conditions, scientific conditions. Da Vinci invented perspective and we live within perspective, our whole way in which we actually perceive the world is a scientific formula that was invented four or five hundred years ago. It can temporarily be broken down through the use of certain drugs. Acid (LSD) totally alters the way one see's things. You don't see how you normally see things. There are forms of meditation and yoga which do the same thing. You can alter the way you actually see things, only temporarily. You eventually have to go back and deal with the common theory that that's there and that's there, but on one's own that can cease to be over there and be wherever you want it. There is another world, another dimension, of course there is, there must be, there is living proof of that. If you stick twenty people in a room and say 'Draw that', they don't draw the same thing. If they've all been given identical training, it would still be totally different. A different scale, different details, all the various flavours and colours. All those flavours and colours, on a common level, are the system. You can transcend those

things by various forms of activity. If you don't sleep for a week you start seeing the world in a very different light, you actually start to believe in your own thing. Last night, when I wasmixing, I was so tired that everything was bouncing around, I know that's because I was tired, but it was real. The only way I could deal with it was to accommodate this dimension that I was on, like the person with bound legs, if I was born in that area of oscillation, if they had been presented to me as reality, like this static life has been, then I would accept it as real, like, if I spent enough time and money on advertising and promoting a theory, it wouldn't be long before the whole fucking world believed it. Why do men think women are a pussy for their pricks? It's because men are promoting it for men.

A SHORT INTERVIEW WITH ANDY T. – ROCHDALE 1981
PUBLISHED IN 'ANATHEMA' FANZINE #2

I was hitching around on a Crass tour, so was Andy T, and we soon became friends – I've written about Andy in other parts of this little book. Andy was, and currently is, a stand-up anarchist poet. We'd hitch individually to various gigs, including the Perth gig, and would meet up whenever we arrived at the next destination – the next small town, large town, or city. It was either between gigs, or after the tour (I can't recall now which tour it was), that I stayed for a few days with Andy at his flat in Ashfield Valley, Rochdale, in Lancashire. I did this interview with him for my 'zine, just before he released his single 'Weary of the Flesh' on Crass Records – he'd already done a track on 'Bullshit Detector' (an album released on Crass Records featuring bands and poets from around the UK, mostly home-made recordings.) He has also just released an album 'At Tether's End', well worth a listen and is available from All The Madmen Records.

Lee: What inspires you to write poetry, and why do you write it?
Andy: Life itself inspires me. I write poems to get it out of my system, also to communicate with others of similar feelings. As long as there are bad things in this world I will oppose them. If one person on this planet, or one animal, is denied basic freedom, then everyone has no freedom.
Lee: Why are you releasing 'Weary of the Flesh' on Crass Records?
Andy: Because Crass are the only people I really trust to make a record with at the moment. They really believe in what I'm doing, they've been asking me to do a single for years and it was only last year that I felt my material was worthy of a single.
Lee: Are you recording it in a studio?
Andy: I recorded it on a portable cassette player like I always do, but Penny said the sound quality was a bit poor on some tracks, so he persuaded me to go into Southern Studios. We will be doing everything in the control room, so I don't feel totally isolated. I don't think studios are really necessary, but it all depends on the sound quality you want on the finished product.
Lee: You obviously believe in peace, but do you support CND?
Andy: I totally believe in peace, but I don't support CND. They do a couple of rallies or marches a year, print a few shitty leaflets that say nowt, crawl up Labour's arse all the time and generally do nowt constructive. The only good thing is that they are against the bomb. It

costs a few quid to join; they have benefit gigs all the time, where does all that money go, eh? Michael Foot's bloody fallout shelter! In the 60's on one of the famous marches an anarchist group started walking down a country lane. The CND leaders went mad. What were they afraid of? The anarchists had discovered fallout shelters belonging to CND leaders and they had documented proof.

Lee: Since your appearance on 'Bullshit Detector' you've apparently influenced quite a lot of people with your approach to music. Is that what you wanted?

Andy: I just wanted to show people that you don't have to be in a band to get a point across. If people are learning from me then that's good, but my approach to music is only one of the many alternatives to a band. I wouldn't like to say that those using my ideas are copying me, if that was true then anyone who picks up a guitar is copying Chuck Berry. Another good thing is to form a theatre group; there are lots of things like that springing up all over the place, doing really anti-system material.

Lee: Why don't you eat meat?

Andy: Visit a slaughterhouse and see for yourselves, the cruel bloodbath people call humane. They make their profits out of death. You keep yourselves alive by eating corpses that you don't actually need in order to survive. I don't eat meat 'cos I don't need it, and neither do you.

A poem from 'Weary of the Flesh'-
You disguise the truth with pretty names
A living thing is now a joint of beef
You shift the blame but you can't hide
The sickly smile on your blood-stained teeth
You are the butcher not the man in the shop
But you haven't got the guts to kills your own meal
If you saw the pain it would make you sick
Just think how the animals feel...think how the animals feel

Lee: You are currently unemployed, so am I. How do you feel about all these people who find themselves in a state of despair 'cos they haven't got a job, and do you believe in the 'work ethic' that so many parents support?

Andy: People who believe work to be the be-all and end-all are stupid. There is more to life than being exploited by an employer. I feel pity for those who see no alternative for work, but suicide is no answer. I don't support the right to work because it means the right to be exploited. Fight for the right to choose for yourself.

Lee: What things do you enjoy in life?

Andy: Good food, good company, sitting at home with Pam and Ziggy, going for walks on the moors, music, books, writing poems and things, nature and animals in their natural environment. The things I hate are zoos, violence, Manchester city centre, London, sexism, capitalism, and you! (laughs)

Lee: Do you feel anything in common with other stand-up poets, like Annie Anxiety or Seething Wells, and do you like what they're doing?

Andy: I love Annie, haven't heard much by Seething Wells, would like to very much, but I don't really feel anything in common with them 'cos we have different ideas about poetry.
Lee: How do your parents feel about what you do and your opinions?
Andy: My parents believe in what I am trying to do and help me anyway they can. They respect me and I respect them.
Lee: Do you consider yourself a pacifist? 'Cos most pacifists, to me, are just passive and they get walked all over.
Andy: I don't believe pacifists should be passive. I only use violence when any other method fails to work. Stand up and defend your rights, but don't be on the attacking, physically violent side.
Lee: Do you support direct action, i.e. glueing up locks, graffiti, raids on laboratories where animals are experimented upon?
Andy: I support direct action to a point. I would love to trash a lab, but not the people who perform the experiments 'cos it's just a job to them. I don't believe in that kind of physical violence. Glueing up locks is great, but only on big chain-stores or banks, not small businesses.
Lee: You live in Rochdale. Are you happy with that? Or would you sooner live in London?
Andy: I am happy with Rochdale, for now. There's nowt going on but it's a very friendly place and I've lived here all my life. I would love to live in the countryside with like-minded people and be self-sufficient, live off the land, etc. I don't like London at all. There's lots going on and so people get complacent. It's safe to be based in London but it's a lot harder up north. It's a struggle to get anywhere. I would never base myself in London.

Another poem from 'Weary of the Flesh'-

I had a dream of tomorrow
I dreamed there would be peace
People living together as one
I dreamed that wars would cease
I had a dream of tomorrow
Of flowers, birds, and trees
Of life as nature intended
With everything set free
I wish it could be tomorrow
For today there is no peace

Lee: In my fanzines I've written stuff about the machismo culture, and feminist ideas. What do you think of feminism?
Andy: I think I am a feminist in that I oppose all the levels of sexism and I believe in total equality. Until men become feminists the women will be divided, separate. Educate everyone, including men, and work together. Don't isolate the sexes.
Lee: Is it easier working on your own, compared to working in a band?
Andy: I have been in many bands in the past but I still worked on my own. Now, I've

concluded that I can only have total control on my own. I have no wish to form another band; I just work with other individuals on things.

Lee: What do you intend doing after the single?

Andy: After the single is right now. I try to be active all the time. I should be gigging soon.

Lee: Would you go on tour with Crass? Are the people who attend Crass gigs your kind of audience?

Andy: I wouldn't go on tour with Crass 'cos their audience are only interested in seeing Crass as a punk band. Annie Anxiety gets a lot of stick and so would I. Crass are just preaching to the converted, most of the time, any-road. If the audience are faced with owt different, they don't want to know. It would be safe to gig with them 'cos you've got a readymade audience. It would be better to find my own, no disrespect to Crass, of course.

Lee: One last question. Summer will be here soon. Did you support last summer's riots?

Andy: I oppose all acts of physical violence, but I do identify with the rioter's reasons. People have been shit on for far too long and last summer made a lot of people stand up and take notice. The rioters made a mistake, though, smashing up the wrong things, like small shops, they're on your side, smash Tesco or Asda, the big chain-stores who don't care about owt but profits, but don't fuck-up your own kind. Another bad thing was it gave the police a space to re-think and get more equipment and to get tougher. Think about the copper who saw his mate get bottled by a black youth, is he going to support racial harmony? Before you repeat the riots, stop and think. Don't repeat the same mistakes.

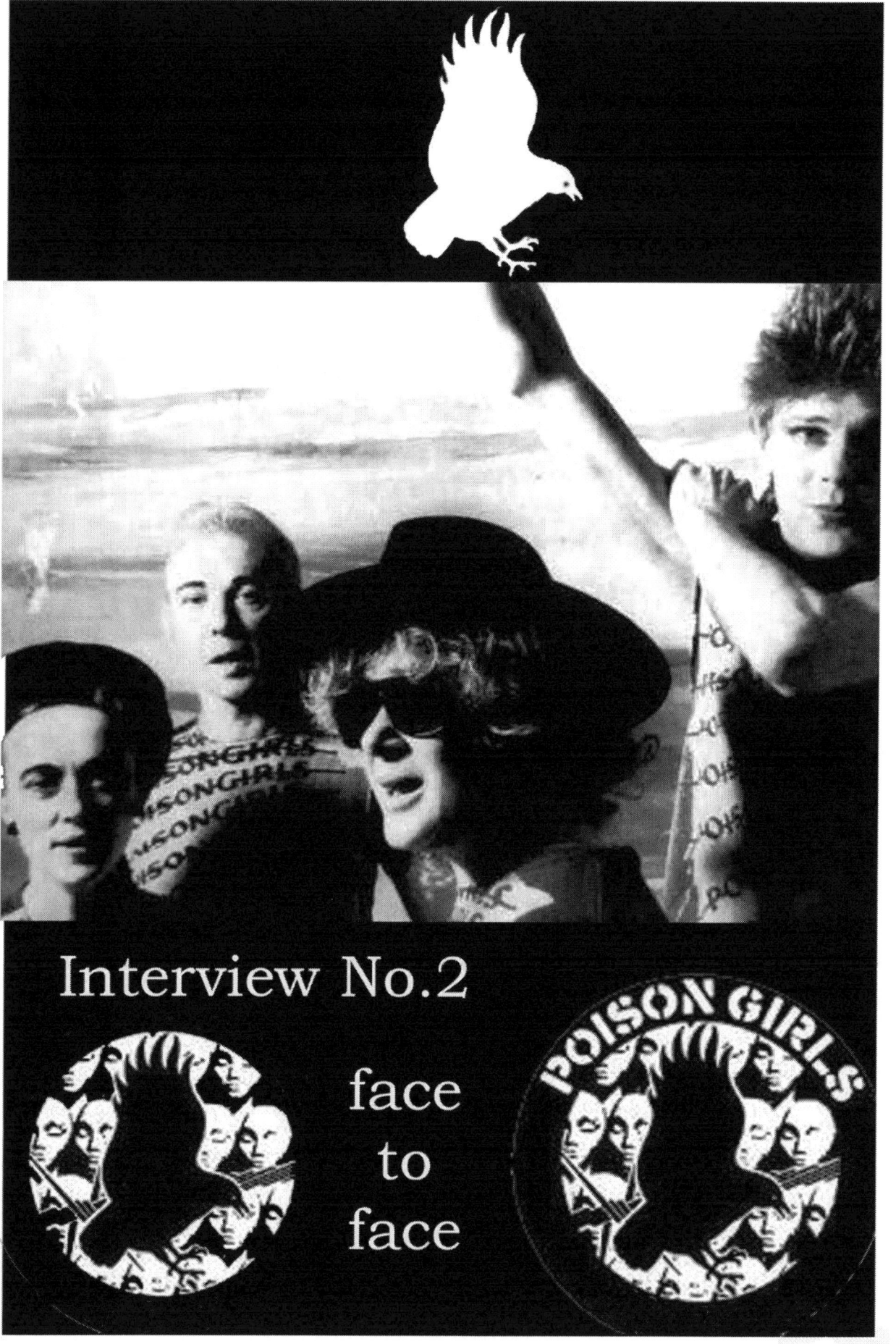

SECOND INTERVIEW WITH POISON GIRLS
LEYTONSTONE, EAST LONDON – EARLY 1982
PUBLISHED IN 'SPITTING PRETTY PIKKTURES' – A SOLITARY ISSUE.

This interview was conducted with Vi Subversa, Richard Famous and Lance d'Boyle.

Lee: Why are each of you in Poison Girls?
Vi: Because we are Poison Girls. Sorry, flippant, but existentially accurate.
Richard: Well, I think when we first started it was just a gas to do it, to get up there and brazen it out, y'know, and really exciting. Before the band, after a period of quite a long time, when a lot of creativity got stifled, I personally was in a position where somebody described me as a hobbyist, 'What are you doing now? What's your latest hobby?', and that really got to me.
Vi: When was that?
Richard: That was in 1975.
Vi: Ahh, aha!
Richard: The band is definitely not a hobby.
Vi: It probably is different for all of us in a way. I just decided it was about time I went public. I'd been living this private sort of existence up till then. There was a lot of creativity going on but it was all privatized and in people's houses, people were talking about all sorts of things. Ever since I can remember there's been exciting thoughts going on, but there's never been any possibility for the bit of it I was in to be anything other than private, and I define the reason I wanted to be in a band, I wanted to get out of the house. I think that's very important. I didn't realize how important it was at the time, one of the most important things behind one of the most exciting political changes to come about recently, like the action at Greenham Common. It isn't so much the action which results in women getting arrested but is the action of getting them out of the house, making issues that were private, public, in a situation that's open for anybody to come in and confront, and this is why I wanted to be in a band, and here you are.
(Note – Greenham Common Women's Peace Camp was established to protest against nuclear weapons being sited at RAF Greenham Common in Berkshire. The camp began in September 1981 after a Welsh group, Women for Life on Earth, arrived at Greenham to protest against the decision of the British government to allow cruise missiles to be based there. The first blockade of the base occurred in May 1982 with 250 women protesting, during which 34 arrests were made. In December 1982, 30,000 women joined hands around the base at the Embrace the Base event. On the 1st of April 1983, about 70,000 protesters

formed a 14 miles (23 km) human chain from Greenham to Aldermaston and the ordnance factory at Burghfield. The women's peace camp attracted significant media attention and inspired the creation of other peace camps at more than a dozen sites in Britain and elsewhere in Europe.)

DIRTY WORK

Bombing cities pulling switches - We won't do your dirty work
Bombing cities pulling switches - We won't do your dirty work
We won't do your dirty washing - We won't do your dirty work
We won't sterilize your dishes - Screw your dirty work

Bombing cities pulling switches - We won't do your dirty work
Making death is full employment - We won't do your dirty work
Bombing cities bombing people - While you eat your dirty meal
We won't serve you at your table - Screw your dirty deal

We won't make your dirty weapons - To defend your dirty law
All that's left is dirty water - Watch the automatic door
We won't clean the dirty basin - Blood that sticks to stainless steel
We won't do your dirty washing - War machine is bloody real

Contribution to appeasement - Pay the economic whore
Flesh and blood on dirty linen - All that's left is dirty air

We won't make your dirty weapons - To defend your dirty cause
All that's left is dirty water - We don't want your dirty war

Ask yourself what else
Ask yourself.

Lance: I think for me it's something to do with finding something that actually sticks, like Richard referred to a hobby; the band hasn't been like that. It seems like every part where it could have just stopped and been quite nice to do it for a bit, it was never like that. It seems to have a very strong impetus somewhere very deep within it that just kept it going through all sorts of times where discouragements were so large that normally you would stop doing it because it wasn't worth it, there's something about it which just keeps it going.

Vi: Well, basically, I suppose it's don't let the bastards grind you down. Every time you feel you can't do it, or is it worth it, there is that thought that having got so far and pushed so hard for so long, another twist and turn and you survive for another level or era of it or whatever.

Lee: Do you feel stronger?

Vi: Oh, yeah. It's taken me forty odd years to get over having been a child in the last world war. I worked this out last night. I've been badly scarred and hung up about a lot of things which could be summed up as having been a child in the last world war. Even if the last world war didn't happen, it would probably have been the same, the upbringing I experienced. I think I've got over it now. I realized yesterday, the air raids were over, to do with the past.

Richard: Where it connects for me being in a band and what I'm doing is that everything I do I can focus on being in the band, where before I was in the band I was doing the same amount of things but there was no focus to them, so they were all individual events in their own right. I was doing this and this and there was no connection between them. You get into a band and suddenly everything you want to do, every area of creativity, you can actually do under the heading of being in a band. The band is only 10% making music.

Lee: What's happened to Xntrix (Poison's independent label), and why did you sign up to Illuminated Records?

Lance: Xntrix records has run out of money and owes money on the projects it has done, chiefly 'Where's the Pleasure' (Poison's 2nd studio album). There isn't any money to do anything else and as we had to find some other source of income to carry on doing the things we are doing, making albums and singles, we need a lot of capitol at a certain time and so we decided to look around and ask if there was anybody who wants to give us the money and Illuminated said they would…they were lying, ha ha.

Lee: What's it been like with Illuminated so far? 'Cos usually people sign to a record label and they screw you for everything you've got and twist it up and corrupt it.

Richard: I don't think they're screwing us up, I think they're screwing themselves up, I mean, we have this effect on a lot of people we work with.

Vi: We'll come out of it alright, but they're probably going to collapse, ha ha.

Richard: Illuminated is an independent label and actually their level of efficiency isn't a lot different to what ours was, except they've got finance and people who are doing a record company full time, which we weren't able to do 'cos we are actually in the band, and I think Xntrix still exists as an umbrella, but we haven't got any money in Xntrix.

Vi: We haven't got any money and we haven't got anyone to run it.

Richard: I think a person to run it is most important.

Lee: If you get financial security with Illuminated records, could that turn into complacency?

Vi: Well, it isn't financial whatever you said it was, I always have difficulty with that word.

Richard: From Social downwards.

Vi: They haven't given us a living. They're financing records, but they haven't given us a living.

Richard: The situation we were in at the beginning of this year was, having brought out 'Where's the Pleasure', if we were going to do it ourselves we wouldn't have been able to because it would have meant increasing our debt. It costs an awful lot of money to keep a band like Poison Girls actually existing, that's not paying anyone wages or anything, that's just to keep going on the level they've been going on.

Vi: Like what? That sounds very indulgent.

Richard: Like Martin who is doing administration with us now.

Lee: What does administration entail?

Richard: He's talking to the record companies. He's organising a lot of gigs, he's working with us, just doing a lot of work that has to be done. I think the problem of working with another company is that you lose control, and you lose control 'cos you don't have actual contact with them, therefore you still have to have somebody who has contact with them regularly to make sure they're doing it the way we want it done, that's the sort of role Martin has with us…he comes round saying he's got a phone bill for £250 for setting up tours, for business which he's done about Poison Girls, y'know, that's gotta come from somewhere. We did that gig at Chats palace in Hackney and got £8 at the end, which I don't mind doing, but it actually costs us money to do gigs. We bought another van 'cos the other van was worn out, £750, that's gotta come from somewhere, we have to have a van.

Lee: A lot of your gigs have been £2.50. (Note – I was digging the band out for playing more expensive venues).

Richard: No they haven't, how many?

Lee: Most of the last tour, places like the ICA, the Venue, the Ace, they've all been £2.50 or £3.00. (Note – that was a bit more than the usual Crass/Poison Girls gig at that time).

Richard: Apart from the ICA, there's always been provision for people to get in for less than two pounds, and if people can't sort themselves out with a UB40 by now, then it's about time they could. At the Ace, there was a bloody ticket in City Limits, (Note – a magazine like Time Out that eventually folded), for people to get in for £1.50, there were 1,000 vouchers for £1.50 going round that were still available on the night, and I thinks it's a bit unfair, you saying that.

Lance: I don't think there's any danger of us becoming complacent. I think there's a danger of our audience being complacent, expecting the gig price to remain the same forever. People say 'You've signed to Illuminated, you've sold-out', and they don't even buy our fucking records. What are we supposed to do? I mean, if people actually really want us to stay independent, they should all send us £50.

Vi: Well, they should have all bought two records instead of one record, then we could have kept Xntrix going and we'd have paid those debts. We only recovered half those costs. If everybody bought two we wouldn't have had to sacrifice or compromise our virgin white politics.

Richard: I don't think we have compromised.

Vi: No, but in terms of what that question's supposed to mean.

Richard: When we originally pegged our price at a pound, when we first started working with Crass in 1978, petrol was then 68p per gallon. If you talk about it in real terms, petrol is now £1.80 per gallon, which is well over two-and-half times as much, and I don't think that £2.50, in real terms, is any more than £1 was back then.

Vi: 'Where's the Pleasure' came out last November, so you could have bought two, kept one for yourself and given one to your mum, which is where I think the record belongs in a lot of people's cases.

Lance: Most of this criticism that we get from this seems to me to come from disgruntled consumers who want cheap product, and if all they want is a cheap night out then they can all fuck off.

Richard: The other side that is we are actually dealing with a dual quality. We are actually doing a gig at the Phoenix in Charring Cross Road where it's going to cost £6 or £8 or £10 to get in, and that's great I think 'cos I don't expect the people who can't afford that to come and see us at that gig, similarly, I didn't expect, and was quite right in not expecting any of our old audience to go and see us at the ICA, where it cost £3 to get in. I wasn't at all sorry not to see them there.

Lee: Why do you play those sorts of places?

Richard: Well, there are people who go to the ICA and Charring Cross Road who would never go to Chats Palace in Hackney, or never go to the free concert we did in Brixton, and actually, if we only played in those places we would never play to those people, I think that's real, y'know? Those people that never go to see us unless we play at the Venue, or go to see us at the Venue and nowhere else, and I know those people exist 'cos they turn up when we're playing in those places.

Lee: It's the whole thing of expanding, isn't it? Trying to reach more people?

Richard: I mean, there's a very complacent bit which says we should just be playing to the sort of people that we have been playing to or who think that we are their band, I mean, I still like them and we're definitely not going to abandon them.

Lance: If it were to come to that, in a years time they'd say 'Oh, Poison Girls, that's boring, they don't do anything', then they abandon us. The way we conduct ourselves is public property, and the way our 'fans' conduct themselves is not. It's a very uneven thing. Everyone can see what we're doing and can criticize it, but we have no way of knowing what they're doing and we can't criticize them. They criticize us anytime they like and then disappear and go and work for ICI, we wouldn't know, would we? It's not a community of people who are all acting in full knowledge of what everybody else is doing.

Vi: What we need are certain special people who might be called spies, but which shouldn't really be called spies, checking up and telling us about the bad behaviour and ideological unsoundness of our fans.

Richard: Go on, Lee.

Vi: Which we can then make public. We do set ourselves up, and I did say at the beginning that I wanted to go public, and it's good to have these discussions.

Lee: Well, these are doubts that people are having and I feel these doubts have to be confronted.

Richard: I think if we'd stayed in the 'Total Exposure' mode of Poison Girls, which was very much an option, we could have done it, stayed playing that sort of music to that audience, and it would have been a sham for us and for an audience who thought they were getting something real from us.

Vi: Why?

Richard: Because what we wanted to do, and have done, is move on from there and attempt to push back some of the barriers which we were up against. If an audience can't see that it's always about pushing back barriers.

Lee: It's like a continuous revolution, gotta keep moving, isn't it?

Richard: If you don't keep moving, then it's over really, once you get stuck into nostalgia.

Vi: And a fashion. I think fashions have a definite time cycle. They last just about long enough to get somebody through their rebellious stage, and just as the fashion peters out, they're just about ready to settle down. I'm sure that's true of the punk fashion.

Lee: And a lot of people line their pockets on the way.
Vi: And how does that happen? Who is manipulating that? I think that what we are doing has never been particularly fashionable. I don't think Poison Girls were ever the leaders of the punk fashion, we were there, we were real in it, but I think the fashion aspect of revolution is manipulative and destined to make everybody redundant and obsolete within that sort of five to seven years or whatever it is that fashion lasts, probably less than that, and so you blow it, you blow your rebellious energy identifying with the latest rebellious fashion. You shock your parents. You have to get out of the house. You do it, but by the time you're really maybe poised to start something a bit really dangerous, the fashion's over and you've been negated, and I think it's very important that that is understood, 'cos I don't think we're anything to do with that.
Lee: Part of that must come from, like the hippy generation, 'cos there are so many similarities.
Vi: Yeah, that's absolutely right, there is a life cycle, it starts off with good raw energy and things do shift, and then it peaks and then it starts to go decadent, and out of both the hippy and the punk, the most lasting thing to come out of it are business men, and the kids just disappear. I mean, that isn't true 100%, but the extent to which it isn't true is the extent to which people can survive fashion and not have to remain loyal to it so you go down with a sinking ship.
Lee: Talking of the fears that people have with Poison Girls at the moment, a lot of them feel frightened that you want to leave behind the alternative scene; this is building a barrier as well. I see the point of breaking away from it 'cos people are too secure with it.
Richard: I don't think we are leaving behind the alternative scene, I think we are the alternative scene.
Vi: We have to remain it.
Richard: The people who are still stuck in leather jackets, snakeskin pants, etc,
the people who, in their heart of hearts, want it to be 1977 again; those are the ones who left the alternative scene behind.
Lee: The people who want it to '77 - '78 weren't there in '77 – '78. It's the nostalgia trip, isn't it? I grew up then and I just want to keep it moving forward, 'cos going back is giving up.
Richard: I honestly don't think we are wanting to leave behind the alternative scene or get out of it, unless it like the same way with rock music, there was progressive rock in '68-'69, then in '74 progressive rock meant something that was really, really boring, and they're still doing it now.
Lance: Like the things they put on The Old Grey Whistle Test. We've been here a long time, especially Vi and me. We've seen it all before, lots and lots of times, and we know what the pattern is. This is the first time many people have experienced a phenomena which has grabbed them, but we've been grabbed, exploited and dropped about six times, so it's clear how it all works.
Lee: So, could you define an alternative to the alternative?
Richard: I think it's people who are continually looking, not content with what's being offered.
Vi: I think one of the dangers is precisely in your question. Once you define something too

clearly it then becomes possible for someone to grab it, exploit it and drop it, manipulate and use it to diffuse the next wave of revolutionary passion. As soon as you said that, I realized that we don't spend much time defining it and we've always had this problem in a business that requires you to define yourself very precisely all the time. What sort of music do you play? What sort of clothes do you wear? And all that sort of thing is a way of defining and packaging something in order to make it obsolete, to dispose of it. And I think we've always had great difficulty in defining it, what we are, in a way, is too real to define. It's very much a mixture of all sorts of strands of life that are going on in a context that is trying all the time so suppress life, so it might be that we are a mixture of all sorts of things, like, using terms which have already been defined; feminist, anti-sexism, anti-war, or whatever, but basically I see them all as strands of disobedience within ours system and you can't really define it. There's a danger in defining it, also in forgetting what it's about. When you're basically disobedient, it doesn't matter what you want, the important thing is what you don't want. I can't define what I want half the time…I know passionately that what I've got isn't good enough. It's the old thing; can we lay down blue-prints for an anarchist society? In a way you can't 'cos it's like permanently half what's in your imagination and in your desires and half making do with what you've got with basic raw material. How can you define a statue when all you've got is a block of stone and you haven't actually seen what you want to make?

Richard: That's right. The act of defining it means that that's the process it goes through. You have to be a 'real punk', wear the right clothes or listen to the right music, and if you don't then you're not a punk by someone else's definition of what punk is.

Lee: That was the thing in '77 – do your own thing.

Vi: It was also the motto of the hippies in the '60's. It was very much a part of the beatnik scene that one of the bloody papers is trying to resurrect as this week's thing.

Lance: I think if you look back through all these movements that we've been associated with…punk came along as a reaction to degenerate hippiedom, in fact, the spirit is very similar, it goes back to the beatniks and the beats…

Vi: The bohemians, dada's and surrealist's…

Richard: The flapper's…

Lance: It's a long strand that's been called all kinds of different things, but I think the intention and the spirit is the same, and I think you have to learn to recognize it when it's happening, but not really be able to define it before it does.

Vi: I think it has to be frightening in some ways, in the way that Quentin Crisp was frightening when he appeared in the street with eye make-up on. I saw him in the '50's and he frightened me, I was fascinated, mind you, 'cos I like that. There's a connection between fear and excitement that is part of what we're talking about. The other thing is staying with the 'Total Exposure' mode, which is what we were doing, but it was becoming really comfortable, it wasn't frightening us anymore.

Lee: Why did you decide on using a synth at your gigs?

Vi: We'd always used the synth in recording and if we were doing it in recording then it should be part of what we're doing live.

Richard: Again, it's taking chances. We wanted to expand the actual style of music that we were doing and it's quite difficult. I don't think we'll ever get away from being a guitar-based band, but actually being able to add another instrument and another vocalist just expands the possibilities of sound that we can use. I don't think we've lost the ferocity of our performance.

Lee: I think your performances are a lot more emotional now. Do you pick up on the feelings that you generate at gigs? Does that come back at you?

Vi: Yeah. I used to be afraid of audiences and some of that was productive, it got you keyed up and feeling that you had to do something. The other side of it is that there's too much fear…

Lee: The Crass audience is mostly male, isn't it?

Vi: I was going to say that, it comes back to that. When I said I'd got over the fear of my upbringing, a lot of that was as a child. I didn't know many boys or men and certainly it was quite protected and I went to a girls school, and coming as it did as a reaction to the hippy thing, I found the clothing and the style and the militaristic aspect of it frightening, but that's all in brackets…the other bit of that fear is that it inhibits you and I was frozen with fear, paralyzed with fear a lot of the time in the beginning. I've just found out lately, since we've broken away and done more of what we wanted to do, I've got more confidence. We've taken a few risks that seem to have worked, like 'Where's the Pleasure', I'm now a lot more confident to actually feel what the audience is feeling and working with that.

Richard: Coming back to saying it's more emotional. The success of any band is how it mirrors the emotions that it's dealing with. What you're picking up on now is that we're dealing with more emotions than just anger. The base of all punk music was always in anger, we're still of and in touch with that anger, but I think there's other things as well that are coming through, which are much more difficult, musically, to portray.

Vi: It always that even in the heart of hard core punk audiences, like one gig we did recently in Manchester, which was 100% really punked-up audience, y'know, and it felt quite frightening. There were a lot of issues we were dealing with; management of the place and the way the gig had been advertised and how much the beer was and everything, it was all quite confronting, the whole scene. It was one of the best gigs we did on the tour and what happened was that all that anger got broken through, where there was so much trust that I felt coming from the audience that I was able to give more of that emotion.

What is proved by that is that all the tender sort of emotional stuff, or more complex than raw anger, is very much felt by the audience, and people do want recognition that they're feeling more than just wanting to get up and fight and shout. There's a huge amount of energy there which is to do with wanting to love and take risks and be vulnerable and admit and be honest about all that, that I think was suppressed, and it was quite oppressive, all that hard core punk stereotype stuff.

Lee: Since your music's sort of changed, let's say from 'Where's the Pleasure', that's like a changing point, since then your audience has changed a lot. There's less leather jackets, it's more of a mixed audience, and the music is tenderer. I've seen people crying at your gigs, is that what you actually wanted, did you want that change to happen?

Vi: Yes, I think the aspects of leather jackets, which is armour, was a barrier to us getting through, to do what we wanted to do with an audience.

Richard: We have always played the tender songs.

Vi: I just want to say, that bit about armour. The writing on the inside of the sleeve of 'All Systems Go' says 'Outside the system there's only you and me and our mutual nakedness'. I think that's always been part of what we're doing, like the slow songs on 'Hex'; 'Bremen Song', and 'Other' (on 'Chappaquiddick Bridge' album), and 'Tender Lover'.

OTHER

You're so other
You turn me on so strange
You plunge me in so deep
Lurch me out of my made up mind
You're such another kind
You're so other
You turn me on so strange
Plunge me in so deep
Plunge me in to the heart of me
You creep me in my sleep
You're so other
You fall me or did you push
You shook me off my tree
Lurched me out of my made up mind
You swam me out to sea
You're so other
You're so white so pale
As you lie on my dark skin
You're from the other side
No familiarity to ease me in
You're so other
You turn me on so strange
You move me along my skin
You're from another side
Sensuality to tease me in
Will you be my lover
I have loved another
But none so other

Lee: 'Who sleeps with who tonight' is a line from your song 'Ménage Abattoir', is that song based on personal experience, and have you ever seen the lover's triangle work?
Vi: I think it's what's in a lot of people's minds a lot of the time…yeah? No?
Lee: Yeah.
Vi: In my personal experience it has been an issue going back through from whenever, it's entirely nothing to do with fashion, is it? I think it's a basic human thing. The song is about jealousy and that's certainly from personal experience. There's a lot of people trying very hard. I've never seen it work, but I've seen a lot of people try, and it depends on what you

mean by 'work'?
Lee: It working means that everybody is happy.
Vi: No, I've never seen that, but maybe you should ask others.
Lee: I've been involved in that situation; it's either jealousy or possession that screws it up.
Vi: It's very important, a lot of energy is wasted and tied up in that whole area. It's not a side issue, it's fundamental; it's part of ownership patterns or security needs that we're all struggling with. I know it's not scientifically correct to bring in other species, but I've seen jealousy operate in animals and bird life, not always. There are life forms that don't have it at all, and the snail doesn't have any problems! It's both male and female.
Lee: That's probably the solution, isn't it?
Vi: And as far as I know, in occurs in heterosexual and it occurs in homosexual and it occurs in lesbian relationships as well.
Lee: I think it's important for people to keep challenging the concepts of so-called normality, the same with the family as well…are you pleased with the way your kids turned out?
Vi: Yeah, well, most of the time…er…I think I didn't have great expectations in terms of what they ought to be, the only strong desire I had was that my relationship with my children would be a lot better than my relationship with my family, which was really bad and still is really bad. That's another thing I haven't been able to solve. My relationship with Dan and Gemma is, I think, very good, especially my relationship with Gemma, and I think the quality of the relationship with Dan is very close, but there are resistances and issues that I can't help him with in the way that I can with Gemma 'cos of him being male. For example, I went to Greenham Common with Gemma just recently, for the first time, for both of us, and there was a whole lot of stuff about the expectations she's been living with on her as a young girl, to do with boyfriends, etc, etc, and she hadn't had any first hand experiences of being in women only groups or situations, and we went there, and it is basically a women's only situation at Greenham, whatever else it is, that's fundamental, and what happened was we sat down there and were just listening and being with everybody round the campfire, and suddenly Gemma turned to me and said 'It wouldn't be anything like this if there were men here', not even saying better or worse, just that something was happening that couldn't possibly happen if there were men there. Well, there aren't any places like that for boys, maybe you don't feel the need of it, but I know that when I was talking to Dan the other day, I realized a lot of what he is struggling with in terms of his relationships, sexual or otherwise, is to do with his difficult feelings about himself as a male, 'cos he's grown up with me and I've said a lot of really heavy things and done a lot of really heavy things which have attacked his manhood, in inverted commas. I've slagged-off male ways and I've left him at times with nothing to identify with. Well, I think that's very sad. I feel sad about that, because of my own survival it was necessary, but he's got a lot of mending to do and a lot of things to sort out for himself, and I think they'll have to be sorted out with other men, or other boy's who have experienced similar feelings. I can't do that with him, and there isn't a Greenham Common, a place for that to be sorted out. I think it's important that it's clear that this has to be done.
Lee: Yeah, for a female to change, I mean, there's a thing where people say a woman has it worse 'cos it's a male society, which it is, and I know it's hard, but people don't often realize

that it's just as hard for the male to un-condition himself with his sexist ways, like you said, Dan hasn't been left with much. I think every male has to go down to that level where they're not left with much, and then you start re-building yourself, 'cos that's how you find yourself.

Vi: And do you think that's something you can do on your own, individually?

Lee: I think I was halfway there when I moved here to London a year ago, but the experience of living and sharing with people (in East London squats), to be able to communicate every sort of feeling, well, I think that's necessary as well. You can't totally sort yourself out without other people, I think it's impossible.

Vi: Well, maybe it's not necessary for there to be a public place like Greenham Common, which is somewhere to go, out of the house, out of the private situation and work through all those things that everybody's feeling in a way, where you've got to be really open. I'm not suggesting a male peace camp, just that this is important. (Tape runs out)

Part Three: The South
1982-88 – A Throw of the Dice

CHAPTER 5

Two weeks after receiving the phone call from Martin L. asking me if I wanted the hotel job in London, I moved out of our house in The Gables and headed south. I took a few belongings with me, as usual, I was travelling light. I've travelled light through my whole life. I broke up with Mandy, ending our relationship of almost three years. Splitting up was messy, to be honest. She came to visit me in London shortly after my move, along with my parents. I told her it was over, it was very awkward for her and my folks, but my mind was made up (She later married a soldier!?). I also had a good heart to heart with my dad and we stepped-on, moving beyond the ills of my childhood. All sins were forgiven and the future remained open and completely unwritten, that's not to say that certain mental scars have been or ever will be erased. My dad has since said that after our chat, in some bar near Trafalgar Square, he knew that everything was going to be ok betwixt us and I'm glad to say that it has been. We got over the past and we got over ourselves and we transcended many things – if only the father/son thing could work out like that for other people, but in my experience, that's not usually how it pans out.

A few days after my arrival in London I began work as a porter at the Eden Park Hotel in Bayswater, West London, just a few streets away from Hyde Park. I didn't know anyone, but at least I'd escaped Stockton and the police pressure that was slowly but steadily building up. London was an easy place in which to vanish. I was also much closer to Camden Town for the printing of my next fanzine. No more 250 mile train journeys each way and camping out on their city farm with the hogs and the horses. No more cops bursting into my room and trying to bust me as a bloody terrorist. I'd finally achieved a state of invisibility and that suited me just fine.

Martin L and his partner (can't recall her name) helped me settle in and we used to go out for a drink. His sister, Lorraine, also moved out of The Gables and moved to London and we had a brief, electric affair. Martin showed me the ropes with the job and I quickly found my feet. A fellow porter was a Jamaican guy called Thomas. He used to make me laugh. The South-African Apartheid regime was still in full swing at that time and whenever we got white South African hotel guests, many of them would refuse to let him handle their bags or even let him get into the elevator with them. When Thomas recognized these bigoted types, he would nimbly step into the lift with them just before the doors closed, and then, much to their horror, he would proceed to breathe all over them.

Another porter was called Hassan. He came from Iran. All the time I knew him he was living in a suppressed state of fear. He was trying to get immunity so that he could stay in the UK – he knew that if he returned to Iran that he would be tortured and probably killed.

The hotel work was easy and we ran a good few scams to increase our lowly wages. I lived in a small room in the basement of the hotel – my rent was deducted from my wages – it's not like they gave me a free room. Within a few months I was working behind reception, doing various shifts. Night shift was a dead zone. During the day, we often received a coach full of female Spanish visitors, they were all over here to abort their unborn children; being Catholics, it was the only option for them at that time. When the women called home, we'd charge them less than they should have paid, but we wouldn't log their calls and we'd keep their cash. It was a good deal for everyone, apart from the hotel.

Whenever a daytime shift finished I would go for a swim in a nearby pool on Queensway, where I would swim until I was exhausted. Eventually I was doing 100 lengths in a single bash although I doubt I could do five lengths now without needing a cigarette break or an oxygen tent! After a swim, I would buy a large bag of fruit from a local store and go walkabout. I saw many homeless people in that area of London and I felt pity for their plight. I used to walk about and give any beggar on the street some fruit, knowing that if I gave them cash they would just buy another can or bottle of booze – I don't know who I thought I was, judging them like that – so what if they'd spend it on booze, it's not like I was going to help cure their alcoholism or their mental issues. When I handed out my apples I always received a puzzled look. No doubt they were thinking to themselves 'What good is a fucking apple to me?' Eventually I stopped doing that and just pretty much ignored them, like everyone else. Looking back, maybe I should have just wandered by and simply not given a fuck, or perhaps got down with their basic reality and given them a can or two of Special Brew (Brain Juice), to help kick-start their day.

Whenever I had the afternoon off work I would always take a wander around Hyde Park. I found a spot near the Serpentine that had a lot of squirrels hanging out in the trees and I would take food for them. I soon made friends with a squirrel that only had one eye. It happened in a moment – the little dude jumped on me, hung on for a while, and then he jumped off my shoulder and scrambled up a nearby tree. After that, every time I walked by, he would cling to a low-hanging branch with his rear legs and then lower himself until he could rest his front paws in the palm of my hand and then he would eat his fill – it was a gentle touch of nature in the midst of a frantic city.

At night I would buy a bottle of cheap sherry and just set out walking the streets, taking in my surroundings, watching the bright lights of Soho and Piccadilly, oftentimes staggering my way through all that shit and barely watching my back, (London streets were – and still are - full of scum just itching to exploit anything and anyone – same as any town, any place), immersing myself in the hectic pulse of the city and the fakery of it all; the drunken tourists, cops whose only purpose was to give directions to lost tourists or bust them on the spot and 'liberate' whatever drugs they might be carrying...gliding past rich tourists eating in posh restaurants, the endless flow of traffic, sirens always howling (do they ever reach their final destination?).

Around that time I started receiving quite a few letters from people who read my fanzines, peaking out at about 30 letters a week, so I would spend time each day drinking sherry and writing back to people. I wrote back to anyone who wrote to me. Some days, by the time I'd finished responding to my mail, I'd be utterly drunk. It was strange - although I was alone in London, I never felt alone. Sometimes people I wrote to would travel into London to meet up with me and we'd just walk the streets, two virtual strangers, and chat about everything under the Sun, then we'd go to see a band and afterwards go our separate ways.

I started going to see bands in London on my own. At first, it was rather big gigs at large established venues, such as The Lyceum, Brixton Ace, and others whose names I can't recall. I remember taking LSD one evening and I went to see The Virgin Prunes and The Birthday Party at a venue in Victoria. I saw Nick Cave for the first time on the street before the gig; black suit, pointed boots, white shirt and wild, black, back-combed hair. I was too shy to go up to him and say hello.

The gig, like most Birthday Party gigs, was intense and primal, with each member of the band dancing on the edge of a chaotic abyss. By the time the gig was over I was sweating from my time in the mosh pit and tripping, bug-eyed, out of my skull. I made my way to the tube station, thinking that no-one would notice, or care, if I was tripping. A tube train was just closing its doors as I stepped onto the platform so I grabbed the black rubber edging of the doors and held them apart before jumping onboard. I took my seat, still sweating, thinking that no-one could see the things that were swimming around inside my head and shimmering before my eyes. They didn't know that their faces were melting like something from a dream by Salvador Dali; like clock faces made of soft cheese.

It was only when I finally made it back to my little room in the hotel and looked at my face in the mirror that I realized I'd blown it. I looked at my face. I looked at my hands – they were covered in black rubber from the tube doors. Because I'd been sweating on the tube, I'd been wiping my face. My face was covered in black streaks. I looked like a soldier, blacked-up in cammo, like a very skinny Arnie Schwarzenegger getting ready for a mission in a deep, remote jungle someplace. So much for tripping, undercover, in the public arena – I must have looked like a complete madman, no wonder my fellow passengers averted their gaze, and perhaps concealed the occasional smirk.

*

In the 1980's there were only a handful of American bands that I liked; I preferred American writers and novelists. Among the few I liked were The Ramones, Talking Heads, Patti Smith, some Iggy Pop stuff and even Blondie, but my favourite U.S. band of the time were the Gun Club, founded by Jeffrey Lee Pierce, who at one time ran the Blondie fan club. It would be a few decades before I began to appreciate the likes of Johnny Cash, The Residents, and a wide range of early and modern hillbilly stuff.

The Gun Club, from Los Angeles, carved a unique niche for themselves, playing a dark blend of punk, rockabilly, swampy slide guitar, country and blues, with notable songs such as 'Sex Beat', 'Jack on Fire', 'She's like Heroin to me', and 'For the Love of Ivy'-

Gonna buy me a gun just as long as my arm
And kill everyone who ever done me wrong

I first saw the Gun Club the second time they played in London, at the Lyceum, April 1983, supported by The Sisters of Mercy, New Model Army, and punkette poet, Joolz. From the get-go Jeffrey Lee Pierce, singer/lyricist/guitarist, was off his face – at the time he was addicted to speed, smack and gin, and it was that unholy trio that eventually led to his demise. JLP died in 1996, aged 37, he was HIV positive and also suffered from chronic cirrhosis of the liver and hepatitis. I recall he sang and wailed and hollered and mumbled his way incoherently through much of the gig, and at one point he vanished behind a huge curtain that hung at the back of the stage and continued to sing – rumour had it that he was also busy shooting-up smack.

The general consensus is that the Gun Club never received the proper recognition that they deserved. Even to day, their albums rock, as does JLP's solo work – highly recommended.

On a small tribute Gun Club web site by Kris Needs, who was a drinking pal and friend of Jeffrey Lee Pierce while the Gun Club were based in London, observes-

The Gun Club at London's Lyceum has since gone down as one of the great gigs. Jeffrey wore an admiral's jacket and hat, for some reason, and caterwauled through a set which bristled and smoked with evil heat. He was staggering – in more ways than one. 'I don't know about anyone else, but I had a ball,' he giggled later.

*

On 20th July 1982 I was taking one of my regular solitary strolls through Hyde Park when a sudden explosion shook the ground and nearby buildings and knocked my off my feet. I knew that a bomb had gone off and quickly proceeded to walk away from the source of the blast, not wanting to bear witness to any scenes of carnage, and also fearful that another explosion might follow.

I found out later that day that the IRA had detonated a large nail bomb. The bomb was hidden in a blue Austin car in the park's South carriage Drive and was deliberately remotely detonated as members of the Royal Household cavalry (the Queen's bodyguard regiment), travelled from their barracks toward Buckingham Palace.

The soldiers were killed instantly and a fourth died later from his injuries. The other soldiers and members of the public, along with visiting tourists, were also badly wounded as nails and shrapnel prayed into the crowd. Seven horses were also killed, or later had to be euthanized due to the severity of their injuries.

In 1987 Northern Ireland electrician Gilbert 'Danny' McNamee was charged with making the Hyde Park bomb and he was jailed for 25 years. He served 12 years before being freed under the terms of the Good Friday peace deal. In 1998 he conviction was quashed at the High Court, deeming it 'unsafe' because of withheld fingerprint evidence that implicated other bomb makers.

*

As I started getting used to living in London and the way that no-one really bothered you for the way you looked, I began to like it. In Stockton, for example, people seemed to be looking for a fight seven days a week. London was different and everyone seemed more intent with getting on with their own thing. It didn't seem to suffer from the small-town, small-mind syndrome. Obviously that was a misperception by me, and even today, London is locked into a small-town, small-mind headset, with kids stabbing and shooting each other because they live in a different post-code area or in the opposite tower block (Block Wars, like something out of the Judge Dredd comics).

Andy T. And Pam (his partner in crime at the time) came down to stay with me overnight in my room en route to a gig. We decided to print out 200 small stickers each and split the cost, and stick them all over the place – I recall that mine read something obscure from the Bible, something to do with Do What Thou Wilt. Andy's was more practical and down to earth, like him, and read: 'If you follow the sheep you'll only get slaughtered.'

We also talked about collaborating and creating a one-off fanzine together, writing and designing our own pages and then putting them all together into one 'zine. Being awkward buggers we both agreed that it shouldn't even have a name. We decided to use black for the written text and red for background images. We also wanted to step above the usual 500 copies and opted for 1,000. We also decided to do a glossy cover, just like a 'real' magazine.

That particular collaboration eventually came to fruition because, like me, Andy T. had a fire in his belly and wanted to make things happen. We were helped out by Andy M. (The Apostles), who worked at a lithographic printing press in Wapping. Crass donated a black and white photograph for the front cover; Steve Ignorant, naked, wearing an animal mask and hanging upside down from a butcher's hook. So, no title, no clues as to what lurked within the pages, just some guy hanging like a piece of dead meat on the cover. Once the fanzine was written and printed, Andy took 500 copies and I took 500, and over the next few months we sold them all as we hitched to various gigs around the country, hitting different kinds of audiences as we had differing tastes in music beyond the Crass/Poison Girls scene. That was the great thing about the two of us, me North-East, him North-West; between us we covered some turf. Wish I had a copy of that zine for myself, if only to count the spelling mistakes and see what the hell we were writing about at that time.

*

I started reading Crowley's 'Magick' and seriously began to study various aspects of occultism, (a study that went on for ten years before I actually performed my first ritual). I bought my books from Atlantis bookstore near the British Museum (an old occult bookstore that Crowley actually frequented), and from Mysteries on Bloomsbury Way. I also purchased my first set of Tarot cards and started to use them on a regular basis, getting to know them. I did, for a time, use the Tarot as a fortune telling device, for myself and for others, and I got pretty good at it, but eventually realized that the true power of the Tarot lay in their use as a self-reflective tool, especially when working with the mystical Qabalah, and as a gateway to meditation techniques. Each card is a doorway. My interest and growing obsession with occultism did put some distance between me and the hard-core anarchists/activists. It also put a little distance between me and Andy T. - over the next year or so we kind of drifted apart and lost touch with one another. Like lots of friendships and relationships, life just got in the way. But life is strange, and even stranger is how the circle becomes complete. After we did our fanzine I didn't see Andy T. for 24 years until the circle finally decided to fulfil its cycle and we met up once again, just last year, and together with my son, Felix, we attended a clandestine gig by The Mob in Shoreditch, East London, as part of a stag-night for Jamie Hince (The Kills), before he got hitched to Kate Moss.

*

During those early months in London, and perhaps before I even moved to London, I began writing to Kim C. She lived in Harrow, North London. I think we actually fell in love with each other through our mutual correspondence. It got to the point where we were writing three, or more, very honest and open letters a week to each other. Eventually, we agreed to meet-up at a gig.

Our coming together was certainly written in the stars; you couldn't make this stuff up. That first time we met for a 'date' in a bar, we both had our Tarot cards with us and we ended up back at my place and made love that same night. Kim was and still is a writer, singer and artist of great talent, she was also into Wicca. We had an on and off relationship that spanned over twenty years, weaving through my twenties, thirties and forties.

We collaborated on the creation of two fanzines – I provided the words, Kim provided the artwork. We worked well together. One of the 'zines was called The Sensation Rebellion, the second fanzine included a great sketch that transformed the spire of a church into an erect penis, and she also painted my portrait with a 'star' in the background.

Later her band, DeSirius, used some of my lyrics for their songs and I made a video of them rehearsing. We also both worked together, along with Neil K., on a 3 song demo for my tattooist mate, Paul C aka The Confuzer.

Our path was deeply interwoven, erratic, erotic, magical and sometimes deeply confusing, and the spark of fire between us could sometimes prove dangerous, even reckless. I crossed more lines and broke more rules for Kim than I ever did for any other female of the species. Kim later got married and has two sons. I have no idea where she now lives and I doubt that our paths will ever cross again, unless the Devil has other plans?

(Note/addendum– Kim and I recently collided via the medium of Facebook and we've communicated with good humour – so another circle or cycle has ended/begun. This is something that seems to be a common thread for many people who were creatively active during the punk/post-punk/anarcho-punk eras, using a technology that didn't exist back in those days to re-connect/e-connect and kick-start another wave of protest for a younger generation; something that has been happening a lot during the writing of this re-call.)

Kim has sent me a few scanned pages from one of the 'zines we did together, and she's also informed me that she'd written her own flashback, some if it regarding our relationship. Kim used to call me Merlin and she once did a portrait of me called @Merlin with his Star' – the star is a UFO. Kim has given me permission to enclose the following piece that she wrote just recently – so here goes:

*

Merlin (by Kim C.)

I met Merlin via the 'zine scene, which is important because it was the first in a series of key, karmic-style, turning points in my life all triggered by writing.

Irrationally perhaps, I've always believed that meeting him was pivotal in leading me to where I am today; one of those "if not for" moments. He was my path into the abyss. □

Merlin bought a fanzine and liked my writing. I guess he read between the lines. We wrote to each other while I was still living at home and he yet to escape the desolate wastelands of the North East.

When we first met I was vain and silly and ill-prepared to penetrate the mystery. The next time I was ready and eager to take it on; he was the epitome of tall, dark and handsome after all. Our third meeting was a proper date, and by then he was living in London; there was nothing in the way.

Although it wasn't my first time, I discovered sex that night. I surprised us both.

Who knew that beautiful things could happen the basements of slightly seedy West End hotels?

I fell in love, and my obsessive side seized upon it. I lived in a kind of fraught teenage bliss for about three months until Merlin unexpectedly broke it off and introduced me to The Dark Night of the Soul. At the time I believed that I hadn't done anything wrong, but hindsight has revealed a bad case of erotic parasitism.

Retrospection, however, has never eliminated the influence of a certain Mr Vex from the equation. At our first close-up meeting, there was an atmosphere of mutual hostility and sourness in the room that bell-ringing could not banish. I had had a premonition of the approaching fight over the choicest parts of the crab.

After a day or two's bed rest at Heartbreak Hotel, I discovered that the black lake of my fathomless despair had a bottom. The lesson initiated the first steps taken on a new journey, laden with excess baggage though it was.

I won't say it was easy, and there were days of slipping backwards and clawing forward, but it was better than the black tarn, and I began to be content.

I left home, I had adventures and met new people, I allowed my creativity to protect me.

But Merlin wouldn't go away. So much of what I did during that time was to impress him or get his attention and I made or took opportunities to be with him that were detrimental to health and bypassed self-respect. That was some sense I had yet to knock into myself.

I convinced him that I was mended so that we could be friends and encouraged him to use me, whereby I had in turn used him. We didn't have the term 'fuck buddy' back then, but its bluntness may have been enlightening. It was a confusing time for both of us and, as became the norm, hard to say who was summoning what. Always, at the back of the room observing the proceedings, was Vex, the toxic gnome.

We levelled with the writing: did a 'zine together, words for pictures and pictures for words. That was a good time. There were other times that were painful and negative; there were harsh words and fights.

Those eighteen months are a big jumble in my head; events and timelines indistinct; years later I came to see that it was all part of the process, whatever that process was for.

As with many a midsummer day's nightmare, the course of true love never did run smooth.

Actions beyond my control, bringing about the end of my time in North West London, then led me to darkest Hackney.

Straight, of course, into the path of the oncoming train crash that was Merlin and me.

Brougham Road needs a book all to itself. Although it had positive elements, I didn't do well there. In part this was down to the proximity of the flame to the never-settling moth.

Merlin was on some kind of slippery slope and I was fully prepared to follow him down. Some of the most shameful and messy things happened during this surreal, precarious and murky period.

Vex was a big part of it. He was big in The Street, having ingratiated himself with a lot of people, all of whom eventually saw him for what he was. In the big picture it might be hard to decide who was worst for Merlin – me or Vex. Most likely, we all got what we deserved.

Nature, of course, has a habit of having spring follow winter.

I got to be a singer in my first proper band, which was something I'd always longed for. That, and the subsequent changes, like moving out of The Street, played a big part in knocking me from the gravitational pull of planet Merlin.

At the tail end of The Great Insanity Merlin left London for the North West to live with his parents; I think for a multiple detox. I was absorbed in my life and I didn't care that much about him anymore. But

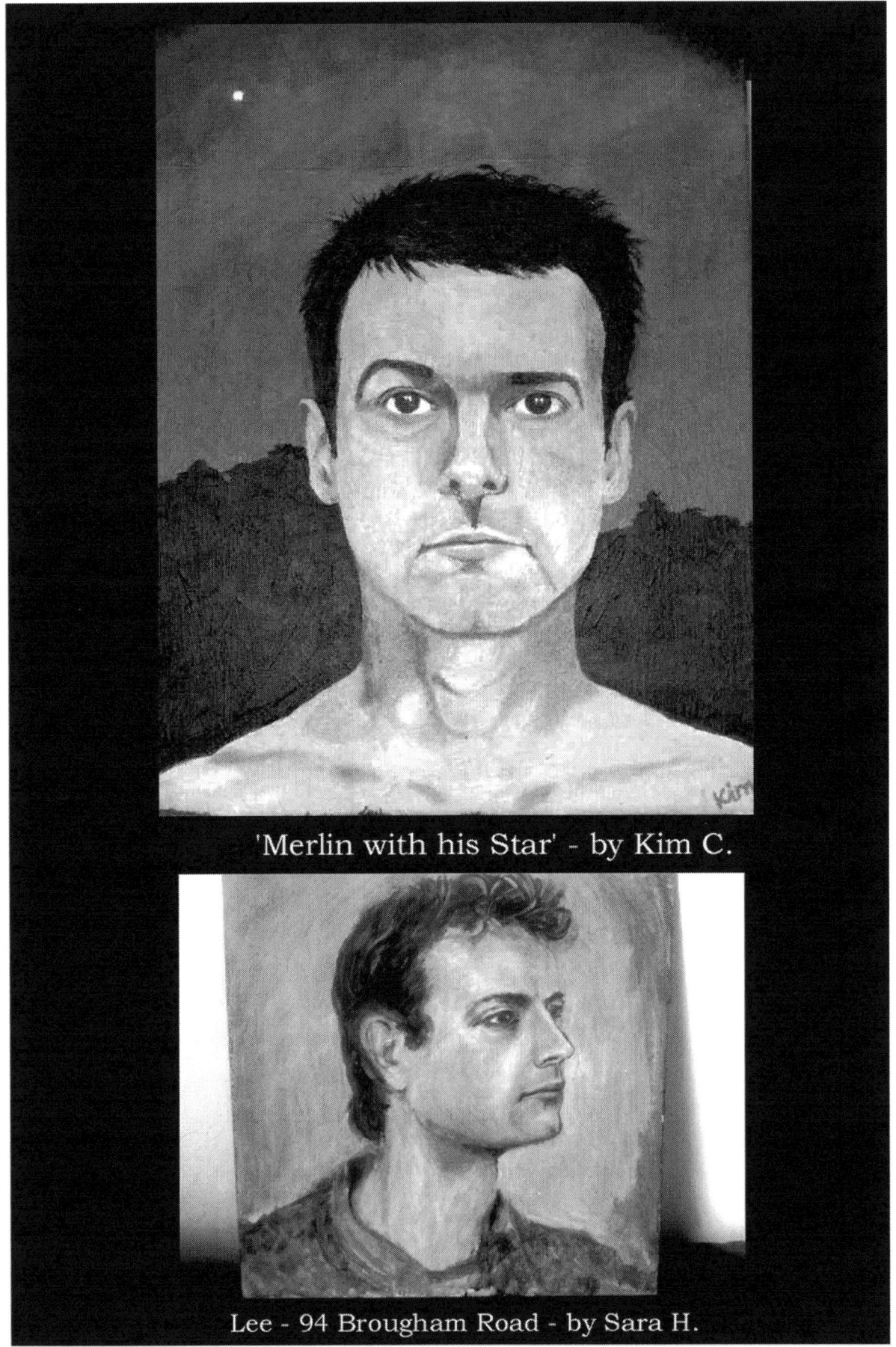

'Merlin with his Star' - by Kim C.

Lee - 94 Brougham Road - by Sara H.

one day, he rematerialized to put a different kind of spell on me. In the middle of an ordinary afternoon, a single glance exchanged across a room full of people resurrected the spark which exposed the nature of the darkness.

A day or two later he wrote to me and told me he loved me. I wasn't impressed, but then my curiosity took the lead; part of me wanted to attend to that unfinished business. We began another affair, the one, if all was in fact just and sound in the world, that we should've had in the first place. The one we probably deserved.

The good times. Emotional, intellectual, sexual, magical – all tuned in and connected. There was no one but us, and neither of us was unhinged. The second time around, I knew I was worth having. We went to so many places which remain with me as really great memories: a day at High Force falls; racing through the North York moors on an empty train; the ruin of Whitby Abbey; and what Merlin called afterwards, 'The lake of death and the river of life' near Bangor.

What was essentially a holiday romance was not meant to last however. Eventually I had to go home, back to the everyday, and this time it was I who walked away.

I moved house again, to a nicer part of Hackney and, after a long relationship with someone else, was free and restless and long overdue for some playing of the field. Merlin still liked me, I got to be mean and nice to him at the same time. We were old friends, yet we weren't friends at all and never had been, and with the help of time and tide all the lines had become blurred.

Merlin once said that we'd probably get married when we about thirty ('cos thirty seemed, like, really fucking old at the time). We didn't, but what we did do when we were about thirty was become parents. I heard that he and the baby's mother had split up but he was a very dedicated dad. By then were out of touch altogether, with paths leading in different directions into a new era.

I starting writing to Merlin again when the babies were school children and saw him a few times during visits I made to London for a music project. The chemistry was still there, but the compatibility way out of time. My home life was in turmoil, there was madness afoot, but Merlin was not equipped to rescue me. At that point I was in need of the completely new, clean and untarnished love that came my way, naturally, through writing.

Today Merlin and I are pen pals again and behaving like friends, although how such familiarity will work out is subject to the customary unpredictability.

Footnote: It's hard to turn away from someone whose life seems so twisted up with your own, irrespective of the percentage of real time involved. Time can be expanded by intensity. As we get older there seems much more behind than before, and behind is a fund upon which you can always rely.

*

I started rooting out smaller venues, where the gigs were cheaper, the bands lesser known and the atmosphere more intimate and involving. I went to see dozens of bands such as Alien Sex Fiend, Ritual, Flux of Pink Indians, Omega Tribe (their singer/guitarist, Hugh V. would later become a music teacher, actually teaching my son, Felix, at primary school), Flowers in the Dustbin (their singer/songwriter, Gerard, would become a good pal), and many of whom I'd never heard of before and can't remember now. I would wander about the venues, meeting random strangers, selling my fanzines and getting merry.

I saw Poison Girls a few times when they were supported by the stand-up poet Benjamin Zephaniah. I would usually turn up early in order to help them unload their gear and set it up on stage, afterwards taking it all apart and re-loading the van; a big old-style ambulance. They invited me to visit them at their house in East London and I started travelling across London on the Central Line to visit them on a Saturday or Sunday afternoon at their house in Leytonstone to chat and hang out by the pond in their garden and maybe later eat a communal meal.

Poison Girls were all older than me but we got on fine. With Richard I shared a love of the sci-fi novels and the strange pre-cog world of Philip K Dick, with Lance I shared an interest in art, surrealism and film, and with Vi I shared an interest in the magical world, such as that explored by Carlos Castaneda. They were always receiving many visitors, from all walks of the counter-culture; musicians, artists, writers, even stand-up comedians like Tony Allen and Green Nigel (who starred in Terry Gilliam's movie 'Time Bandits'). I remember answering the door once and Richard's mate, Howard Devoto (Buzzcocks and Magazine), was standing there. I was a little bit gobsmacked and gestured for him to enter the house. I liked the set-up in the house; everyone who lived there created a communal vibe, taking it in turns to the cook the evening meal throughout the week. Working together, looking after the pond, the garden and the cacti in the greenhouse.

Every now and then I would buy several tubes of superglue and walk, usually on a Sunday morning, from the hotel where I worked in Bayswater and head along Oxford Street to Tottenham Court Road. On the way I would superglue the locks of any store that sold leather or furs, just to cause them a little aggro come Monday morning. This was one of my little routines during the nine months I lived and worked in the West End of the City.

I remember my first winter in London. I took LSD with Martin L. and we took a ghetto blaster to Hyde Park after midnight, when the park was closed. We climbed over the railings and walked through the virgin snow, playing 'Low' by David Bowie. It was hard to believe that we were in London at all. On the way home, we saw a guy who stood bare-chested on a rooftop, playing a melancholy tune on a saxophone to the icy stars, it was surreal and wonderful, like moving through a film noir scene, and we cheered him on. I shouted up to him and asked him his name – 'Lee', he shouted back to me.

During that winter I went to a gig, can't recall which bands I'd gone to see, but as I was selling my fanzine I got chatting to two guy's, Rob C. and Rob V. I'm pretty sure that I'd already exchanged a few letters with Rob C. After the gig they accompanied me back to my meagre room beneath the hotel to talk and consume more alcohol. Rob C. produced a good fanzine called Enigma, and later he ran WOT records distribution. Rob V. was involved in a band called This Bitter Lesson. They were both squatting in a house in Hackney, East London, and invited me over to visit. They didn't have a phone but they wrote down their address; 96 Brougham Road; easy enough to find with a London A-Z.

That meeting proved pivotal in my initiation into the underground anarcho-scene in London. A week later I took a tube to Bethnal Green and made my way to Brougham Road through the snow. It was time for me to have my eyes opened to a truly alternative lifestyle. Like Poison Girls and Crass, the people in this house also lived in a communal fashion, taking it in turns to cook an end of day meal. I met Paul W. (from Oxon) and J.C. (from South Africa) for the first time. For all we were strangers, it seemed that we were all speaking the same language; we were all on the same page, as they say. However, where Poison Girls had a shared mortgage, people assumed that Crass owned Dial House (in fact they didn't at that time), 96 was part of a squatters housing group, in fact, most of the houses in the street were occupied by squatters. The electric and the gas were being fiddled in most of them. Later that night, as I lay on the floor of Rob C.'s room in a sleeping bag, warmed by a two bar electric fire, watching through the window as the snow fell from the sky, I thought to myself, I wouldn't mind living somewhere like this and being part of a scene like this.

In a matter of weeks my not-so-idle wish was granted. During my spare time out of work hours as a hotel receptionist in ironed uniform, I was visiting Brougham Road more and more, wearing my alternative punk uniform; all black, a bit of red, chains and black laces hanging from my belt – it took me a while to get away from any kind of uniform or blatant identity. I'd also had enough of the hotel job. My feet were itching, I'd settled, kind of, in London, and I was restless and ready to dance the random, sacred jig of the merry Fool. Card zero in the Tarot; the circle, the cycle, the roundabout way.

The way I ended up moving to 56 Brougham Road was rather weird. A family was due to move out and the housing co-op was going to take over the property. They had a waiting list and I wasn't even on it, but there was something of a rift going on in the co-op, essentially between the older hippies and the Spanish anarchists and the younger anarcho-punks, several of whom wanted to help to get me on the street. With the help of J.C. we staged a kind of squatter's coup.

The night after the family vacated the house; I accompanied J.C. and saw firsthand how the squatting thing worked. He broke the front door lock and I held a torch while he changed the lock for a new one. He handed me a key. That was it. I was in. Rob V. also moved that night from 96 to 56 to live with me, and with J.C. we held an all night vigil as the angry Spanish anarchists gathered outside the house, angry at our underhanded manoeuvre. The low lying rift had just escalated into full visibility. Eventually they gave in and I had to join the co-op. That was fine by me. I'd moved into my first squat. I quit my job at the hotel and hauled my few belongings across town; a cheap stereo, a box of vinyl records that weighed a ton, a box of books and fanzines, plus a few clothes (mostly red and black). I remember carrying my stuff from Bethnal Green tube station. I was wearing a black beret that I favoured at the time. The wind was howling and eventually blew away my beret. I watched it roll on down the street and I just kept on walking, not missing a step – not missing a beat. It was time to let things go and cling to nothing.

For a time, life in 56 was good, if a little chaotic. The houses in Brougham Road were all built before WWII. They survived the Blitz, but now they were creaky and draughty places, perfect for conducting a bohemian existence. The place had three bedrooms upstairs, and a kitchen, toilet and two small living rooms downstairs, plus a garden that backed onto an abandoned bus garage, where members of The Convoy would park their vehicles and set up camp during the winter months, before heading back out on the road for the summer festival circuit. We had no central heating, just small two-bar electric fires and a real fireplace.

I was busy writing and designing my fanzines, Rob V was working on reproducing music tapes of a This Bitter Lesson recording session and designing the tape cassette covers as Crass Records had decided not to take them onboard, essentially because they thought that one song could be interpreted as an anti-abortion song.

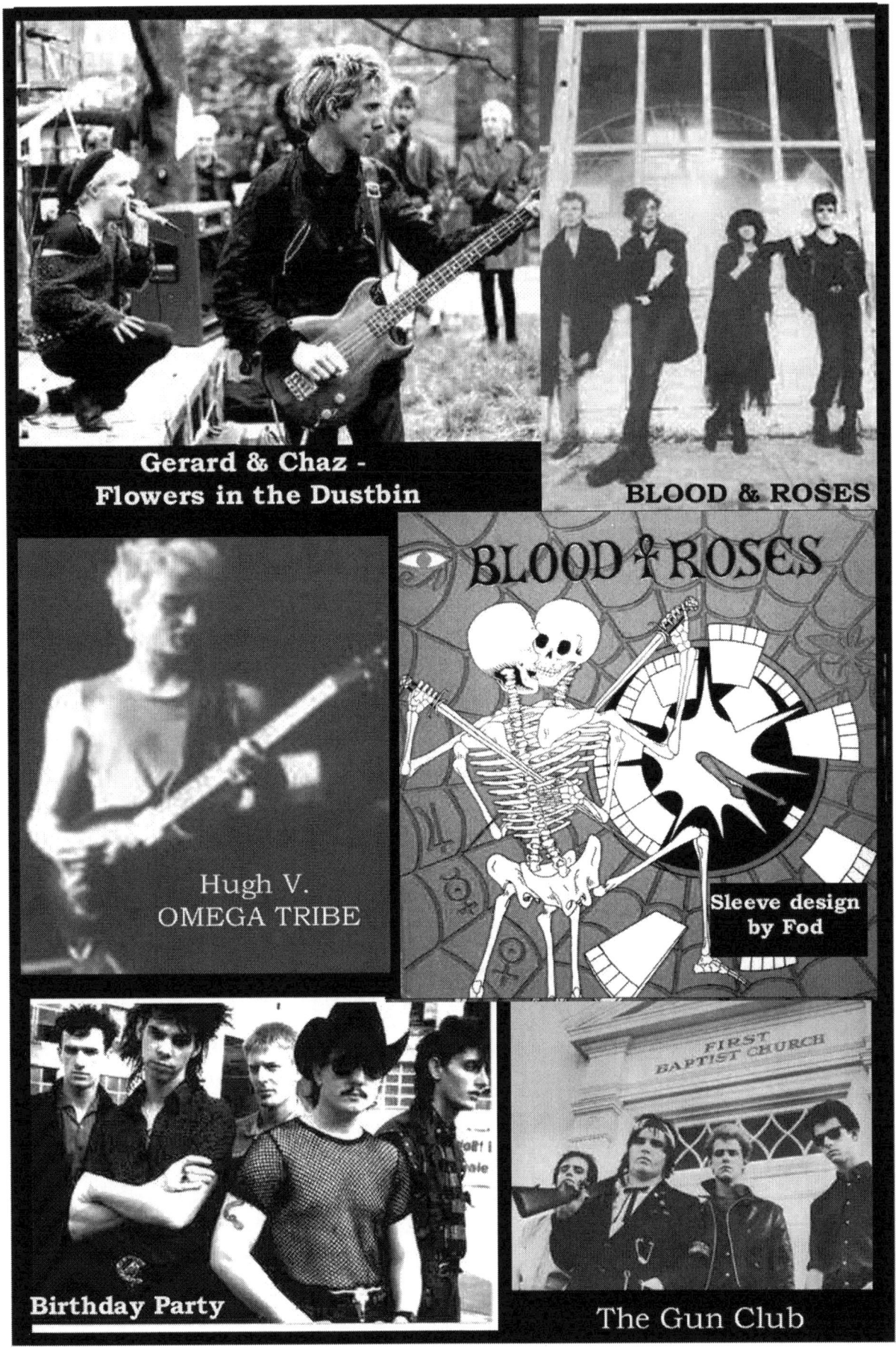

Personally, I have an open mind about the issue of abortion – I think it depends upon the circumstances and I totally believe that a woman has the right to make her own choice either way; the right to express her own will. This is one aspect of Catholicism that I question, as the people who make decisions on issues like this are predominantly men, the same with their attitude toward any form of contraception. In years to come, as our planet overpopulates, growing like some out of control virus, and as our resources dwindle even further, I think governments will enforce contraception, and perhaps even enforce abortions whether people want them or not, strictly limiting people to one-child families. We see the start of this in countries such as China and Nepal. I also wonder if the abortion issue would be an issue at all if it was men who became pregnant. Can you imagine? Most men can't even manage fatherhood!

At 56, usually Rob V. and I would be working on separate projects and always listening to music, staying up until around dawn before crashing out, then waking up some time before noon and starting all over again. I recall my favourite record during the time I lived there, it was released that year, 1983, by The Birthday Party, a 12" E.P. called 'The Bad Seed' with four great tracks; Sonny's Burning, Wild World, Fears of Gun, and Deep in the Woods *(Love is for fools and all fools are lovers/ it's raining on my house and none of the others/ love is for fools and God knows I'm still one/ the sidewalks are full of love's ugly children).*

Rob V. was into speed at that time, but I generally didn't go there, but my time spent in Brougham Road did get me into sampling marijuana and dropping more acid – it was a druggy street, no two ways about it. Brougham Road was also a creative, alternative street overflowing with musicians, artists, poets and some great characters you probably wouldn't find anywhere else (I'll talk about some of these later).

Unlike the rest of my schoolmates, I never smoked cigarettes, essentially due to the asthma problems I'd suffered from as a child. When I lived in Brougham Road I was still suffering from other childhood ailments like eczema on my throat and in the crook of my arms, and severe hay fever in the summertime, always looking for a remedy and finding none. The quacks failed me. Then, when I tried dope, and found I liked it, the eczema vanished and so too did the hay fever. I've never suffered from them since. The herbal remedy seemed to work, the only problem I had with smoking dope was that I started putting tobacco into the mix. As a result of smoking dope I became addicted to the more evil weed called tobacco – I don't do dope these days, but I still smoke roll-ups, and quite heavily when drinking or writing, too heavy. So I blame dope for my tobacco addiction. Dope was ok, and I did a good twenty years smoking that shit, but I don't like the skunk they do these days – you don't know what you're smoking. Dope back than was a different ball game – today it all seems to be about heavy funky skunk, with mixed-in chemicals and the inevitable psychosis and paranoia that it can induce.

There are so many ways to smoke Mary Jane. The ones that I tried were the basic joint; Rizla papers rolled around tobacco mixed with herb. Have you ever wondered why major supermarkets around the UK sell King Size Rizla? Ever seen anyone roll a pure tobacco King Size cigarette, without adding some dope? Basically, major supermarkets are selling drug paraphernalia at a store near you. I also did blow-backs, water-bongs, pipes, hot-knives, chillums, and hashish-cakes and cookies. I never did a bucket, bongs were usually enough to send me into another dimension and I figured a bucket would wipe me out forever.

I recall we had a problem with a huge rat in Brougham Road. It was such a beast that it had already killed two cats. One night I heard it rummaging in the kitchen below my bedroom and resolved to hunt the critter down. I made a spear out of a long stick and sharpened one end with a knife, then climbed up onto the sink and sat and waited. I waited patiently for hours, half-wondering if this was the right thing for a vegetarian to be doing? Then I saw the rat. He came up from a hole in the hallway floorboards and made straight for a black refuse sack that was full of a day's worth, or possibly a week's worth, of trash. I hurled the spear at the giant and I completely missed. The Great White Hunter I am not. The rat bolted back down his hole. I simply nailed a board over the hole in the wooden floor and we never saw the critter again.

*

Kim C. Used to come stay with me at the house, sometimes bringing along other punks she knew from the Harrow scene. They all still lived with their parents and wanted to see how the squatting thing worked. Things were sometimes a bit tense and confused between me and Kim, and Rob V. was transforming into something of a subtle manipulator, if not an outright head-fucker and utterly sly, devious bastard – well suited for the Vatican!.

One time, when Kim and I had fallen out and I hadn't seen her for about a week or more, I was walking past the public telephone box that stood at the end of Brougham Road. The phone started ringing. I decided to answer it. I picked up the receiver and it was Kim. I don't even want to think about what the odds might be on my walking by at that given moment in time as she decided to ring that public phone box at that given moment in time, and me deciding, on a whim, to answer the call...a million to one? Who knows? Despite the randomness of it all, despite both out tears, the call didn't go well.

A short time later I received a letter from my brother Wayne, who is twenty months younger than me. He wanted to come for a weekend visit. At that time, he was still living at home and working in a small factory on an industrial estate that made metal saw blades; his hands were always getting cut to ribbons.

Wayne made his way to Brougham Road, and as soon as I greeted him, I handed him a cup of tea; magic mushroom tea. What are older brother's for? We had a wild night and watched the stars from the nearby Union Canal. I also recall that in the early hours of the morning we laid in the middle of Brougham Road, watching the stars and cosmic vapour trails, and not a single vehicle manifested, which is just as well, otherwise we'd both have ended up as road-kill.

After the visit, Wayne went back up North. A few weeks later he quit his job in the saw-blade factory. He moved out of our parent's house and came to live with me at 56 Brougham Road. I guess the mushrooms had truly worked their magic!

Like I mentioned in the first chapter, if hallucinogens are taken at the Right Time, with the Right People in the Right Place, the trip can be beautiful, mind-blowing, cosmic, illuminating and utterly transformative. Break any one of those cardinal rules and you can expect psychosis, the horrors, the fear, ultimate paranoia because they are all out to get you, and the Devil himself will be trying to fuck you up the ass...after that, well, things can get really bad.

These days, if I mention magic mushrooms or LSD to someone, they often say they'd be wary, or even afraid, to try them. I always say, if you have that sense of apprehension about hallucinogens, then definitely DON'T. You need to be comfortable in your own mind, and be willing to experience what happens to your mind when it opens up in all its amazing glory. If you have a hang-up, and you focus upon that hang-up, that hang-up will hang you for sure. On the other hand, if you can ride and surf the waves and 'gently drift upstream', you can actually break through that hang-up and suddenly find yourself laughing aloud at the folly of it all. Sometimes you learn a thing or two about a thing or two, most notably, when our perceptions get blown open wide, we realize that reality is not what we have been educated and indoctrinated to believe it to be. Reality is infinitely stranger than most folk can imagine. And that is the thing with hallucinogens – you know, at the time, that you are witness to a deeper, richer form of reality – deeper and wider than anything you've experienced or perceived before, like reality with a capital, glowing R. After that, you have to find other techniques to put you into the same state of reference. Things like meditation, yoga, or ritual magick, just to test out that capital R and check out its boundaries, if you can find them, at the same time finding that inner, radiant light that reveals the soul when you are totally drug free, and then you Know.

A glimpse behind the illusion of reality might obtained by the use of hallucinogens, but there exists a multitude of methods that can whack you out without using a druggy high. There are dozens of ways to feel, connect, interact and use the energy we are taught doesn't even exist; and just as many ways to make it work for the benefit of others.

A few months later things came to an end at 56. I'd travelled up north to see my folks for a few days, but on the train journey back to London I began having doubts about continuing to live with Rob V. He was manipulative and something of a head-fucker. Anyhow, I was seated at one of those tables on a train, crammed in with three other people I didn't know. I thought 'Fuck it' and got my Tarot cards out of my backpack. I consulted the cards, laying them out in a ten card formation known as the Celtic Cross. The decision was made. The way I read the cards – they said move out – immediately!

When I got back to 56, I walked through the door and saw Wayne. I told him that I was leaving, right then. I had no idea where I was going to go, I had no back-up plan-B, none at all, but the vibe I got off the Tarot was urgent. Wayne was a little taken aback, but then he turned around and said 'Well, don't leave me here alone with him. I'm coming with you!'

I told Rob V. that I'd done a Tarot reading on the way back to London and they'd told me to leave the house. I told him I was out of there, with no idea where I was going to live. I was literally walking out onto the street, realizing that I'd quit a job and a room in the West End of London to move into the squatter scene in the East End of London, and now I was moving deeper into random uncertainty. I was very scared by this turn of events, but deep down, I trusted the cards and the Way of Things – the Path of the Fool.

The way I saw things, I had no choice – I had to follow the magical path, not knowing where it might lead. By then, I didn't have any other path to follow but my own.

Wayne and I packed up our meagre belongings and together we walked out of 56 Brougham Road into the big, bad, beautiful, Great Unknown.

CHAPTER 6

Wayne and I carried our stuff out of Brougham Road. We rounded a corner onto Shrubland Road and happened to bump into Neil K. I'd met Neil a few times in Brougham Road but had never really got to know him that well – he was just another face on the scene. He knew that I wrote fanzines and I knew that he wrote a comic-type 'zine called Ka-Ka Komic (which I thought was very original for the zine-scene at that time) – I think the first time that we met we just paid mutual respect and we didn't really pay each other much heed to be fair – too busy scoring dope and getting stoned.

(In retrospect, this was a very auspicious, random meeting. Neil proved to be a smart and humorous guy who became a lifelong friend – he's a clever musician by nature who has a genius for cutting thru the crap and getting the sounds he wants. We've shared many musical ventures, from sofa drumming to working in a studio. We've seen hundreds of movies together and even made a few Zero Budget movies together – he played at least 3 characters in my 40 minute UFO spoof 'Buffoon' that we scripted together. I won't even begin to talk about beer and narcotics…..)

Anyway, we told Neil we'd left 56 and were going to look for somewhere to live, although we didn't really have a clue about how to go about doing so. It was all a little vague and slightly desperate, to understate it. Neil said that his mother, Sara, was on the verge of throwing him out, so he went and grabbed his stuff and he joined us. Now we were three…three homeless amigos in the middle of Hackney desperate for somewhere to live. Landlords were not an option; we had no job, no money for deposits, rent and bills.

It's a funny feeling, standing in the middle of a park with your few wretched belongings, wondering where, or if, you might live someplace else. Wondering if this is the end of the road? Wondering if you've finally reached rock bottom and feeling helpless, like the God's are having a laugh at your individual expense. At the same time knowing, deep down, that you can only go with the flow, the tidal wave, the tsunami, or whatever else comes at you. I guess, without even knowing it, we all had faith in the Universe and trusted in that old saying that everything happens as it should. Or maybe we were just stumbling blindly into life as it hit us in the face like a car crash?

We walked to the end of Shrubland Road, crossed a street, and walked into London Fields, where we stood for about fifteen minutes in the sunshine, wondering what the hell we were going to do. Then J.C., the guy who'd opened up 56 Brougham Road, happened to cycle by. He stopped to chat and we explained our situation to him.

J.C. was our random saviour; an angel manifesting itself in the guise of a huge, strong, stubborn as an ox when he needed to be, sharp-minded, surprisingly caring, white South-African with a very dry wit and an inbuilt instinct for survival outside of the system. He usually walked around barefooted no matter what time of year it happened to be. He was nick-named J.C. because he had the same initials as Jesus Christ, but unlike Mr Christ, J.C. was also an expert in judo; I recall seeing The Art of War on his bookshelf in his room at 96 Brougham Road. (Further down the line, the first time I graduated from writing stuff using a typewriter to a computerised word-processor was in J.C.'s room – then my Tipex days were over.)

J.C. suggested that we try squatting a house on Queensbridge Road, Hackney, as he knew some people that had just moved out of the place. We said OK – hell yeah! We were out of options and instantly grabbed the first opportunity that presented itself to us.

What we didn't know at the time was that the people who'd been living there had moved out because they thought the place was haunted by an ugly spirit. And so we moved in with a somewhat scary ghost.

J.C. took us to the house, cracked the lock and changed it. Now we had a set of keys and somewhere to live. The building was huge. It had a basement and three floors above it, plus an attic kind of room. Each floor had its own bathroom. We jacked the gas and jacked the electric. Neil, Wayne and I had a whole floor each to ourselves, but we spent most of our time hanging out in the basement.

In the basement we had sofas and a TV set (black and white – that we bought from a TV repair shop down on Richmond Road, cheap as chips), and a fridge that was usually more full of chocolate bars, cheese-cake and fizzy drinks than food – this was our dope-fridge; the munchies fridge. The munchies fridge was usually better stocked than the food fridge in the kitchen. It was our way of life. We were always pale faced, with dark crescent moons hanging beneath our eyes, happy as Larry and stoned out of our gourds.

The ghost in the house took a while to manifest, but when it started making noises it definitely creeped us out. We should have tried to communicate with the spirit or entity or whatever it was by using a Ouija board (Oui/Ja = Yes/Yes in French/German), who knows, if we got lucky, we might have contacted Captain Howdy; the demonic entity in The Exorcist. Anyway, the first signs were random, such as loud banging sounds that seemed to manifest from all over the house. Sometimes it sounded like someone was in the room with you, whacking a hammer against the wall. Thinking about it now, the sounds often reminded us of a hammer – perhaps a hammer had something to do with whatever energy-force was stuck in that house. Maybe something bad happened and a hammer was involved?

At first, we joked about it, but gradually we all had our own individual experiences, especially if you happened to be alone in the house with 'it', and we were sometimes really spooked out.

For myself, I recall that one night Wayne and Neil had gone out. I was alone in the house. I was sitting in the basement when all these disturbing bangs began to occur. The sounds were not coming from next door or anywhere else; they were in the room with me. I

Brougham Road E8

Val's photo of JC carrying stolen timber – the shadow reveals his true identity.

Jane E.

Neil K.

got so spooked that I grabbed hold of a claw-hammer and waited until Wayne and Neil returned home, tho' I'm not sure what good a hammer would have been against a spectre who was probably handier with a hammer than me.

It was only when they got back that they both revealed their own weird experiences in the house, and then we knew something strange was lurking there, unknown, unseen, but not unheard.

The next day I did a thorough search of the house, looking for some kind of clue, but not really expecting to find anything. Beneath a carpet on the second floor (the one floor that we never used), I found a letter and an un-cashed cheque from long ago. The cheque was made out to some guy's mother who had died about 15 years earlier. I couldn't figure out why the cheque had been hidden under the carpet and never cashed.

The day after that, we were taking our black and white TV back to the repair shop, for the umpteenth time, when we bumped into a bunch of punks. It turned out that they had been living in our place just before we moved in – one of them was Mark Mob's younger brother.

The first thing they said, once they realized that we'd moved into that house on Queensbridge Road, was 'Have you seen or heard the ghost?' That freaked us out. Yes, we'd heard it, but No, we hadn't seen it, and I'm not sure that we wanted to, unless a camera was rolling.

Shortly after that we received an eviction notice from a housing corporation. We had just a few weeks to get out and find somewhere else to live. We started looking for an empty house. It was time to go and get gone – someone else could keep old Spooky company.

Before we left, we did something that squatters were often accused of, but rarely did. We put the plugs in every sink and bathtub in the house and set the water running full blast, then grabbed our stuff and moved to another empty house that we'd found just around the corner.

Usually, when squatters were evicted by a local council, the council would send in workers to seal the doors and windows. However, before securing the premises they would often smash up the toilets and sinks to make the place inhabitable, then they would take a series of photographs and display them in the press, 'informing' people that this was how squatters lived and behaved. Needless to say, if you're squatting in a house, the last thing you want to do is smash up the khazi. We just happened to flood the house on Queensbridge road out of pure bloody-mindedness because we were effectively being made homeless by a left-wing housing co-op that was supposed to help people like us.

Anyway, we left the house and let the water fall. The place was not occupied by anyone for more than a year, and I seriously doubt that was due to water damage. I blame Spooky.

After moving into my third squat, I began to help J.C. out when he opened up squats for other people.

The people that he was assisting around that time were mostly white South Africans who had fled from the apartheid (apart-hate) regime that was in place at the time and headed for the UK. They didn't want to serve their obligatory two years in the army. They didn't want to fight the ANC (African National Congress, whose leader, Nelson Mandela, was in prison – the same guy Margaret Thatcher labelled a 'terrorist'), nor did they desire to carry a gun for a hate-filled racist establishment which they despised. South Africa, back then, produced a lot of anarchists.

We would wait until it was dark and then cycle to an empty premises. J.C. would bust the door and change the lock and I'd keep an eye out. We'd sometimes spend the first night in the place and then the next day hand over the keys to a bunch of guys and basically give them a house. Back then, if you squatted a place, you knew you were secure for at least six months. If the property owners wanted to kick you out they had to go through the courts and then employ some bailiffs to evict you, and that process took a while, usually three months or so. If you got served an eviction notice it usually gave you enough time to find somewhere else to squat and live.

One evening, as J.C. and I were heading toward an empty property, we passed a church and I noticed a large Jesus on a wooden crucifix that was fixed to the door. I pulled up, and using a screwdriver I helped myself to Jesus. I took the Saviour home and painted him bright green, like an alien, and hung Him on my wall. Years later, when I was out of my head, I ripped Jesus down from his cross, thinking he'd been hanging there for much too long. I broke his arms and legs and left his feet and hands still pinned to the cross by nails, and then put it all in the bin.

*

The Scala cinema in Kings Cross became one of our favourite haunts. It was the best cinema in London, far better than the West End movie houses with their red carpet blah-blah. The Scala showed a different double-bill every day of the month. On Saturday evenings they would do a late show, usually showing 5 films on the trot, running from 11 at night until 7 in the morning. We would usually sit at the back where we could smoke dope without getting spotted by the usher. We saw hundreds of films there, including very early Robert De Niro movies, the works of Kenneth Anger, twisted comedy-porno-noir Thundercrack!, and film oddities such as Salo, The 5,000 Fingers of Doctor T, The Trip, and Faster Pussycat Kill! Kill! and a whole range of obscure, cultist films you just couldn't see anyplace else.

One afternoon I went to see Eraserhead, directed by David Lynch, with Andy M. I'd seen the film once before and found it very funny. We smoked some skunk-weed on the fire-escape stairs and then settled in to watch one of the oddest films ever made. About halfway through the movie I broke out in the sweats, getting the 'fever'. I decided to go to the toilets at the back of the cinema to splash my face with cold water in an effort to cool off and get a 'grip'. I made it to the top of the stairs but as I was walking behind the back row of seats the floor suddenly hit me in the back of the head. I came to and my money had fallen out of my pockets. I gathered up the coins and staggered into the toilets, and then the toilet floor rushed up and whacked me in the back of the head. It was the first time I'd ever been mugged by a toilet floor! I regained consciousness and as I came to I saw my coins scattered everywhere. I gathered my coins ('my precious'), washed my face and then walked back into the cinema. I found Andy and told him to call an ambulance. I was totally freaking out. He walked me outside and I came to my senses. He told me that everyone in the cinema heard a bang coming from behind them, but when people looked around, including Andy, they couldn't see anything; I was laid unconscious on the floor behind the last row of seats, out of sight and momentarily out cold. Was it the dope? Was it Eraserhead? Or was it a combo?

One Saturday night Neil, Wayne and I had planned to go to see an extreme 5-film horror bill at La Scala. Before we left I cooked a pasta meal. I laced it with magic mushrooms. When we'd all cleaned our plates I told them about the magical ingredients. I knew it wouldn't be a problem; they were both experienced 'trippers'. The horror films were fun and we ended up laughing through some pretty heavy splatter chop-chop scenes.

However, The Scala eventually shot itself in the foot when it showed the film A Clockwork Orange (which they billed under a faintly disguised title). At the time the film had been withdrawn from UK distribution by its director Stanley Kubrick and the copyright holder (Warner Brothers) sued, at Kubrick's insistence. As a result The Scala closed down in 1993. It re-opened a few years later as a music venue.

*

In the basement in our squat in Queensbridge Road with the fridge full of munchies, we would watch black and white TV. At that time most people were watching colour TV, but once you start watching black and white TV you soon get used to it. That TV set became a nightmare. It kept on glitching and breaking down and we'd have to carry it back to the little ramshackle store we bought it from to get it repaired by the old guy who ran the place, then wait a day or so and go collect it. We must have had that old black and white idiot box repaired more than a dozen times. Maybe the ghost was interfering with our transmission?

*

After moving out of 56 Brougham Road, under guidance from the Tarot, I hadn't been in touch with my folks, and nor had Wayne since leaving home and moving away. As the months slipped by they grew concerned. They had no way of contacting me – I'm still rather elusive that way – I have minimal friends on Facebook and only half a dozen people have my mobile phone number, and I'm double-hard to reach because most of the time my phone is switched off.

The reason for my reclusiveness is obvious to me now. When I was a child I would sometimes answer the phone at home and I would receive sexually abusive threats from an adult guy who knew my name – he wanted me to suck his cock and so on and basically freaked me out. My folks bought a whistle to blow down the phone to discourage him if ever I answered his calls, but eventually they had to change their phone number to an unlisted one – my folks have been unlisted ever since. I never found out who the mystery caller was, but I do recall he rang me on the day of my 14th birthday – he knew my name and he knew it was my birthday and he talked nasty before I slammed the phone down and broke down in tears. I'd like to meet the fucker now. I'd enjoy putting his lights out and I know the perfect place to bury a sack of evil human shit and I've got friends who would gladly help me with the task. Whoever the fucker was, he did succeed in marking me, psychologically, for life. Thanks pal.

Anyway, my parents were getting worried about me and Wayne and they decided to drive down to London from Stockton-on-Tees in order to find us. How does a parent drive over 200 miles from up north to seek out their squatting sons somewhere in the murky depths of east London and hope to find them? How they actually found us is still something of a mystery but my mom has always had a strong extra-sensory psychic ability.

I think my dad pulled up in Brougham Road and basically knocked on a random door, asking people if they knew where Wayne and I were living. He might have spoken to Dead Kev (a bespectacled, rake-thin, long-haired druggy), or Biker Dave (who built great customized bongs out of coconut shells and bamboo), or speed-dealer Chris (who had one corner of his room full of empty silver-foil wraps all ready and waiting for the inevitable bust, knowing that the cops would have to open each wrap; a task that would take them a few days). Whoever they spoke to suggested they try Queensbridge Road. Somehow they found us and late one morning we got a knock on the door.

I answered the door, kicking a broken plate and some half-eaten spaghetti that lay on the floor to one side. It was a shock visit for sure, like an electrical shock. Fuck! The folks! Fuck! Fuck! I woke Wayne up, he was still stoned as well, and he'd dyed his long back-combed hair bright green. My dad was still standing there on the doorstep. He said he'd wait for us in the car. My dad has always been a no-bullshit man, but at that moment on the doorstep I knew that he knew that both of his sons were totally out of it – completely out of this fuckin' world.

We took a ride, away from the east end, with my dad commenting that he felt like taking a bath after driving through Brougham Road.

We hit the west end. We hit a bar. We had a chat, and all was kinda good.

The next time my folx came down to London to visit me they stayed in a hotel. My mum and sister went to see a rom-com movie together. I took my dad to a bar and after that we went to a small cinema in Soho to watch Taxi Driver and Midnight Express. That cinema had been showing Taxi Driver for seven years. Dad said that the latter film disturbed him the most. I didn't tell him that I'd seen the former film nearly twenty times and knew every line off by heart. I didn't tell him that Taxi Driver was wrecking my mind and that my eyes were secret cameras, why should I?

*

Squatting didn't just apply to opening up empty houses for people to have someplace to live; it also involved taking over larger, empty premises and using them to create an event. In December of 1982 a bunch of us squatted the Zig-Zag club and put on two days of free music.

This kind of activity definitely harked back to the 60's and probably beyond that. It was also a forerunner of the squat-rave scene that took place many years later so that people could party and dance all night, wired to the mains on E, guzzling mineral water to stay alive, or dropping ketamine and tumbling into the abyss of the K-hole. (I made a 40 minute film of that scene – usually filmed while I was on acid – perhaps I should put it on You Tube?)

Around midnight, along with more than a dozen other people, I met up with several members of Crass. An earlier attempt to squat The Rainbow had failed. We walked to the Zig-Zag club, broke in and some smart people managed to switch on the power without zapping themselves. Crass brought along walkie-talkie radios and had people monitoring all sides of the building. It was a well organized operation – dare I say it was run on military lines? Crass army anyone?

When the police eventually turned up they seemed rather caught-out by what was taking place; uncertain how to react. I remember Andy Palmer from Crass talking to them, nice and polite, explaining that we had squatter's rights. The cops were confused as we gave them no cause to be violent (and I think the smarter of them were already thinking about the overtime they could make from the situation).

Winston Smith wrote an article that appeared in the Sounds music news-rag on January 1st 1983. (I found this via the Kill Your Pet Puppy website, where you can also find free downloads of the bands who played the gig; Faction (from 96 Brougham Road with Rob C. (WOT Distribution & 96 Tapes), and Paul W. (Fack Fanzine), D&V (Drums & Vocals; two guys from Sheffield – they were like Northern Rap and in my opinion much better live than their awfully produced Crass Records single – if anyone out there has a decent live recording of D&V I'd love to hear it), Omega Tribe (their guitarist, Hugh, taught my son, Felix, at infant school in Hackney), Lack of Knowledge, Sleeping Dogs, The Apostles, Amebix, Null & Void, Soldiers of Fortune, The Mob, Polemic Attack, Poison Girls, Conflict, Flux of Pink Indians, Crass, and D.I.R.T.) –

THIS IS SQUAT WE WANT!

Crass beat the system and play for free at London's Zig Zag Club.

Word was out early last week Crass (accompanied by several experienced squatting organizations) were occupying the Rainbow Theatre at Finsbury Park, and an all-day event was being planned for Saturday the 18th December. Short, but sweet . . .

Wednesday morning things had changed; Crass had been evicted and were searching frantically for an alternative venue. A hotline was set up and three days later, on the morning itself, the ansa-phone message was bold, clear and full of optimism: they were now squatting in the disused Zig-Zag club in London's Westbourne Park, and from midday until late it was round to Crass's new place, for the party of our lives . . .

'Squatting this venue is not a last ditch stand to get a gig, the music business would love us all to be down at the Venue paying their bar prices: On the contrary, we hope that today's gathering will provide inspiration and impetus to people everywhere to take similar opportunities and open up and take back the property that belongs to us all . . . We hope that today we will be able to demonstrate that together we can begin to reclaim that which is ours . . . Freedom, free food, free shelter, free information, free music, free ideas . . . Freedom to do whatever doesn't infringe on the freedom of others.'

By 2.00pm things were beginning to happen: a large group of people had already arrived and the free vegetable soup was on the boil and being distributed to hungry, happy young ragamuffins. Meanwhile down the Portobello Road, word was spreading like wildfire.

With no admission charge, no age restrictions and no dress regulations, the partygoers arrived in their hundreds; bags of chips, biscuits and all manner of booze piled up high in their hugging arms and rotting rucksacks.

As the first of many bands came on and the party really started to swing, police were waiting around outside, no doubt wondering just what the hell they ought to be doing about it all. Someone went in and gave them a leaflet, which they did seem to be genuinely interested in.

'. . . We have not employed security today, and we believe that no security will be necessary . . . It is up to us together to make it work. Treat others as you would expect to be treated and leave the place as it was

when you arrived. We can only claim the right to use places if we are prepared to take responsibility to see that they are well looked after. We are here to be creative; we can leave destruction to the authorities.'

Everywhere the emphasis was on responsibility: posters cropped up all over the place encouraging the crowd to pick up litter, refrain from vandalism, and generally be sensible. It all seemed to impress the police who, putting an end to rumours of an imminent (unlawful) eviction/break-in, wandered off back to their station, leaving just a couple of friendly coppers behind to keep a (very) discreet eye on things.

... As the day turned into night, more bands took to the stage, some of them terrible and some excellent. People staggered around sharing food with complete strangers and getting drunk on free beer. When the Mob came on, the event became The Event.

Everybody stood up for the Mob, and 'No Doves Fly Here' was the moment to treasure — the highlight of the day; They were wonderful.

By now the 'house' was packed, though not uncomfortably so. A rain of shredded Zig-Zag club tickets fell from the sky and the Poison Girls were doing whatever it is they do, which seems to be quite an acquired taste; although through the jubilant alcoholic haze 'Persons Unknown' just sounded so good, especially whilst persons unconscious lay slumped in exhausted heaps around the floor...

'Anarchy In The UK' exploded from the midst of Conflict's opening tape, and my God, never before had it sounded so magnificently right.

The drunken hordes floated to the front and had a bloody great time, but this killjoy just couldn't see the appeal apart from the brilliant intro to 'Meat Means Murder', and even the subtleties of that soon disappeared beneath the bewildering Conflict wall of noise.

So off they went while Flux of Pink Indians walked on and plugged in. An unusually murky sound tarnished their short set but, even so, the urgency and dynamic flexibility they've always possessed didn't go amiss.

And so with the last of a genuinely harrowing succession of anti-nuclear films already screened, and with those mighty rows of peace/love/freedom banners hanging victoriously, proudly over the stage, it was soon time for Crass.

A woman's voice boomed from the speakers denouncing the sacrifice of young soldiers to war and then, like the legends they most definitely are, Crass were bathed in a flash of dazzling white light while they exploded straight into a dizzy 'How Does It Feel...' For the crowd this was it, this was pure heaven.

Sure, with some notable exceptions, 'Big A Little A' being one of them, it was mainly a monotonous racket but, Christ, Crass were impressive, and so utterly spellbinding, even when making the most horrendous of dins. Style, charisma and sheer impact: believe me. Crass had it all, in bundles.

'Do They Owe Us A Living' sent the hordes into a final frenzied boil, and then it was all over. The phenomenon had become even more phenomenal, and the dream, the dream only Crass and their companions had held any faith in, had come completely, magnificently true...

Nobody was hurt, no-one suffered, nobody ruled and no-one was governed. For 24 hours Crass had achieved their much-ridiculed vision of a peaceful, creative Anarchy in the most fantastically triumphant, clean, efficient way anyone could have ever imagined possible.

This was truly a Christmas on Earth.

It won't be forgotten.

*

I started getting seriously into amphetamines, aka speed, sulphate, whiz, 'Billy' – so-called after the character Billy Whiz in The Beano comic. I slipped into the white-line-fever so fast

I didn't get time to look back or reflect. I loved the buzz, the instant rush that speeded everything up and I loved waging the war against sleep. I loved tooting line after line and being awake all night like some kind of nocturnal creature, like an inner-city owl with a brain working overtime and giving off sparks. I carry a psychosis to this day that can still catch me, and those I love, by surprise. I blame speed for my self-destructive impulses.

I really enjoyed London in those pre-dawn hours when the city grew quiet, when traffic briefly stopped bustling by, just listening to music, writing stuff, or sketching when I was on a come-down, always chain-smoking like I was in a 1950's movie. During those hours the city became another place – like a palace of silent magic, a place where you could hear your own thoughts and focus and really lose yourself in even more mad thoughts; the train-line buzz.

I rapidly submerged into the rabid depths of the speed-freak zone; pale faced, wearing black eye-liner for added contrast. I often bought it from a punk speed dealer in Cross Street, Islington, and found myself constantly cycling back and forth from Hackney to Islington to score some more…and then some more…more, more. I did some really fast cycle journeys during that time, all buzzed-up and wigged-out, like a speeding punk ghost passing by…a spectre dancing ever closer to the whirlwind of psychosis and meltdown.

The way I figure things, anyone who chooses to dabble with drugs and thinks they can handle them all with ease will always find the one drug that will fuck them up. They might be cool with just about every drug under the sun, but then, out of the blue, comes The One. I'm talking about The One that fucks you up and maybe steals your life or your soul away. The One that takes over your life. The One you cannot walk away from. The One that drags you under, and under…

THE ONE (TASTE)/HINDSIGHT

The One will light up your life like no light you ever saw before; brighter than fireworks or Jesus in your bedroom on Halloween or a UFO in your back garden or your step-mom in panties (indulge my indulgence).

The One will take you over before you know you've been taken over.

The One will drag you places you've never been.

The One will take you places you never dreamed you dared to go.

The One will take you places you wish you'd never seen.

The One will take you beyond the map.

The One will drag you down to the depths of the Pacific Basin and laugh at you, knowing that you want just one more taste…one more taste…

The One will spend all your money and cost you precious friends.

The One will flip your lid and then flip you back again, like a pancake in the Devil's frying pan.

The One will show you a glimpse of Heaven.

The One will eventually turn Heaven into Hell and you won't ever see it coming.

The One will distort all your visions and corrupt your truth.

The One will make you feel like a genius – like a spark of God.

The One will comfort you and make you feel invincible – like a Tyrant.

The One is the Tyrant – The One is invincible.
The One will make you wish you'd never been born
The One will make you believe that Hell exists in your own heart and mind.
The One will break you, for all time.
The One can teach you vital lessons.
The One is a powerful master/mistress/god/goddess.
Never underestimate the power of The One.
If you are wise and survive The One, you know never to visit that house again.
If you don't make it past The One, then you are dead and gOne.

*

During my speed indulgence I became obsessed with the movie Taxi Driver. I often went to the movies alone and must have seen Taxi Driver in cinemas in every quarter of London. Like a man possessed, or driven to partake in some kind of un-holy mission, I once cycled to a cinema somewhere in the ass-hole of North London to watch a late night showing. I took a rather large and heavy ghetto blaster with me, carrying it in a backpack, and inside the cinema I recorded the entire film soundtrack onto tape cassette. I played that cassette so many times that it got to the point that someone could hit me with any line of dialogue from the film and I would know the line that followed it.

The only other film I'd heard of where people had a similar obsession was The Rocky Horror Picture Show, which I really didn't like at all, but I respect the fervour of the 'cinamaniacs' (a phrase coined by Neil K); crowds used to turn up to screenings of Rocky Horror, in full costume, and recite line after line and sing along with all the songs and generally have a camp, transsexualized ball, and why the hell not?

I didn't realize it then, but I was slipping deeper and deeper into speed addiction and the psychosis that always accompanies addiction to the sneaky white powders, be they amphetamines or cocaine.

The first time that my psychotic behaviour manifested was when Neil, Wayne and I were packing up our stuff to leave the house we were squatting. We'd been served an eviction notice and had all joined the Brougham Road Housing co-op in the nick of time – we were going to move into number 66. For some reason, I got pissed-off and threw a huge mirror down the stairs in Neil's general direction. Glass exploded everywhere and it's a miracle he didn't get cut to pieces. I was the oldest out of the three of us, but certainly not the most level-headed.

I also started really getting into the novels that Raymond Chandler wrote during the 1940's and 50's, particularly the character of private-eye, Philip Marlowe. I read all 23 of his books. Those novels were the first to define noir, and they were written with wit and verve. Raymond Chandler was 50 when he wrote his first novel; The Big Sleep – a novel so full of plot holes that when Chandler wrote the screenplay for Hollywood, he later admitted that he had no idea who killed one of the characters (a chauffeur, I think). I always find the thought that he started writing at 50 somewhat comforting, certainly more inspiring than so-called child prodigy's (as they tend to suffer from mild forms of autism), just because a person has reached half a century, it doesn't mean their game or their creative output is over, does it? It strikes me that the older a person gets, the more they know what they like and what they

LEE GIBSON

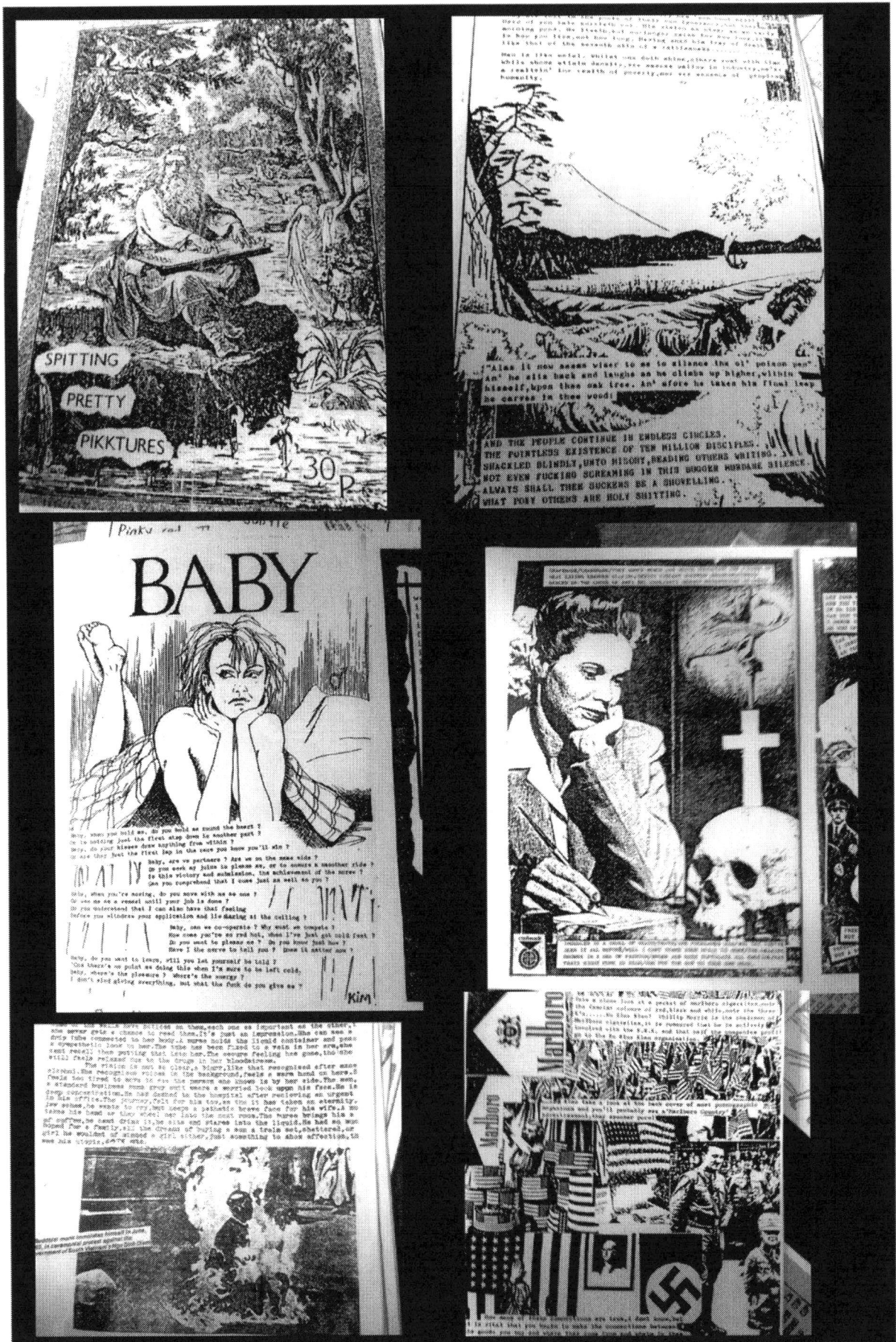

don't like, what gets them off and what bores them or brings them down. Maybe, being older, they understand the currents of energy and inspiration that flow through them in a clearer, sharper light? Maybe their creative path is more defined, dare I say, more enlightened? But perhaps, being older, the raw energy and devilish drive they possessed when they were seventeen and full of fire has been tempered and soothed in the furnace of time? Do they see the way of the world with a clearer vision or through tired, worn-out eyes? Take your pick.

Like many writer's, Chandler had many occupations before he became a writer. I always liked the fact that he once tried to kill himself with a .38, but the bullet bounced clean off his skull and just left something of a bloody mess in his bathroom. Like many a good (and bad), writer, Chandler suffered/enjoyed alcoholic tendencies.

I so fell in love with the fictional world of Raymond Chandler that I got myself a trilby hat and a few pairs of baggy 1950's style suits from Oxfam — basically old men's suits that never fitted my slim waistline, hence the need for braces. Then my obsession took a step into a darker, murkier realm.

I sold all my vinyl records and bought two replica hand guns from a store on Hackney Road, just opposite Brick Lane. The store specialized in all manner of weapons, including a wide selection of knives ranging from short 3 inch blades to 12 inch Bowie knives, from lock-knives and flick-knives, to stiletto blades and double-edged knives favoured by fishermen (or the fishers of men on the local streets) — the type with a sharp blade on one side and a serrated, tooth-like blade on the other. The store also sold brass and silver knuckle dusters, replica machine guns, air-pistols and air rifles, high-powered binoculars, and cross-bows, some of them so dinky you could strap them to your wrist like something out of a Mad Max movie. I opted for a snub-nosed .38 Special 6-shot revolver (as favoured by Philip Marlowe), and a Magnum pistol with a six inch barrel (like that favoured by Clint Eastwood's renegade cop in the Dirty Harry movies — 'You feeling lucky, punk?'), plus a few boxes of blanks. In fact, they were both weapons used by Travis Bickle (De Niro's character), in Taxi Driver.

When I fully entered my Travis Bickle phase, I bought a green army surplus combat jacket and had my head shaved into a Mohican cut. I used to walk around the West End, speeding off my tits, carrying the guns, pretty much looking for an excuse to shove one in someone's face and play out my role in the movie I thought I was living in. However, I never overstepped that particular line and I was never stopped or searched by the police. But I had entered a psychotic phase for sure, my eyes were like a camera as I walked around the West End — I think, to a certain degree, I'd lost my own identity and slipped into an actor's shadow, or perhaps tapped into a dark undercurrent that was broiling beneath the surface of the collective psyche of the city, one that would manifest itself more blatantly years later as knife and gun crime increased exponentially, not just in London, but across the entire country.

Either way, I certainly wasn't the only one to be hexed and spellbound by the dark undercurrents that permeate Paul Schrader's script of Taxi Driver. The entire film oozes psychosis — De Niro, Scorsese and most of the cast and crew were all using cocaine on a pretty heavy scale during the movie's production, and, as if to emphasize the point, the soundtrack to Taxi Driver was created by Bernard Hermann (just before he died); the same guy who created the musical score for Hitchcock's Psycho.

In the USA, John Hinckley went that extra mile; he was obsessed with the movie, and in particular with Jodie Foster (who was 13 when she made the movie, playing a naive child prostitute). Hinckley ended up trying to assassinate the President of the United States, Ronald Reagan (Ray-Gun) – however, Hinckley only wounded Reagan instead of snuffing out his existence.

Do I sound sorry that Hinckley failed in his self-appointed mission? Hmm ;-)

There were many things that I loathed about Reagan – here are three of them.

1- Reagan was a cowboy President who managed to portray a similar level of smirking ignorance/arrogance/dumbness as George W Bush.

2- When he was a mediocre/crap actor in Hollywood, Reagan testified against his fellow actors in the witch hunt of the House of Un-American Activities. (When J Edgar Hoover, head of the FBI, was rooting out Commies and 'Reds under the bed' instead of rooting out the Mafia – but Hoover couldn't root out the Mafia because they possessed photographs of him cross-dressing, and who knows what else?)

3- Reagan was a fascist, he was pro-war, he loved nuclear weapons and I'm sure he nurtured dark fantasies that involved performing cunnilingus on our Prime Minister of the time, namely Margaret Thatcher (herself an ally of mass murderer General Pinochet and friend of Jimmy Saville). (Note: Thatcher died 8th April 2013, just a few days after I wrote the above. I hope she enjoys her tour of Hell.)

The only thing I ever kind of liked about President Reagan was the fact that he'd witnessed UFOs on two occasions and had gone on record regarding what he'd seen, the same as his predecessor, President Carter. There's a curious (perhaps revealing) quote from Reagan that he made before the United Nations General Assembly in September 1987 – 'To think how quickly our differences worldwide would vanish if we were facing an alien threat from outside this world.'

Perhaps it is more than a coincidence that during his time as President of the United States (POTUS as the security services say), Reagan initiated the Strategic Defence Initiative (SDI), also known as 'Star Wars'. Maybe he knew something the rest of us suckers don't?

Anyhow, as far as my Taxi Driver obsession went, things finally came to a head with the (replica) guns and amphetamine psychosis when I attended my final Crass gig. I'll refer to that in a while, in its proper psychedelic drag-queen context.

*

Neil, Wayne and m'self moved into the end house on Brougham Road, number 66, and quickly settled in. Numbers were always valid in Brougham Road, they identified where a person lived. It was still in a cool period where front or back doors didn't really have to be locked, where you could knock on a door and walk into a house and have a cup of tea in the kitchen and a friendly chat, or turn up later in the day and be offered a vegetarian meal. We had all kinds of people living in that street, including Andy M of the Apostles, Dave F of the Apostles (who also produced a unique magazine - Harlequin), we had an ex-con, ex-biker called Biker Dave who built insane bongs out of bamboo and coconuts, Wolfen, Andy Ashford, we had hippy remnants like Dead Kev, we had school teachers and last generation

Spanish Anarchists including Spanish Elizabeth, and some who were probably old enough to have fought alongside George Orwell during his time in Spain when he took up armed resistance against the fascists and got shot in the throat. Above all else, Brougham Road had children who were living there, growing up there, in a weirdville world completely outside of the box. I always envied those children, in a soft way, wishing that I could have experienced such a fluid, ramshackle, creative, flowing space when I was their age.

I suspect that Brougham Road is built upon a ley-line. It possesses a curious energy and the street has a long and powerful history going back to the 60's. I'm not suggesting it was perfect. Far from it. Of course it had its schisms, its rifts, its star-crossed lovers and their multiple star-crossed relationships, it's fuck-ups, its casualties, its dealers and drug abuse, drug deaths, its busts by the cops, its filth and squalor, its sporadic acts of violence, but it always had more than its fair share of writers, artists and musicians, its mystics and healers, its wise priest-like figures and high priestesses, as well as its fake-gurus, its head-fuckers, and wannabe leaders – it was a hyperactive, dynamic microcosm of society, and let's not mention the bands associated with Brougham Road, bands like The Astronauts, Zounds, The Mob, The Apostles, Faction, Blythe Power and such friends who visited like D&V and the Subhumans (a band I dig a whole lot more now than I did back then). I remember waiting up to the early hours 96 Brougham Road, waiting for the guys from The Mob to turn up, brandishing freshly pressed copies of their first album; 'Let the Tribe Increase'.

That aspect of Brougham Road has rarely been matched in my time on this planet. Outside of Brougham Road I only ever really experienced that honest vibe/vibration of giving and sharing when I used to visit the folx who lived in a Black Sheep co-op house on Grosvenor Road, near Islington, where I encountered the powerful individuals of Val (who let me use her pix from Brougham Road), her brother, Tony D (Kill Your Pet Puppy Fanzine), Alaister (another writer for KYPP), Mark Mob, Josef Porta (drummer for Zounds/The Mob/founder of Blythe Power), Nicky, Fod (who created the groovy sleeve for Blood and Roses 12" single), and a whole spectrum of characters who revolved around each other and interconnected like wheels within wheels within radiant wheels in a fireworks display.

I also experienced that genuine vibe whenever I visited Poison Girls – I was always intrigued by the individuals in Poison Girls and I always felt a little shy; I didn't possess their confidence. I was full of so much doubt and insecurity and had real problems dealing with crowds because I felt like I could hear everyone's thoughts (I had a few years suffering from acute shyness, despite my outward rage and manifestation of writing/fanzines – perhaps a result of speed psychosis.) We were from rather different generations, different places and spaces, and I found that interesting. Poison Girls possessed a wide range of knowledge and they were more than happy to share their wit and wisdom with the likes of me.

*

While I was living at 66 Brougham Road I produced a few fanzines, such as Kiss The Earth - Fuck The Corpse (two issues) and Spitting Pretty Pikktures (a one-off issue). Shortly after releasing SPP, Kim informed me that a band from Harrow were performing a song at their gigs called Spitting Pretty Pikktures – the song was about a punk writer who was also a heroin addict. Obviously the barbed comments were directed at me and I was not happy with being called a smack addict.

I've never done heroin, never been interested in trying it. I did once try a heroin substitute in the form of pills called DF1-8's – I didn't enjoy the sensation of being numbed out to the point where I didn't care about anything – It was like my mind and body were wrapped up in a duvet. I always preferred drugs that activated my mind.

I found out when the band were playing next and accompanied Kim to see them. I wasn't quite sure what I was going to do, but if they played the SPP song I was certainly going to confront them about it. However, I didn't get the chance because when they found out that I was in attendance they bottled it and didn't play the song.

*

After living at 66 for a few months I started hanging around with a bunch of punks who lived in a squat on Holloway Road. I got to know Alex T and Matt M – they were looking for a place to live. 94 Brougham Road became vacant when a family moved out, so I squatted the house and the three of us moved in. Neil and Wayne were a bit narked at me for leaving on such short notice, but it wasn't like I was moving a million miles away, I was just several houses further down the street, next door to 96 and in the end things worked out well for Neil's family as a result my restless nature.

CHAPTER 7

The scene on Holloway road was debauched. I remember a guy from Yorkshire called Dave who lived there – his skin was yellow because he had hepatitis B. For his birthday his parents had sent him a crate of various alcoholic spirits. Because of his illness he couldn't drink a drop and he insisted that we drink it all on his behalf. We had some very smashed days. A gay couple lived in a room at the top of the house. Whenever someone took them cups of coffee, they would usually return carrying a tray full of empty cups and used 'works'.

I remember I was laid on the carpet one evening; everyone was a bit drunk and heavily stoned. I had my eyes closed. Suddenly I felt someone kissing me. It was a girl called Sue. She sang backing vocals on 'Necromantra' by Blood & Roses. We began a brief affair. One time I hitched up North with her, she originated from Middlesbrough and was going to see her dad. Alex T joined us. By the time we made it up north it was very late. I suggested they both stay the night at my parent's house. My parents let them stay overnight, but the atmosphere was colder than Alaska at midnight. Alex had a huge mop of black spiky hair, he was always wasted. Sue had long blonde hair, she was very thin. It was obvious that among other things they were both druggies. My mom especially was horrified and she sat there knitting like a mom possessed. The next morning they pulled me aside and told me, 'Don't ever bring your friends home again'.

Matt M came from a rather well-to-do family. As a youth, he and his younger brother, Jake, would sit in the basement of their house and sniff glue. Jake eventually got heavily into the Krishna scene, Matt, on the other hand, got into Aleister Crowley, William S Burroughs, music, writing and taking drugs. When Jake walked out on the Krishna's, they came actively looking for him, trying to drag him back into the fold. They received short thrift from Matt, myself and others who were around at the time. Matt was out of it at a house party one night. He decided that he wanted to take heroin. He rolled up his shirt sleeve, leaned against a fridge door and shouted 'Do it! Stick it in!' Someone obliged and they jacked-him-up. He said later that he just wanted to try it, to see what it was like. He never did try it again – I would never have lived with him if that was his inclination.

I once walked past Ray Winstone on Holloway Road – the only film I'd seen him in at that time was Scum; a violent film set in a boys detention centre. I have to admit that I was a bit shy and more than a bit wary, to say 'Hello mate – liked the film', in case he turned around and asked me 'Where's your tool?'

*

I enjoyed my time in 94. It was a chaotic, ramshackle and creatively productive period. I produced a few fanzines while I was living there, including 'Let All the Children Boogie' and 'Operation Mind Fuck'. OMF was my 13th and final publication – the front cover had an in image of a sinister guy inviting the reader to sit in a vacant electric chair. I created OMF it in the form of a newspaper. I only wanted to do 1,000 copies, but it worked out cheaper to print 3,000. In all, I think I sold about 1,600 copies, which is way more than I expected. The remaining bundles of OMF gathered dust in the basement and were used on occasion to kindle a fire in the kitchen fireplace. I didn't really contribute that much to OMF and I think, in hindsight, that it could have been much better if I'd taken a little more time in its production. OMF was part-financed by Rob C who ran WOT Distribution – I probably still owe him money.

At the time I think I wanted OMF to be about the people in Brougham Road as much as anything else and so I welcomed contributions from anyone who could be bothered to make the effort. Matt M. contributed some cut-up writing stuff and Elaine R. (who used to be in Hagar the Womb), also contributed a page. Elaine had moved in with Martin C – after me and Val D got them together – and they now lived with Neil and Wayne at number 66. It is funny how our lives' criss-cross with each other; Martin C was the guy who offered me a place to stay at his squat in Stoke Newington when I travelled down to London to print my early fanzines. Years later I was partly instrumental in getting him involved in a serious long-time relationship, and now he'd moved into the room I vacated at Brougham Road. If ever anyone drew a map illustrating how all our lives interconnected on that scene I think you'd need a powerful dose of LSD to follow all the sparkling threads.

Genesis P. Orridge (Psychic TV and formerly Throbbing Gristle), contributed a page for OMF. Gen didn't live in Brougham Road, he lived just a few streets away in Beck Road. I used to pop around sometimes to visit him, and also Min when she lived there for a time. I used to know John G who was in Psychic TV for a while, but then he left the band and became a boxer – I recall he had three fights in New York and won them all.

Joseph Porta created what I think was the best page in OMF. It included an illustration; his interpretation of the Mad Hatter's Tea party from Alice in Wonderland, with the Mad Hatter brandishing a handgun. The page also contained an-unbalanced drawing of yin-yang – 'The Tao of Hate', along with a poem written in rasta-slang about domestic abuse – I can recall the odd snippet from the dusty, cob-webbed archives of my memory; 'I and I don't want no trouble or strife/ I and I just like to beat up the wife/I do it dub-wise-stylee/it makes me feel ire'.

OMF received a brief mention in the song 'It's a Curse' by The Fall on their album 'The Infotainment Scan' – and bit of a critical bashing by Mark E Smith; 'Operation Mind Fuck/I do not like your tone/it has ephemeral whinging aspects.' If MES knocks you, consider it an honour that you even crossed his radar or stepped into his rifle sights. At the end of the day, I think MES was probably right.

*

In my bedroom at 94 I slept on a mattress on the floor, Bohemian style. The mattress had bed bugs and so I had to get rid of it and get another one. Bed bugs are a drag. You go to bed, check the sheets and everything looks ok. Then you wake up in the middle of the night, itchy-scratchy, click on the bedside light, throw back the bed covers and see all these critters on your body. Earlier, they were invisible, but now they are so full of your blood they are bloated and can hardly move. Some try to escape from the light of discovery and scuttle up the wall. When you crush them against the wall you leave a bloody smear on the wallpaper. After a few weeks of this you finally realise that you need to acquire a new mattress in order to obtain a blood free, stress free night of slumber.

One night I was at a house party somewhere around the corner from Brougham Road when Mark W handed me a small lump of opium. I'd never tried opium before. I smoked it and then headed off home. On the way I gathered up a stack of timber and carried it up to my bedroom and set to work. When I woke up the following late morning I discovered that I'd built myself a five-legged bed that rose almost five feet off the ground. The bed was solidly constructed – the fifth leg was positioned underneath the centre of the bed – the legs were positioned like the five points in a dice. I was impressed by the structure but had no recollection of building it. If people ever mention opium to me, I can't help but think of a 5-legged bed.

*

During that first winter in 94 Brougham Road I spent much of the daytime in the front room with Matt M and my brother Wayne. We had a real fire burning. The wooden window shutters were closed. We passed around the spliffs as we read our way through all manner of books on the varied aspects of occultism. It was a very intense reading period, our minds soaking up stuff like sponges, reading about the magical order of the Golden Dawn and the O.T.O., reading Crowley's magical diaries and pondering the mysteries of ritual magic and sexual magick.

I recall we'd wake up on Sunday mornings and rake through the ashes of the fire looking for the roaches of the previous day's joints in order to salvage last fragments of dope and tobacco and get a morning high before lighting a fresh fire and getting back into the books. That was a magical winter.

Occultism began something of a magical revival during the latter years of the 1960's and it continued to grow during the 1970's. By the time of the 80's the (under) current of magical energy was flowing through the post-punk/anarcho-punk scene like a river of fire; some people knew it and surfed on the energy of hidden knowledge once more coming into the light, but some people chose to oppose it and reject it, including Annie Anxiety who denounced Aleister Crowley, and those who were 'resurrecting' him, during one her performances. A schism was taking place between hard-core political activists and hard-core spiritual activists. I succumbed to the latter, based on my out of body experiences as a child. That's not to say I abandoned the political aspects of anarchism completely or stopped being an agitator. I just felt that the whole scene was in danger of boxing itself in with limitations about who, or what, we could be.

That winter's intense book reading sessions proved to be very transformative. Wayne decided to leave Brougham Road in order to follow his path. He moved back up north, to Stockton, then over to Manchester, then back to Stockton, then over to Spain, and back once more to Stockton. During that time his occult studies continued, he became a member of an occult order and then became a Reiki Master – healing and helping alleviate the suffering of hundreds of people, including those diagnosed with severe forms of cancer. He was a servant of the Light.

Another schism taking place was that between Crass, who lived in a rather secure environment when compared to the squatters and the people who attended their gigs and had to deal directly with the skin-head/fascist violence that often took place. We couldn't just walk away from it. My friend John, for example, had his nose slashed with a razor by such thugs – he was caught in a double conundrum; he was Asian and he was a punk – double-fucked.

*

Whenever I woke up in my room before Matt, who slept in the next room, I would hear him start to moan and wail the moment he woke up and frankly wondered what the hell was going on. I mentioned this to Alex and he said he'd been hearing the same thing. We both wondered what the fuck was going on. Then one day, we confronted Matt and said 'What's with all the moaning and the groaning and the endless wailing first thing in the morning?'

Matt simply replied, 'It's when I wake up and realize that I'm still alive.'

*

94 had a basement with a low ceiling, so if you were down there you had to stoop. We turned the basement into a music room. We had a few guitar amplifiers, a microphone, part of a drum kit, the back of an old piano and a few large metal boxes and containers that formed an 'industrial drum kit'. We would go to a local pub for a few beers and games of pool, then stagger back and make a racket in the basement, swapping instruments, whatever. It's a shame we never recorded any of it – I think we were too out of it to be that organized.

Sometimes one of us would go to the all night garage on Mare Street and fill a container with petrol. Then we'd stand in the street and do a bit of fire-breathing. I used to like breathing fire, but the petrol was a bit risky – you never knew if your lungs were going to suddenly fill up with flames and the petrol usually brought you out in a rash of spots around your mouth and chin. However, despite the risk and the folly of our actions, the flames did look fantastic in the black of night.

The all night garage was something of a Mecca for the dope fiends of Brougham Road. Quite often there would be half a dozen of us in someone's front room getting stoned, and then the munchies would begin to kick-in. Whoever was the most skint at the time would make the journey to the garage with a shopping list as long as their arms and return with a carrier bag full of chocolate supplies.

*

One day, fairly early in the morning, we had a knock on the door. The next thing I know, two young punks walked into my bedroom and woke me up. It turned out that they'd hitched all the way from Glasgow to come see me. I was still stoned. They seemed really pleased to meet me and for the life of me I couldn't figure out why. Why would they travel so far? The first thing they asked me: 'What do you hate most about the world?'

I didn't answer – recently I'd been getting into the Beatles acid-influenced music and trying not to hate the world – I always had more anger in me than hate. There wasn't much that I

hated, but there were a lot of things in the world that made me angry. At that time I was seeking out the things that I loved or the things that fascinated and intrigued me, things that inspired me, simply following my creative path. What was I going to do with these young Glaswegian punks who I came to regard, in a joking way, as my 'fans'? The poor buggers; life in Glasgow must have been ten times worse than it was for me in Stockton.

I got out of bed and made some tea. The two guys stayed with me for about three days. I took them to the West End for a walkabout. We got drunk in Hackney and I probably got them stoned. The whole thing had caught me off guard. It was like they hero-worshipped me or something and that made me feel very uneasy, so I did my best to break whatever ever illusions they might have had about me. They clung to me like leeches (or that's my perception). I tried to be nice and kind and helpful and so on, but I was glad when they fucked off back to Glasgow. I was in no mental state to deal with people I didn't know. I was still psychotic.

*

One of the most radical books I've ever encountered is a work of fiction, written by Luke Rhinehart, called The Dice Man. I'd previously heard the song 'Dice Man' by The Fall on their second album 'Dragnet', and read the accompanying sleeve-note which said something along the lines of 'don't read the book, listen to the song, the song is much safer'.

For those who have not read Dice Man, all I can say is that it involves a psychiatrist who decides to live his life by the random throw of a dice. It is a funny and entertainingly challenging novel that rips into our structured patterns of behaviour and pokes glorious fun at psycho-babble and various philosophies. I would recommend the Dice Man to anyone - like it says on the recent cover of the book that I bought for my Son, Felix (15), 'this book can still change your life'. This book can indeed challenge and change your life. Felix, after reading the book, did begin to dabble with the dice, but only to let it decide which x-box game he should play. Some people think the notion of allowing the random fall of the dice to dictate your decision making process in life is an affront to God.

After reading Dice Man I started to dabble and experiment with dice-living; letting the fall of the die make decisions for me and following them through. I never used it for really major decisions because I generally used the Tarot cards or the I Ching for such things.

Probably the daftest dice decision I ever opted to follow was a health-kick de-tox regime where I had to live on nothing but brown rice for seven days. I managed to make it through four days, but on days five and six I started to cheat by adding a little grated cheese for some flavour. On day seven I went to a pub on Broadway Market, just next to Brougham Road, with Neil and Wayne. After drinking two pints of lager I was staggered-Lee. My system was so de-toxed and pure that the alcohol trashed me in no time. They literally had to carry me home; my legs didn't work, my head wobbled like that of a broken puppet, I probably dribbled too. Praise the Dice.

During that time, Dice Man fever was spreading through Brougham Road and we had all manner of people doing all manner of things. One South African guy walked over a mile, at midnight, to Bethnal Green tube station, wearing a pair of striped pyjamas. Amazingly, he returned unscathed; he wasn't beaten, stabbed, or shot. He just suffered from cold sore feet.

*

In 1993 a bunch of anarcho-punks squatted an empty office building, 99–119 Rosebery Avenue, in Islington. A Black flag was hung from a window, emblazoned with a white painted anarchy symbol; a capital 'A' in a circle. The people who had taken over the empty premises distributed leaflets urging people to 'come and join us'. The leaflet was signed by 'Frieda People, Anna Key and Paz O Fist'.

The squatted office building became known as The Peace Centre, or The Anarchy Centre, and it became a temporary home for over twenty people. It also became a venue for free gigs. The Mob in particular played there frequently. The gig space was cramped, with a rather low ceiling, and usually transformed into a fun and very sweaty experience. People were working together to make things happen, and usually events flowed in a peaceful, albeit chaotic manner. The centre was a cool place to go see some bands play, up close and personal, and it was also cool just to hang around with some of the folks who were living there, such as John, my friend who got cut, for example.

I do recall one evening when things did get a bit messy and a little scary too. I'd gone to the centre with J.C., helping him set up the band's gear. The Mob were playing, I can't recall who else. A bunch of NF skinheads bundled into the place, saying they were in a band called Verbal Abuse and they wanted to play, right then, right now – so right-wing.

I remember talking with a guy who seemed to be their leader, trying to pacify him, even though I knew, instinctively, that their intention was to cause a ruckus. I said that the evening was booked with bands that were already going to play. I did suggest that if they wanted to book another night, then they could probably get a gig in the next week or so (hoping that they would just fuck off, to be honest). A while later it all kicked off. They started punching and kicking people. One guy hit J.C. in the face. J.C. didn't even flinch. I recall that I took one flank aside J.C. and my brother, Wayne, took the other. The skinheads were trying to get on the small stage to wreck the band's gear and we smacked a few faces. The high point for me involved J.C. picking up a heavy amplifier and hurling it into a particularly nasty, violent guy – he threw the amp like it weighed no more than a cardboard box. Eventually the skinheads had to beat a retreat. To my knowledge, I don't think they ever came back. All in all, I don't think the centre lasted a year before it was shut down.

*

1983 also marked the first ever 'Stop the City' demonstration, devised by three anarchists in Hackney as a 'Carnival Against War, Oppression and Destruction', it was to be a protest against the military-financial-industrial-complex in the heart of the so-called Golden Mile.

Their plan was simple; unite the various factions of anarchists, liberals, ecologists, animal rights activists, anti-nuclear activists and such like to create a non-violent demonstration in the heart of the Square Mile; blocking streets and access to London's Stock Exchange, big businesses and major banks, with the intention of bringing a halt to the machinations of the capitalist district that is protected by the Metropolitan Police. Obviously a big concern was the issue of violence – how would people respond against the inevitable police violence? CND were the first group to refuse to be involved with the proposed demo.

The secondary idea, and the most radical of all, was to organise a mass demonstration without informing the police or consulting with them over which routes they could take – something that has rarely occurred in modern British history.

Obviously the police got wind that something was in the air, but they didn't know when or where the demo was going happen, they were completely in the dark. Rumour has it that two plain clothed senior cops turned up at a meeting of London anarchists, pleading to meet with people, but they were met with an angry silence and sent on their way.

The date set for Stop the City was September 29th.

*

I'd heard about the proposed plan for the demo. At that time I was spending quite a lot of time with Poison Girls. Vi Subversa was getting her teeth and lyrical skills into a corporation called Rio Tinto Zinc; a British-Australian multinational corporation with their head office in the City of Westminster, London.

Rio Tinto Zinc are the third or fourth largest mining company in the world, in particular they mine coal, iron ore, aluminium, diamonds and uranium. They have been widely criticized by environmentalist groups for their mining methods that involve environmental degradation, the company's coal operations for their contribution to global warming, and their uranium operations for environmental and nuclear technology concerns.

In 1993, Vi bought a single share in Rio Tinto Zinc. This is a little known fact and one that I love about Vi. She used that single share to gain access to the annual shareholders meeting in Westminster, using it like a key, or a foot in the door. At some stage during the meeting, Vi climbed upon a table and sang the following Poison Girls song to her fellow shareholders before she was removed from the RTZ premises:

RIO DISCO STINK

Do you know what it means when you hear the pain
Of an ugly woman's song
I know the truth, I won't hold my tongue
About what's going on
I know what it means when you look away
When I sing my song
I've got nothing to gain, and nothing to lose
And what you do is wrong
Do you know what it means when you hear the cry
Of the hungry girls in red
It hurts my mind and it hurts my pride
That they come to you for bread
And the company creep will dig them deep
As they lie down on their beds
You make your pile, on their weary smiles
And the hole between their legs

It's not enough to cry when miners die
At Rio Tinto Zinc
Uranium will kill your son
Whatever you want to think

It's not enough to cry that children die
For the leader of your pack
When you hear their screams, you'll know it means
They're gonna get you off their backs

Do you know what it means to breathe that dust
And feel it on your skin
When you're poor and black, with a weary back
And the white man's got a whip
They make white man's power from a hole in the ground
At Rio Tinto Zinc
And the company banks fill up their tanks
But you can't lock up the stink

You make your pile where the miners die
At Rio Tinto Zinc
Do you know what I mean, can you hear them scream
Can you smell the stink?
Of the hundreds dead at the RTZ
To pay for your British fun
The rotting men at the Rossing mine
That digs uranium

I know what it means that they're moving in
With their rigs to Donegal
The greedy men that pay so cheap
To dig their poison hole
I know what it means to want to blow up the Queen
And Rio Tinto Zinc
And take a shot at the creamy lot
That sell us tea to drink

When the music dies in your disco dives
And the news fades on your screens
You'll get no sleep, you'll get no peace
You'll hear them in your dreams
Uranium will kill your son
Whatever you may want to think
Are you feeling proud...of that hole in the ground
At Rio Tinto Zinc

A cancer spreads from a hole in the ground
At Rio Tinto Zinc

The company banks fill up their tanks
But you can't lock up the stink
Uranium will kill your son
Whatever you may want to think...
Are you feeling proud...of that hole in the ground
At Rio Tinto Zinc

As a result, Vi obtained the name, address and home phone number of every major RTZ shareholder in the UK and we concocted a plan to print up thousands of leaflets containing the shareholders details and distribute them, with the help of friends, throughout the upcoming Stop The City demonstration. It was going to cost a bit of money to produce thousands of leaflets with a decent print quality, and I volunteered to put together a fund-raising gig at Chat's Palace in Hackney and asked if Poison Girls would play. Of course, they said yes. I also approached The Mob and they also agreed to do the gig.

I set everything up with Chat's Palace, managed to keep the ticket prices low, and because the gig was a complete over-full house, Chat's got their money, both the bands got paid in full and I was left with enough cash to print out thousands of RTZ shareholders details leaflets.

The gig was hot, in all respects. The Mob played first. By the time they finished their set, hundreds of people had to spill out of the venue in order to grab some air. Everyone was dripping sweat. After a thirty minute break, everyone piled back in for Poison's set to sweat it out some more.

I loved that gig simply for the fact that it was peaceful, pulsing and heaving, so full of energy, and so unlike the first time I saw Poison Girls at the malignant venue of Middlesbrough Rock Garden when violence ruined everything. This time, the magical circle was not broken by little devils and we all got to share and savour our collective power – anarchy in full effect.

*

On September 29th the 'Stop The City' demo took place.

The night before the demo, a large number of riot cops stormed the 'Peace Centre' where many demonstrators were crashing out. The police searched the entire building looking for weapons and petrol bombs and such-like. They found nothing of the sort – if they had it would have been known as the 'Violence Centre' from that day onwards.

The 29th proved to be an interesting day, unlike any demo I'd ever attended before. Firstly, on most demo's, people just walk, holding their cardboard placards, singing and chanting their little harmless nursery-rhyme inoffensive ditties, all the time guided and escorted and 'protected' by the police. This day was different, possibly the greatest British demo that had ever occurred.

Here, people were not being herded like stupid cattle or automated 'hole-in-the-pocket' socialists, instead they were making it up as they went along, running, everywhere, in all directions, like spiky haired rabbits, and the cops just couldn't keep up. You'd hear a cop on their walkie-talkies going 'Where are they going to next?' They didn't have a clue.

The cops made us suffer for causing them so much stress and uncertainty (and for making them run around, therefore missing several donut breaks).

They weren't in control, but if they got hold of someone, then they went overboard to remind you exactly who was in control. I saw cops smacking people in the face – they were hitting people who were not being violent in the slightest (non-violence was a real part of the agenda – we were taking pages from Ghandi's notebooks – that fella who brought down an Empire, before his own people shot him), I saw cops knocking women to the floor and then picking them up, hand right between their legs, making sure they felt some pain, making sure she cried and screamed aloud. I saw truncheons swinging...to the left...and to the right...

That day proved to be a real test for the pacifist-anarchists.

I have to say, the pacifists proved themselves.

On that day the police made 350 arrests.

Not one police officer was injured.

I was arrested exiting the Bank of England, where I'd been handing out the RTZ leaflets. As I attempted to cross the road two cops jumped on me and squashed me flat on the ground, merging my face with the road. They told me I was causing an obstruction. They lifted me to my feet – I was in a daze - they said I was resisting arrest and then they threw me into the back of a van. When the van was full with maybe a dozen fellow demonstrators, they drove us away.

They took us to a police station. I was never informed what station I was being held in, so when I walked out of there at 4:30 in the morning, I had no idea where I was. Was I even in London?

To this day I don't know what station I was taken to. I do know that they were overwhelmed. They'd arrested so many of 'us' that the cell I was in, probably designed for two or three people, contained more than 20 people – it was so hot and airless in our cell that they actually left the door open and then brought in an electrical fan. Most of us were vegetarians and we were being treated like cattle.

After a few hours I was taken out of the cell and frog-marched down a corridor by two PC's (for anyone of a younger generation reading this, PC in this instance does not stand for Politically Correct or for Personal Computer). They pulled me into an upright posture and then shoved me through a set of swinging doors. As I stumbled through the doors I saw two guys wearing suits – one of them took a Polaroid photograph of me. I told him that what he was doing was illegal. He pulled the photograph from his camera, waved it at me, smiled, and said, 'Secret Files'. Then I was taken back to my cell. Who were those guys? MI5? (Or as my mother would say, in her verbally dyslexic way, MFI?) It didn't really matter. When it comes down to it these guys are ineffective, and like most cops, all they do is pick up the pieces after the event. They can't even stop a rainstorm.

Val had also been arrested and taken to the same station – I recall that at one point we were shouting stuff to each other from our cells.

We were both charged with causing an obstruction and resisting arrest – we were also due to appear in court on the same day.

What we didn't know, until Wayne told us the following day, is that over 100 demonstrators had followed the vans we'd been carted off in and had surrounded the police station, demanding our release. We were below ground level and never heard a murmur and missed the station under siege.

Later, when Val and I went to court together, along with many others, we had to pay a small fine for obstruction. All charges of resisting arrest were dropped – hence, they were false charges - lies.

One thing that really pissed me off at the time of the demo was the way that the London Evening Standard reported briefly, derogatorily, on the demo in its early edition and after, all subsequent editions said absolutely nothing, fuck all, like it never even took place – Orwellian bastards.

Not long after 'Stop The City' the Evening Standard also wrote a short, sexist, nasty put-down piece on Vi Subversa.

These days, they give the London Evening Standard away for free, but I still wouldn't read it or wipe my arse, or your arse, with it. On the day of Thatcher's death procession (17th April, 2013), the Standard was certainly kissing the Iron Lady's arse. I went down to Fleet Street that morning and filmed her coffin being carted along – I just wanted to watch Dead Thatcher go by before she was vanquished in the flames of the crematorium – I only filmed one minute of it on my phone, even so, someone shouted out 'Fucking whore! Bitch!' I put that on Facebook.

The Golden Mile in the corrupt heart of London is a an anti-human abomination and the Stop the City demonstrations of 1983 and 1984 were the forerunners of the anti-globalisation protests that have since been taking place, sporadically, all around the western world.

CHAPTER 8

When Poison Girls played a gig at the Brixton Ace Club, Pete M. and I joined them onstage during their performance of 'Real Woman'. We both wore huge, hand carved, painted wooden cocks. Pete had my replica .44 Magnum pistol and I had the .38 revolver. Both guns were loaded with blank ammunition. During the course of the song we masturbated at the crowd and fired our guns over their heads. Some people thought that it was poor taste, some people enjoyed it. I'm not sure what I thought of it. The band thought it was ok as we'd discussed it beforehand with them. I recall that the NME reviewed the gig and it began with the opening line: 'A cock in one hand and a gun in the other...' After that, the NME started calling its live gig review section Live Ammo, accompanied by an illustration of a handgun. Pete also featured on the opening of Poison Girls live album 'Total Exposure', recorded during their tour of Scotland, where he shouts a line taken from Poison's magazine; The Impossible Dream- 'Never mind the bomb, who's got the biggest cock?'

*

The last Crass gig that I attended took place in Camden, North London, just a few months before they packed it in. I went with Jane E. We'd been involved together for a while. We drank a hell of a lot of vodka together; so much that today I cannot drink a single drop of the stuff without feeling poisoned or passing out in a heap. (If I find anyone trying to give me vodka I get really pissed off. I lost one friend because of that, a guy I'd worked with for a few years thought he was clever, trying to spike me, but I told him, never spike a friend.) I was still drinking a lot of vodka at that time and still doing my fair quota of speed. My psychosis was functioning perfectly. I was in harmony with the chaos zone.

I was still dabbling with my replica guns and still obsessed with the Taxi Driver movie. Elaine R. and Jane E. helped dress me up in psychedelic drag, including a set of high heels that were a real struggle to walk in. We had a laugh and a few photographs were taken (I hope none survived). I was doing this because I was sick of the predominantly male, all in black, audience that attended Crass gigs. I thought they could do with a bit of psychedelica. I also thought that I would take along the .38 in my black plastic handbag. Jane knew I had the .38 with me. She'd been with me when I was firing it late at night in London Fields. She knew that I'd knocked on Neil's door and fired it point-blank into his face, freaking him out and burning his skin and really pissing him off – I regret doing that to Neil. I was becoming something of an irritating nuisance with my little black steel toys.

One afternoon, during the summer months, I'd visited Poison Girls in Leytonstone. I did some great acid (purple Om's) with Vi and her son, Dan. We sat in the garden for hours.

The acid was great. The frogs were swimming in the pond and when we started spraying the garden hose they would leap out of the pond and start jumping around the lawn because they thought it was raining. We watched rainbows arcing in the spray from the hose. We could see each other's aura's and the vapour trails from our moving hands were like nothing I'd seen before, but all the way through that trip I was playing with the .38, clicking the trigger at certain points through our conversations, as if to make a point...what point I was trying to make, I have no idea.

Jane and I set off to the Crass gig. She knew I had the .38 in my handbag. She knew it was loaded and she knew that it only fired blanks. We got to the gig and mingled with familiar faces. J.C. was there. Paul W from 96 was there. Lots of people we knew were there.

When Crass started singing/chanting 'Fight War, Not Wars', I took out the .38, hoisted it into the air, and started firing. The gun was incredibly loud (if I fired it indoors it really hurt people's ears), and despite the fact that Jane knew I was carrying it, she passed out with shock.

J.C. was standing nearby.

He saw Jane fall to the floor – he saw the gun in my hand – he thought I'd shot Jane - he smacked me in the face and sent me flying.

Paul W grabbed the .38 and got rid of it for all time. At first I resented Paul for doing that, but gradually his choice of actions made sense to me – he was a good friend of Jane's and he was also trying to save me from my stupid psychotic self.

My psychosis was beginning to rub a lot of people the wrong way and part of me enjoyed that process. My writings at the time were also designed to oppose the status quo that I sensed around me. It's a defect I suffer from to this day (and I always thought Status Quo were a shit band ;-).

I picked myself up and made my way home. I was a mess, battered but not overtly bloody. My clothes were a state and my heels were giving me hell! My face was swollen and my make-up was smeared. My world was a topsy-turvy and I had about 5 miles to walk before I got home.

I never saw that .38 again.

I never saw Crass play live again.

That scene was over.

I did see Jane later that night. She couldn't believe that she'd passed out; she was almost embarrassed by the fact. I couldn't believe that J.C., a judo champion, had beaten me up while I was dressed-up in psychedelic drag. Maybe it was an omen – a sign for me to get my shit together and straighten the fuck out? It was a funny old night.

*

Shortly after that Jane and I did a brief hitch around Europe, travelling around on nothing but our giro payments. We had two weeks and so we hit Belgium, Luxembourg, Germany and France.

Belgium, Luxembourg...nothing much to say about them. My impressions were ones of dull cultures, extra dull peoples, good beers and no sign of rebellion anywhere. Europe looked like a dead zone, a comfort zone of banality.

In Germany people had a little more spark. They were much nicer and kinder than I expected (and I didn't mention the fact that they killed my Granddad who served at Biggin Hill during WWII). We had a few good drinking sessions with some cool Krauts. We didn't go to Berlin; instead we headed for the Schwarzwald (Black Forest) where we camped out in a remote area. We used to hike out of the forest and visit different villages. We'd buy cigarettes, bread and a few bottled beers and also steal pizzas, cheese and a few bottles of wine and take them back to our camp. We'd cook the pizza over an open fire and drink the wine. We never got caught. We exploited the villager's naivety — essentially due to our own state of poverty. If we'd had more cash on us we would have paid for what we needed, but we didn't, so we didn't.

One day we came upon a shrine dedicated to the Virgin Mary. I stepped inside, got my cock out and said 'Suck on this' (a line from Taxi Driver). That night, as we camped in the forest, we experienced a ridiculously scary, massive thunder and lightning storm, plus unknown creatures that relentlessly chewed at the sides of our tent like they wanted to eat us alive. We were both frightened and freaked out during the whole course of that night and I vowed never to cuss the Virgin Mary again — after all, she is just the Christian adaptation of the ancient Egyptian Star Goddess, Isis, symbolic of Sirius, the brightest star in the night sky; her hieroglyphs are now tattooed upon my right forearm.

The German people were cool with us, but the moment we crossed the border into France the whole vibe changed and I began to wish we'd never saved them from beneath Hitler's boot.

Within the space of an hour we were searched twice at gunpoint by French cops. Each time they dumped the contents of our rucksacks onto the highway, motorway or whatever they call it over there (not an autobahn), and then kicked all our stuff into the path of the oncoming traffic. The second time they did that to us, Jane grabbed my hand — she clocked that I was going to grab the cop's gun from its holster. Those French cops really pissed me off — they tipped our rucksacks out like so much garbage, because we were punks and perhaps more so because they knew we were English. In the back of their squad car they started reading through a few letters I was carrying — one was from Robert Smith of The Cure — the cop said 'He writes like a child'. I was just thinking, 'You're lucky to be alive, pal.'

We finally made it to Paris. Because the French cops were giving us so much grief for hitching we decided to blow most of our dwindling cash supply on train fares. We hit Paris very late at night. We knew we were drifting into dire straits. We staggered into a store to buy some wine. Jane fell over. She was weighed down by the weight of her rucksack and the alcohol levels in her bloodstream — she wriggled about on the floor like an upturned turtle, laughing her head off. I was so drunk I could barely haul her to her feet.

We bought the wine, spending the last of our money.

It was raining, real heavy.

We needed somewhere to stay. We had our tent. We both agreed that the cemetery where Jim Morrison (The Doors) was buried would be a suitable place and headed off in that direction.

We had to walk around the cemetery for a while because there were cops patrolling everywhere. Eventually we picked our moment and jumped the fence. We crawled into some bushes and half-pitched the tent, then crawled in and crashed out.

The next morning, the sun was out, we were in the centre of Paris, utterly broke and a long way from home.

After that, we suffered a very grim week. We had plenty of cigarettes but no money for food or booze. Rob C put us in touch with a French artist he knew. She let us stay at her house for a day and then we were moved to another house shared by a bunch of students. The students were happy to take us both out for a drinking session every night, but were never offered much in the way of food.

We approached the British Embassy. All they were willing to provide us with was a metro ticket that would take us to the edge of Paris. I think they expected us to walk a few hundred miles to Calais and then swim for Dover – they were no help at all.

We had to make phone calls, and much to his credit, Rob C bailed us out. By the time we got home we were fragged-up and our relationship soon came to an end. However, recently I happened to bump into Jane at The Clock House bar near Chancery Lane where I work. We said hello and had a chat and got on cool enough for sure. One more person from the past stepping out of the woodwork and into the light of day.

*

While I was living at 94 Brougham Road I got to know Joseph Porter, drummer with The Mob. He'd also drummed for Zounds. He took his name from a character in the Sven Hassel novels about the exploits of a bunch of German soldiers during WWII.

At the time I got to know him, Joseph was living in Grosvenor Avenue, a house that belonged to the Black Sheep housing co-op. He lived there with Mark Mob, Tony. D and his sister Val. D, Fod, Nicky, Al L. and Mick L. I used to cycle to Epping Forest with Val and Joseph and we'd spend the afternoon hiking around. Invariably, Joseph would find a fallen branch and it would become his staff of wisdom, and like a sage he would lead us through the forest. Sometimes he would hand the staff over to me or to Val if he deemed us worthy.

In many respects I think Joseph is a very old soul, certainly medieval, who happens to be caught in our current time vortex. He was growing increasingly frustrated with his position in The Mob, essentially because he was beginning to develop his own lyrical narrative and what he was writing did not really fit with what The Mob were doing. I definitely encouraged him to follow his own path – like I encourage everyone to do – but it's not like he needed much guidance from anyone in that respect. The Mob ended up splitting up; Mark fitted out a truck and moved out of the city, choosing the life of a traveller. Joesph moved out of the communal house in Grosvenor Avenue.

Joseph moved into 66 Brougham Road – well, into a kind of extension to the house that was probably once used as a laundry room. He made a pair of swords and two wooden shields and we used to have sword fights, all very gung-ho. He once swiped a sword blade across my stomach, leaving a mark that cut through a single layer of skin, a few more millimetres and my guts would have spilled out all over the back yard.

Lance D'Boyle, drummer with Poison Girls, was making an 8mm film about men and masculinity. He wanted to film us sword fighting. He invited me and Joseph over to Leytonstone and we went up to the Hollow Ponds; a series of man-made ponds surrounded by woodland. We wore sandals and loin-cloths, like something from Roman times, then waded into one of the ponds and had a swordfight. That was a fun afternoon; the only time

I haven't been nervous in front of a camera.

I once did a slideshow before a Poison Girls gig in Victoria, London, and Joseph did the soundtrack for it; Spartan, military drumming.

When Joseph moved out of 66 Brougham Road my brother Wayne and I helped him build a small home in the back of Spanish Elizabeth's house – I can't recall the number of her house in Brougham Road – years later she had a daughter with J.C.

His new dwelling place was little more than a glorified shed. It was built from timber. It had a wooden door and a single small window. It had a raised bed and a place to stand his oil lamp. And that was it. Minimal to the extreme, like the place a monk or holy man might volunteer to live in. While he lived there, Joseph began to seriously write poems and accompanying illustrations. He was forging his own vision and out of that intense, creative period, Blythe Power was spawned.

The original line-up of Blythe Power consisted of Joseph on drums and doing all the vocals (a true sight and skill to behold), Curtis Y. (ex-Mob bassist) on bass guitar, and Neil K. on guitar. They began rehearsing in the low ceilinged basement of 96 Brougham Road and eventually began gigging, before releasing their first album; 'A little touch of Harry in the night'. Since then the band have undergone many personnel changes, and just as Mark E Smith is the only constant in The Fall, so Joseph Porter is the only true constant in Blythe Power. Like The Fall, the band has kept going.

To call Joseph a train-spotter would be a severe understatement. He's a train-freak! When he appeared on a London Weekend Television show called 'Holy Smoke!' where various musicians discussed their individual religious beliefs, Joseph cited train-spotting as religion of choice. Personally, I never was a fan of trains. It was the 'iron horse' that helped to decimate Native American culture. It was trains that ferried Jews and Gypsies and other 'sub-humans' across Europe before they were fed into the Nazi ovens. I think Joseph understands the history and power and symbolism of the train better than most. Indeed, the band takes its name from a train. (Years later, when I moved back to Stockton-on-Tees for nine months to live in a bedsit and write my first novel, Blythe Power played at the Dovecot arts centre at the end of my street. I hadn't seen Joseph for years, and that gig was the last time I saw him. I recall that in between songs he was asking if anyone in the crowd could get him into the Darlington railway yards. He was a man on a mission.)

During that summer when Joseph was busy writing and illustrating, he taught me Hatha Yoga. Every morning, around 8 O'clock, I'd turn up at Spanish Elizabeth's and we would do yoga for about an hour. He taught me the Salute to the Sun sequence of postures, and other moves, such as The Tree, The Crocodile, The Lion. Eventually, after performing various 'moves' and breathing techniques I would enter a mild hallucinogenic state. One morning I woke up earlier than usual and took a handful of magic mushrooms and then proceeded with the yoga lesson. At some point, Joseph figured out that I was tripping and from that point onwards he was merciless in his mirth. He was hopping around on one leg in the Tree posture, and then pulling the Lion face at me until I was cowering in a corner of the room and laughing like a maniac. Yoga is cool.

After I moved out of 94, Joseph ended up moving into my old room. I recall visiting him there one evening and caught him out slightly unawares. I noticed what appeared to be the outline of a magickal circle beneath the rug on the wooden floor. I voiced my suspicion and Joseph rolled back the rug. In the midst of the magickal circle was the symbol for British Rail. I thought that moment spoke a lot about the deep level of his personal obsession, and it also showed that he totally grasped the techniques of magick; it uses the power of symbols to create a new reality. Symbols work on the deeper levels of mind and they activate and stimulate places where words alone cannot reach. Numbers also possess a similar power.

I recently got in touch with Joseph via the magick medium of Facebook and he kindly sent me a copy of his last album 'Land, Sea and Sky', and I sent him some of my own D-Frag/Mr Hex recordings in return – I'm sure I got the better deal in our mutual barter.

Joseph has written his own 'flashback' in his own inimitable style of wit, wisdom and insight – he's a far better wordsmith than I; it can be found on the Blythe Power website.

*

On March 29th, 1984, the second Stop the City demonstration took place. I did attend, but I played it a little smarter, determined not to get arrested a second time due to my last encounter with the 'spooks' from MI5 and their Polaroid camera. More people attended the second demonstration and the police were once more chasing people left right and centre. Again, the police came in heavy and hard. At the time, the miner's strike was ongoing, but lots of cops were brought down from up north into London for the 'occasion'. The cops had been given carte blanche to smash the fuck out of the miner's, to the point of beating several of them to death, so when the same, rather huge cops turned up in London, they already had the flavour for street violence and they relished their duties as they squared up with unarmed pacifist-anarchists with their telescopic truncheons and steel-toe-capped boots, smashing men and women to the ground – I guess they call it a perk of the job. On that day, over 1,000 arrests were made. After that the police started to instigate what they call 'Kettling'; herding people together and holding them in the same spot for several hours, like stupid sheep in a pen.

*

That year was rather intense due to Thatcher's determined fight against the miners, their unions (and their leader, Arthur Scargill), and the working class population of north England in general, and her nuclear-power, nuclear-weapons agenda. Without a doubt she smashed those communities – her police led miners who were peacefully protesting into a field and then charged at them with horses and batons and broke hundreds of faces. Some of the battered miners from that day never walked again. However, it should be noted that Scargill played directly into Thatcher's hands due to his own lust for power, and it should not be forgotten that the previous Labour government closed down more mines than Thatcher ever did. Left and right, they're all pricks and cunts in suits and not to be trusted with our children's futures.

I travelled around with Poison Girls on a tour that was created to help out the families of striking miners as they had no income. I was also selling my fanzines – can't recall what the current 'zine at that time was called. It was kind of funny talking to some of the miners – here they were, out of the 'pit' and attending a Poison Girls gig, getting pissed with a bunch of anarcho-punks – the kind of people who they had no doubt judged and damned along with everyone else when the mass media declared war on the blank punk generation. Now here they were, waking up to the reality of the harshness of government power and finding themselves, along with us, on the wrong side of the fence. More than a few of them admitted that they didn't want to go back to the mines – they preferred the anarcho-punk hedonistic-revolutionary lifestyle that was suddenly swirling about them, they enjoyed the gigs and the beer and meeting 'folk from all over', and more than one of them said they enjoyed being away from the wife, and who can blame them? Fuck the pit – no man, boy, woman or child ever should have to endure such a chore to fill the government's coffers.

*

Alex T. and Matt M., who lived with me at 94 Brougham Road, used to visit an 'artist' guy every now and then. The guy was fairly well off and he was in quite a successful band. He would give them free drugs and booze and pay them a decent hourly rate if they stripped off naked while he sketched them. The guy also had another interest and he offered to pay them £100 to squat on a glass table – he wanted them to defecate while he lay on his back on the carpet, looking up from beneath the table. I know they got naked for the art, and they took the dosh and the drugs and the booze. I don't think either of them ever went for the £100 jackpot.

Alex moved out and moved to Amsterdam. I've never seen or heard from him since. Matt also moved out, but our paths have crossed several times, once every year or so, at random, on various East London Streets – I put that down to our mutual interest in Crowley and Magick and things weird.

At the same time, Neil's family were looking for someplace to live. His mother, Sara, an artist, and her three daughters, Ali, Rosie and Liz, were looking for a new place to live as they were about to be evicted from their house around the corner – the same house where Wayne and I bumped into Neil before we started squatting places together. Sara and the girls moved into 94 - how time carves its strange circles and never ending spirals.

Living with Sara, a Rudolph Steiner artist and teacher, and her family was a great time. They are all truly fantastic people. Sara painted a portrait of me that I've posted on Facebook. Kim also painted a portrait of me. They're both clever bits of art; I wish I had such skill.

During the time we lived together I had two very strange 'occult' experiences. I do not know the order of the events, like which one came first, but I think they both happened within a few days of each other and they certainly freaked me out for all time.

One night I woke up, it was around 3 in the morning. I knew something strange was happening. I sat upright and I saw the outline or silhouette of something or someone standing there, at the very foot of the bed. Because I was in my slightly raised opium-built bed I realized that whatever was standing at the end of my bed was about 4 and a half feet tall. I didn't see any distinct features, just a black bulbous head – I knew that something was there, and then I just rolled over and went to sleep.

When I awoke the next morning I felt rather unsettled. I recalled seeing something at the end of my bed. I recalled being disturbed by its presence. The one thing that disturbed me more was the fact that I just went back to sleep. Let's face it, if you've got an intruder of some kind in your room, are you just gonna roll over and go back to sleep?

The next morning I told Sara that I'd seen something strange in my room during the night.

She said – 'It was probably your Guardian Angel', and I put it out of my mind until a psychic encounter, years later, with a blue entity. I have wondered if I've suffered from alien abductions (hence spending 7 years writing a non-fiction book called 'A Star Cult Mythos'). There was a period of several weeks when I first moved to London when I awoke every Wednesday morning with a nosebleed.

The second event was stranger still.

I was awoken during the middle of the night by a very loud sound - I thought it was an explosion of some kind, like a bomb had just gone off. I jumped out of bed and looked out of my bedroom window and saw four bright white lights on the ground in our back garden. The top two lights were closer together than the bottom two lights. The lights were so bright that I couldn't see what shape or object they were attached to. Then, silently, the four lights shot up into the night sky, and in the blink of an eye they vanished into the dark heavens above.

The next morning I asked people in Brougham Road if they'd seen anything unusual that night. Ali, Sara's daughter, who's bedroom faced out across the wasteland that was once the bus garage, said that she thought she'd seen a fire, but she was a bit vague.

I didn't know it then, but that was the start of my dealings with UFO's – since then I've had several close encounters in London, Nottingham and Vienna. I've also filmed more than a dozen unidentified objects on my camcorder and spent 7 years writing a book called 'A Star Cult Mythos', a subject way beyond the scope of this particular flashback.

*

Due to the fact that I've lived in well over 25 different places, including houses, flats, bedsits and squats, I sometimes have difficulty recalling the exact sequence of my timeline. I'm pretty sure that I'd moved out of 94 Brougham Road. I basically handed the house over to Sara. Years later she managed to buy the house and obtain a secure place for her family – I recall that she used left-over copies of Operation Mind Fuck that were gathering dust in the basement to kindle her kitchen fire during winter months and I thought that was groovy – burn my words! Love it! Destroy!

I moved into a shared flat (the bottom half of a street house), in Lower Clapton, Hackney, with Andy M. (the guy I first met one night when he was perched in a tree with Pete M.), when he moved from Stockton to London. We didn't live too far from a stretch of Hackney that was known back then as Muggers Mile. These days the same stretch is known locally as Murder Mile.

It was right next door to a store that had a good selection of video rentals. We got into a serious movie mode, watching dozens of movies every week and smoking dope like nobody's business.

During that time I got a job at the old Hackney Hospital as a porter. It was a crazy place to work. One wing was a psychiatric hospital and guys just used to walk in from the street and rape a female patient on the stairwell – if they ever got caught by someone they were just kicked off the premises; the cops were never called.

That's when Andy first introduced me to John H. Aka Sinker (his dad, like mine, was an ICI truck driver and actually a pal of my dad's) and Paul C, aka The Confuzer. They were both from Thornaby, near Stockton, a tough, somewhat deprived area. I never knew either of them back then but we all knew quite a few similar people on the punk-skinhead scene. Our paths just never crossed.

We smoked some dope together and had a few beers. Paul showed me a map and a book of Nepal. He said he wanted to go there and hike around the Himalayas. I hadn't even heard of Nepal but I liked what he showed me, I liked what I saw and said that if he ever got it together to go there that I'd like to go with him. After that initial meeting, Nepal was on my radar, lurking on the edge of my peripheral vision like a future spectre.

At that time I was spending considerable time with Poison Girls at their house in Leytonstone and I ended up living with them for a total of around 7 years. I recall that Lance D-Boyle (referred to as Gary R. from here onwards) had stopped drumming for the band, but he still shared the house with Vi Subversa, Richard Famous and Dan S. who built his own 8-track recording studio in the basement where he recorded, produced and mixed music by Poison Girls, The Omega Tribe, and Rubella Ballet to name a few, plus a one-off project of 3 tracks by Headonastick with Paul C. (Guitar/bass/vocals), Neil K. (drum machine patterns/vocals), me (vocals and lyrics), and Kim B. (vocals).

I also got involved with making a short 8mm film with Gary. We built a large work surface and a cube-like wooden frame, and then built all kinds of 3 dimensional shapes such as cubes, pyramids, five and six pointed stars, octahedrons, tetrahedrons and dodecahedrons, plus planets and silver letters that we suspended from fishing wire. We brought the whole surreal land-space-scape to life using stop-motion filming. 8mm film uses 24 frames for every second of footage, so we'd move things a fraction, then film 2 frames, and then move things again and so on. It was time consuming but the result was interesting. We called the short film 'The Cosmic Egg'.

*

I'm not sure how it came about but a side project to Poison Girls began to assume form. Basically the idea was for a bunch of us to perform a multi-media alternative cabaret show dealing with various aspects of emotional, sexual and narcotic dependency. We worked under the name of The Zany. Members included Gary R. who had stopped drumming for Poison Girls, Vi, Richard, and the three other members of Poison Girls at the time; Agent Orange (Dave), who played drums and was into Transcendental Meditation, bassist Mark D., and Synth Ethics (Sian – keyboards and vocals), plus me, Vi's son, Dan (formerly bassist with Omega Tribe and Rubella Ballet), Vi's daughter, Gemma, (also a former bassist with Rubella), and Tony Allen, one of the original 'alternative' stand-up comedians and occasional script writer for TV shows such as 'Spitting Image' and 'Alas Smith and Jones'.

The show we created was called 'The Naked Addict'. We all worked hard on it and produced some cool material, but we only did a few performances, essentially due to some members of Poison Girls thinking that The Zany was going to totally de-stabilize them as a working band. The potential was definitely there.

We spent time doing various workshops and we each began to work on developing a persona that we would inhabit for the show. For some reason, my character wore a suit, carried a .44 Magnum and sported a De Niro mole on my face. Gary became a strange, almost baby like, 'Professor Lemming', who was worried about 'The Gremlins in Russia taking over'. Tony Allen became a rather sinister clown.

Then we travelled to a remote farm somewhere in south Wales that was owned by some friends of Poisons. On the way there we kind of got lost; the driver, who shall remain unnamed, was heavily stoned. There were no road signs anywhere, just fields and grazing sheep. Vi suggested that we simply follow whatever direction the nearest sheep happened to be gazing. Obviously the rest of us must have been stoned as well because we agreed – it seemed like a good idea, the logical thing to do. As crazy as it might sound, the sheep guided us to the farm. I always knew that Vi Subversa possessed shamanic powers.

For two weeks we lived in a huge barn and slept on the upper levels that had been built for that purpose. In the morning a few of us would roam the nearby fields and gather fresh mushrooms to go toward breakfast – unfortunately it wasn't magic mushroom season, a real shame as the area was perfect for those little devils. Before we started cooking breakfast, which we took turns preparing; we would do a group exercise, usually something different each day. For example, I taught the group a little Hatha yoga, the Salute to the Sun sequence of moves, and solar-luna breathing techniques that I'd learned previously from Joseph Porta. Richard Famous taught us some Tai Chi movements. Sian taught us breathing techniques and gave us singing lessons. Gary taught us some really nice Hindu meditational chants. Everyone had something to contribute. Everyone carried their own weight. It was a positive and creative fortnight. We wrote monologues, dialogues, song lyrics and a rap lyric, plus all the music to accompany the various scenes of 'The Naked Addict'.

When we returned to London, Dan recorded several of the songs that we'd created in Wales. However, as I mentioned earlier, we only did a few gigs; one was a free gig, I think that took place at the Anarchy Centre in Islington, another took place at the Zap Club on the seafront at Brighton – the gig was recorded on video, no idea who has that now. We used live music, pre-recorded music and background film-projection, including a few clips from Taxi Driver.

Sian died a few years later from cancer. I especially enjoyed working with her on a song we did together; '(All the heroes are waiting with a).44 Magnum'. As I was working on the lyrics, Sian was playing guitar and singing and it all fell into place real fast, like some of the best songs do. I recall Joe Strummer once said, in an interview I read someplace that most of the best Clash songs were written in 20 minutes. I think he was speaking the truth.

Poison Girls continued as a band for about another year. They also became involved in two other stage productions, namely 'AIDS – The Musical' and 'Mother Russia was a Lesbian'. They reformed briefly in 1995 to play a gig at London Astoria to celebrate Vi's 60th birthday. I think admission to the gig was a gift for Vi. Gary moved to Spain; Neil K. and I travelled over to see him before we went to Morocco. Vi also lives in Spain, and last I heard, Richard moved back to Yorkshire.

*

My Robert DeNiro obsession was still going on. I have to admit that I commit fully to my obsessions. However, I'd shaken off my speed psychosis and given up playing with replica guns and firing blanks into my mate's faces or firing them off in pals living rooms or firing random shots in London Fields late at night – shots going off and lights coming on in all the nearby blocks. I'd also stopped snorting lines of white powder; I was pale, underweight, hardly slept and was sick and tired of horrible hallucinatory insects crawling around at the edge of my vision. I've never touched speed since.

I found out that Robert DeNiro was going to do a lecture/interview at the National Film Theatre on the South Bank of the Thames. I think I had two days to get a ticket. First, I had to become a member of the NFI as the 'lecture' was only open to NFI members. So I paid the yearly NFI membership. The next day I turned up outside the NFI at something like four or five o'clock in the morning and waited until well after lunchtime. There were only 300 tickets available and by no means was I anywhere near the front of the queue. After hours of anxiety I got my ticket. I was so thrilled that it's ridiculous – I was turning into a Rupert Pupkin; DeNiro's celebrity obsessed character in the classic Martin Scorsese movie 'The King of Comedy'.

I arrived early, hoping to meet the man himself as he arrived at the NFI, because I always meet my heroes. Let's face it, I met Eater, I interviewed Mark E Smith, I interviewed Poison Girls and Crass, surely I'd get to meet the star of 'Mean Streets', 'Godfather II', and 'Taxi Driver'. But no, it wasn't to be. He probably arrived at a secret back entrance, or got dropped off in a silent helicopter.

When I turned up at the NFI and attended the 'lecture' I couldn't believe I was in the same room as 'Bobby DeNiro', breathing the same air! He was interviewed by an Evening Standard film critic whose name I can't recall, Malcolm Somebody. DeNiro agreed to the interview but insisted that it would not be recorded or filmed. He sported a full beard; he'd just got back from filming 'The Mission'. He was shy, but honest and humorous. When it came time for people in the audience to ask him a question I froze. I couldn't think of a single thing that I wanted to ask the person who, at that time, I considered to be the greatest living actor in the entire world. Then a guy who was sitting two or three seats away from me stood up and asked 'Bobby' a question. I recognized the guy's voice – it was Martin 'Marty' Scorsese, director of many of DeNiro's finest films before he systematically ruined his best actor in the world status with a succession of lame 'comedies'.

After the lecture, I just went home. When DeNiro left the lecture he had to deal with a fan hiding in his car, and then another one hiding in his hotel room. Considering my obsession with him and guns and so on, I think he's lucky I never killed him ;-)

*

Once more I got itchy feet. I told Andy M. that I'd decided to move to Ellesmere Port in north-west England; 'The Port' as locals call it, situated between Liverpool and Chester. My reasoning was simple. My parents had just moved there and I decided I wanted to spend some time with them and also start work on another novel. It made things a bit difficult for Andy, but he understood my motives.

When I first moved to Ellesmere Port I spent about month on the dole, getting to know the area. I rarely went to Liverpool and spent more time in Chester than anywhere else. Then I saw an ad for a job that interested me. It was a community project, working in a TV studio in the psychiatric wing of The Countess of Chester Hospital. The 'wing' housed around 600 patients (quite possibly 666 of them!), many of them suffering from Alzheimer's, schizophrenia and dementia – some were lucid some of the time, some were living on the remote edges of a distant galaxy, suffering the cruellest of all fates – that of forgetting who they are, who they were, forgetting the people they knew and loved, losing all their precious memories and all recollection of the journey of their lives; their twisted fates and the paths they chose.

The job involved working as part of a production team, creating a weekly forty minute TV show that was broadcast live throughout the wards; hospital TV.

My obsession with Magick was growing around that time and so I performed a magical ritual and consecrated a talisman, invoking occult forces to assist me in obtaining the job. The ritual/job interview was a success and I worked at the Countess for about 9 months.

I did enjoy the time I spent living with my folks in Ellesmere Port – we got on really well. When I was busy writing, clack-clack-clacking on a typewriter using just both forefingers, just as I do now, my 'old man' started calling me Machine Gun Kelly. In Chester and The Port there were plenty of decent places to drink, and compared to Stockton the level of street violence was minimal. I also met some interesting people, such as a young guy I worked with (he was a presenter), Neil; he sang in a local romantic-gothic type band who had a few decent tunes under their studded belts. He introduced me to a bunch of obsessive characters (I wonder why?), they were really into fantasy role-playing games like Dungeons & Dragons – so far into it that they'd crafted their own swords and chain mail for when they met up with other players in the 'real world'. One of them went by the name of Dice Man – nuff said. Neil's band did a gig in a pub in Chester; they were playing in the upstairs bar. The manager was a short fella and he was short staffed, and because there were barely a dozen of us in attendance to see the band, he spent most of the night working the bar downstairs. We spent most of the night jumping behind the bar and filling our glasses with free beer. Cheers!

Ellesmere Port is not far from the Welsh border. My folks have always been keen hikers and they love the English, Welsh and Scottish countryside, and so we often went to cool places like the coastal town of Rhyl, or the rocky mountains of Snowdonia, and especially the groovy village of Portmeirion, where the 1960's TV show 'The Prisoner' was filmed. The actual location of 'The Prisoner' was never revealed until the very last episode of the series – 'I am not a number! I am a free man!'

The in-house live TV shows that we created at the Countess of Chester Hospital were intended to let the patients know what facilities and events were available to them, both inside and outside the hospital. If it was a patient's birthday we would film a piece on them, chatting to them (which was sometimes really difficult and sometimes really funny in a 'don't laugh now' kind of way), putting them onscreen for their friends, if they had any, to see.

Because the 'show' was broadcast live I learned quite a bit about using cameras, presenting (I did a stint chatting about the films that were showing in Chester – I wore shades and bright Hawaiian shirts – and we showed clips from movies while I gave my brief review, which was probably breaking all kinds of copyright laws – I was often stoned if I had to present.) I soon learned that the worst time to be stoned is when you are the vision mixer, basically cutting between Camera 1 (wide-shot showing presenter and victim), Camera 2 (Close up of interviewer), and Camera 3 (Close up of interview victim). When I was stoned my timing got really bad and I learned to stay straight in order to be on the ball.

I also learned how to edit video, something that has come in handy through the years as an amateur short-film maker working on a low-budget, zero-budget level. I directed a 40 minute UFO spoof-comedy called 'Buffoon', and also a 50 minute film called 'Critical Times', filmed in several underground raves, getting up close and personal with people dancing, high on E. The only reason people let me film it was because they knew I wasn't a cop – I was off my face, filming after dropping tabs of LSD, or licking drops of liquid LSD from the back of my hand, or tooting lines of pure MDMA.

Working alongside two other guys we created what might be described as 'pop videos'. We each took turns to pick a song we liked, and then we'd use the TV stations gear and film our storyline. We did all this outside of work hours, in our own time. We did some decent stuff and created storylines to go with the likes of 'Running up that Hill' by Kate Bush (where I played a guy going into a church, trying to make a deal with god and end up running through a snow covered cemetery), 'Glass' by Robyn Hitchcock & The Egyptians (where we really got into video effects and I end up swallowing Egyptian Ankhs whilst miming to the song and my skin changes through all the colours of the video spectrum), and 'Private Investigations' by Dire Straits (I played a detective who used Crowley's Tarot Cards but failed to see his own murder; I was coshed and kicked to death beneath a bridge in Chester).

At first our bosses/producers were not too happy with our music videos, but the psychiatric patients begged to differ. The phone began to ring from various wards. Patients wanted to see our stuff again. In the three or four years that in-house TV had existed, requests had never happened before. I suspect it was a few of the nurses making the calls, just to have a bit of decent music playing on the dead TV. Either way, the request empowered us and we got busy. We created quite a few videos – we were just keen to experiment with camerawork and editing and learn through play. We got away with a few videos and then got squashed flat.

We made a 7 minute war-based video, essentially a montage of clips ripped-off from the 'The World at War' TV series. We edited it on a magical level, working through the four elements of Earth, Air, Water and Fire. Thus we had war scenes that were filmed on land, then in the air, then at sea, culminating in explosions and fireballs and burning cities. The music we chose to accompany the 'pop-video' was 'Mars: The Bringer of War' by Gustav Holst. Our 'producers' took one look at the video and simply said, 'No Way.'

After that things seemed to slip into decline. I became disillusioned with the entire psychiatric TV show. The producers were all about their own ego's. One of them had once experienced his five minutes of fame when he appeared on the TV show 'Liver Birds' – he was so talentless, yet so full of himself. They were just creating mediocrity – sedative TV for sedated patients who were already living on planet Zorg.

We did one legitimate assignment where we spent the day on the roof of a building, drinking and filming the Chester horse races that were taking place below. One guy was filming the horses and stuff, but another camera dude, Scouser Steve, a shrewd and funny guy, just happened to be keeping a close camera-eye on a pretty woman in the crowd, (always good for a 'drop-in' shot'), and then he found a few prostitutes who were in attendance and working the crowd. The highlight of our afternoon was watching as he filmed a uniformed police officer getting a freebie hand-job from one of the hookers. Afterwards we thought about sending it to the media, but eventually the tape got erased. Even cops have mates, so why mess?

*

While I was living with my folx in the 'Port, Kim C. contacted me to let me know about a forthcoming DeSirius gig at Chat's Palace in Hackney, East London. On the day of the gig I caught a train down to King's Cross, where we'd arranged to meet up. However, as I stepped off the train I was stopped on the platform by a female police officer. 'Are you Lee?' she asked. I told her that I was, wondering what was going on. She explained to me that Kim had been assaulted and was waiting in a nearby office for me. The cop said she knew who I was because of Kim's accurate description of me; tall, lean, dark hair, dark clothes, dark soul.

It turned out that while Kim had been waiting outside King's Cross station some black guy started hassling her. Kim eventually told the guy to fuck-off and the prat responded by punching her in the face, knocking her to the ground, and leaving her face in a bloody mess. He then walked away. The police assisted Kim, but failed to find and arrest her attacker.

Later that evening the DeSirius gig went ahead as planned. Kim was determined to do it, not wanting a mindless, cowardly thug to ruin her day. During the gig her nose kept leaking blood and spattering her white T-shirt (emblazoned with black letters; BOLLOCKS TO THE POLL TAX, if I recall correctly). Kim finished the gig. I thought she was rather heroic. If she was a guy, I'd have said she had balls ;-)

*

Gary (Poison's drummer) came to stay in the 'Port with me for a few days. That was the first time I'd had a friend stay my folx place since Sue and Alex stayed at my folx house in Longnewton and freaked them out. It was interesting to me because Gary was about the same age as my dad. My mum caught us getting stoned one afternoon – we were in my room, smoking away, then my mum popped her head in and said 'Hi'. She said 'It's really smoky in here.' I said 'It's the incense.' She looked at my incense burner and like any sharp-eyed mom she saw that it was clean, not an incense stick or cone in sight. I think then she knew that we were stoned. Later on, we were watching a film together and Gary totally crashed out halfway through it. Sometimes you just have to put your hands in the air and say 'Fair cop. My older mate is stoned out of his head.'

Shortly after that, when Gary had gone back to Leytonstone, he phoned me - he was stressed out. His father, who had worked all his life in a Cadbury's Bourneville factory in Birmingham, was beginning to suffer from increasingly frightening episodes of senile dementia. Gary was spending more and more of his time travelling up to 'Brum' to care for his dad. His sister actually lived in Birmingham but she never seemed to have the time to really give much of a damn. The burden of care fell right into Gary's lap. Some nights he'd find his dad collapsed in the bathroom, covered in blood and shit because he'd fallen over and hit his face on the sink or the toilet. It was a really hard time for him as the renegade, yet loving, son. Gary once taught psychology at a college or university in Brighton but he got fired for encouraging the class to teach themselves.

The reason he phoned me that night was because he'd had a really stressful day dealing with and caring for his father. He left the house and went browsing around the shops. Not thinking what he was doing he walked out of a bookstore carrying a book that he hadn't paid for – he wasn't even trying to hide the book in a bag or beneath his jacket, his mind was simply elsewhere.

The police had arrested him and were charging him with theft. I knew Gary well. If he was going to steal a book he'd never have been caught. If he'd stolen the book he would have said so. Flashback: I recall going to see one of the 'pricey' Poison Girls gigs at the ICA in Whitehall that I mentioned to them about in our second interview; I think their stance was solid and valid. The ICA ran a really expensive bookstore – I walked out of there with several books by Jack Kerouac and William S Burroughs, all free of charge, and then went to watch Poisons play. Flashback: One other thing I'd like to mention about Poison Girls, distorting the timeline somewhat – does anyone have a straight timeline, I wonder, and is it all true? - during one Poisons gig I'd been talking with Vi Subversa before they played – I was having a tough time with certain aspects of my childhood, stuff that pre-dates the timeline for this biog-thang – Flashback: I was cutting my arms with a scalpel, usually just drawing blood and cutting just deep enough to create a scar, but one day I was messing around with a Stanley knife in the kitchen of 66 Brougham Road with Rob and pretended to slash my forearm. Fool that I am, I cut my arm real deep. I am the Homer Simpson of knife crime! The flesh peeled back with a horrid sssissssing sound. That was too much for me - I had to have a little sleep, probably in shock. When I woke up I went to the hospital and had 12 stitches. Back to the previous Flashback: During the gig, Vi looked me square in the eye and dedicated a song 'To the children whose parents don't understand them'. She made me cry. That open power of understanding completely blew me away. Vi Subversa is a priestess of the highest power.

Sometimes we forget how fantastic it is to be really understood by another being and how that mutual understanding fills us with light and a brilliant, blinding, wonderful sense...whatever. Sometimes I forget how fantastic it was to partake in a Poison Girls gig...to sweat in the crowd, to jostle at the front, to stand at one side, to stand at the back, or stand right next to a humungous bass speaker that rubberized the brain...to watch Poison Girls play live with all their collective power; pure heart and soul.

That particular gig was very special to me. Vi touched my heart; the one I'm always hiding and losing and finding and trying to save. That night I knew what it was like to be swept up in the rapture of the sacred wings of a black crow; the Poison Girls symbol. I like the fact that a group of crows are not called a flock. Crows do not follow; they're called 'a murder'.

Anyway, flashbacks within flashbacks aside and ongoing, Gary wanted to know if I could help him out, using Magick. He knew I was a dabbler, with a penchant for so-called 'Forbidden Knowledge'. I initiated myself into The Great Unknown on September 2nd, 1986.

I wasn't looking for a guru, or for any particular deity, and I didn't have anyone who knew how to guide me, so I decided to guide myself and basically took the occult Path of The Fool, stepping into a potential Twilight Zone in search of 'The spaces between the spaces', as my favourite artist, Austin Osman Spare, put it. Let's face the music; I've been floating out of my body since I was seven years old...on several occasions my mother has predicted the deaths of friends and family a few weeks before they have suddenly died. Maybe there's glitch in our family DNA? An occult strand...perhaps encoded in everyone's DNA, just waiting to be activated when the time is right.

CHAPTER 9

I'm not going to meander through all manner of magickal theories and ritual 'experiments'; some things maintain more power when they remain silent. Nor am I going to completely evade the third part of my triangle of recollection; As this book covers a specific period of my life, I can't help but put the three corners of my triangle under the same reflective light, namely Punk Rock (music-rebellion), Creativity (art-writing-rebellion), and third, Occultism/Magick.

After several years of reading and studying various aspects of occultism it was time to step into the Circle, so-to-speak, or off the ledge, perhaps. I began testing out different forms and techniques of magical ritual. From the get-go, I wrote my own rituals, fusing astrology, the tarot, numbers, colours, ancient Egyptian, Hindu, and Sumerian texts, plus ritual methods of the Golden Dawn and Crowley's Magick of Thelema; Current 93.

'Does 'it' work?', 'Is 'anything' there?', 'Is 'it' dangerous?'

I was curious enough to find out. I know some people fear shifts in perception or assumed levels of 'control' over what they perceive; I suspect that deep down many of them already know, on a deeper, intuitive level, that something 'else' is already here...has always been here, right now standing at your shoulder; probably sucking out your soul even as you doubt 'its' very existence.

*

The Hermetic Order of the Golden Dawn flourished in Great Britain from 1888-1900. Women were admitted into The Golden Dawn on an equal basis with men – this was well before the British Suffragette movement began in 1906. The Order's headquarters were located in central London close to the British Museum, where the Post Office Tower, or Telecom Tower as it's now called, stands like a post-modern obelisk. The Golden Dawn had barely 100 members, and despite the fact that it only existed for a dozen years before disintegrating, it proved to be one of the largest single influences on the revival of 20th Century occultism.

Known members included Allen Bennett (1872-1923), best known for introducing Buddhism to the West, perhaps lesser known for teaching Aleister Crowley yoga and meditation. Algernon Blackwood (1875-1951), English writer of supernatural stories. Bram Stoker (1847-1912), Irish writer best known for his vampire novel 'Dracula', which he wrote in the north-eastern fishing town of Whitby; the place where Dracula first lands upon

English soil. A.E. Waite (1857-1942), Freemason and co-creator of the Rider-Waite Tarot Deck along with fellow member Pamela Coleman Smith (1875-1951). Arthur Machen (1863—1947), a leading London writer of the 1890's and the author of occult-based novels such as 'The Hill of Dreams' and 'The Great God Pan'. There's a printed version of the latter novel that contains illustrations by my favourite magical artist; Austin Osman Spare. Florence Farr (1860-1917), London stage actress, musician and author of books on ancient Egyptian magical practices. And last but not least, The Great Beast 666; Aleister Crowley (1875-1947), Prophet of the Aeon of Horus. Crowley was an occultist, writer and mountaineer who created the magickal-philosophical system of Thelema; 'Do what thou wilt shall be the whole of the Law', 'The word of Sin is restriction', 'Every man and every woman is a star'. He was also the world head of the O.T.O, and friend of Ian Fleming, creator of 007. Crowley and the Golden Dawn are both mentioned in David Bowie's song 'Quicksand' on his 1971 album 'Hunky Dory'. Crowley also appeared on the front cover of The Beatles 1967 album 'SGT. Pepper's Lonely Hearts Club Band', alongside such notables as Marlene Dietrich, Carl Gustav Jung, Sigmund Freud, W.C. Fields, Diana Dors, Bob Dylan, Aldous Huxley, Lewis Carroll, Edgar Allan Poe, Karl Marx, Oscar Wilde, H.G. Wells, Marlon Brando, Stan Laurel and Oliver Hardy.

*

Random thought – 'I'm not sure what messed me up most, Punk Rock, Anarchy, LSD, Magick or UFOs? I'm just thankful I got messed up.' – I wonder if that might look okay as a quote for the front cover – ha!

*

How does one initiate oneself into a cult or religion of one?

I just had a go.

I dabbled and blew bubbles into the wind.

I built a small pyramid-shaped framed-structure as a replica of the Great Pyramid, built it so that when I sat cross-legged and meditated within it, my head would be one third lower than the pyramids tip; experiments have proved that inside a pyramid, one third down from the apex of the pyramid, a curious energy zone exists. For example – razor's retain their sharpness for longer if kept inside a pyramid. Fruit retains its freshness for longer periods of time if stored inside a pyramid. What happens when you put your mind and consciousness in that zone?

The self-initiation marked a definitive moment where I wilfully began to explore occult techniques. The occult is basically lost, forgotten or hidden knowledge – a knowledge that can also be re-discovered, re-membered and re-vealed. There are so many frequencies to tune into...and just like Austin Osman Spare, I don't believe in 'black' or 'white' magick; all magick is colourful.

The reason I initiated myself was simple. I only had books on the subject to guide me, to bullshit me, or to ill-advise me. The best occult books were mostly written by dead people from the last millennium. Most occult books are crap. All occult books are overpriced. I also knew that various magical groups existed across the UK, heck, they even advertised themselves in magazines - I've never been much of a joiner, always more of an outsider, hoping for the outside of everything; I tend to side with Robert Anton Wilson (co-author of

'The Illuminati Trilogy'), and it goes something like this; I will never join any secret society or magical order that would accept the likes of me.

Putting the timeline together for this book has sometimes been a real struggle, a complete time-space-place head-fuck, but as far as my 'dabblings' go, and despite the fact that over the years I've thrown away or lost a lot of my writing stuff, I still have a slim and curious book – a 'Book of Shadows' as the Wicca-witches might call it, or the 'Magical Diary' as others might say. Anyway, a few extracts from Ritual Zero (0 = The Fool in the Tarot)-

OPUS 0
(Operation Zero)
2ND SEPTEMBER, 1986
SUN IN VIRGO
(God-Solar-Yang-masculine energy in the Air (mind) zodiac sign of the Virgin)
MOON IN LEO
(Goddess-Lunar-Yin-feminine energy in the Fire (creativity) zodiac sign of the Lion)
OBJECT: INITIATION
(With Modesty and Reception, as determined by the I Ching - Book of Changes)
(Using parts of The Egyptian Book of the Dead – The Book of Coming Forth by Day)
(Performed in the mind whilst sitting inside a pyramidal framed structure)
Time: Sunset – 19:45
Facing West – toward Amenti; abode of the dead, the Underworld.
Pay homage to the four quarters of East, West, South and North using the ancient Egyptian sons of Horus;
Tefnut, Geb, Atum, Shu.
Purification: 'Let the Shining Ones not have power over me. I have purified myself and my heart is filled with joy'
(The litany at the moment of sunset – visualizing each god-form)
'I seek protection on all levels – ANUBIS be with me
I seek spiritual construction, PTAH be with me
I seek to know the will of the gods, NEPHTHYS be with me
I seek strength and nourishment, HATHOOR be with me
I seek the path of knowledge, THOTH be with me
I seek joy and fulfilment, BAST be with me
I seek harmony and solution, HORUS be with me
I seek true stellar love, ISIS be with me
I seek the light, OSIRIS be with me.'
(Sunset): 'Hail TEM, thou givest splendour in heaven as a phoenix going in and coming forth.'
(Sacrifice): Mantra 'BA-PUH-NETER, BA-PU HEH'.
(The Closing): 'Swifter than light O Shining Ones return now to the heights of heaven. I have walked besides the Great Ones....'

And so on.

I find the fact that my first ritual of self-initiation was performed facing West, the place of death, where the Sun sets, instead of East, the place of new life and the rising Sun, a little disconcerting, but I'm sure I had my reasons.

*

Anyhow, when Gary asked me if there was 'anything' I could 'do' to help him with the case of the book he'd taken from the store. I said I would happily try and 'do something'.

I already had a magical book connection with Gary. I've only had three occasions, some in peculiar instances, where I've been given serious books on occultism that popped-up, out of the blue (or out of the Abyss), at the perfect unexpected moment. The first was when Mandy gave me Crowley's 'Magick in Theory and Practice' for my 18th birthday. I've had dozens of instants when a certain fictional book has appeared on a charity store bookshelf or, more often, on the ground before me as I'm walking along. Books found on the street include books by Jean-Paul Sartre, J.G. Ballard, Nick Cave, and James Lee Burke. Finding, or being given a book on occultism holds a little more power, but that's not to deny the fact that all books contain a measure of the author's soul. A spirit known as 'the librarian's friend' has helped me on many occasions. Anyone who enjoys reading knows exactly what it feels like to find 'just the right book at just the right time' – it feels like a blessing.

The second occult book handed to me, after Crowley's 'Magick', took place years after I'd moved out of 56 Brougham Road – where I decided to move under guidance from the tarot. Rob V. had moved up to Sheffield. I hadn't seen him for a few years, and then one dark and rainy night he turned up at my door, completely out of the blue. Without saying a word, Rob V. handed me a book and walked away. The book turned out to be a first-edition, out of print, hardbound copy of 'The Magical Revival' by Kenneth Grant (1924-2011), the first book in a series known as 'The Typhonian Trilogies'. Grant's books have probably inspired and shaped the modern occult explosion more than any other writer since Crowley's death.

I've wondered about Rob V.'s silent gesture. What did it mean? What was the purpose of giving me such a book? Was that his way of saying that I'd done the right thing by leaving 56 and taking Wayne, and by the fall of the dice, Neil K. along for the ride? How could I know what he meant by such a gesture of silence? Was it a hex? Had he delivered an occult mind-bomb? Or, as I'm more inclined to believe, was I visited by an Elemental Spirit assuming human shape in a heavy rainstorm, bringing forth knowledge regarding peculiar aspects of reality, for reasons of its own, that it knew might intrigue me. With occult forces, one never knows.

The second magical book was found by Gary in a very different set of curious circumstances. I wrote a short occult horror story 'Demonic Influences' (now lost), partially based around his discovery of a book. Gary had been away with friends, in Dorset I think. One day he set off for a hike, and randomly decided that he would endeavour to walk in a straight line and surmount any obstacles that crossed his path. Later that day, whilst continuing his straight-line hike, he came upon a small building, little more than a shed in a completely isolated area of the countryside. Gary went inside the shed and found an old trunk. He opened the trunk – it was full of books. One book in particular caught Gary's attention. It was black, clothbound and embossed with golden letters; like something from an alien language. Gary picked the book up and took it with him. When he returned to London, he gave the book to me – 'I thought this might interest you'.

The golden letters embossed on the book's front cover were Enochian; the book turned out to be an 'Enochian Dictionary'. The Enochian system of magic dates back to the time of

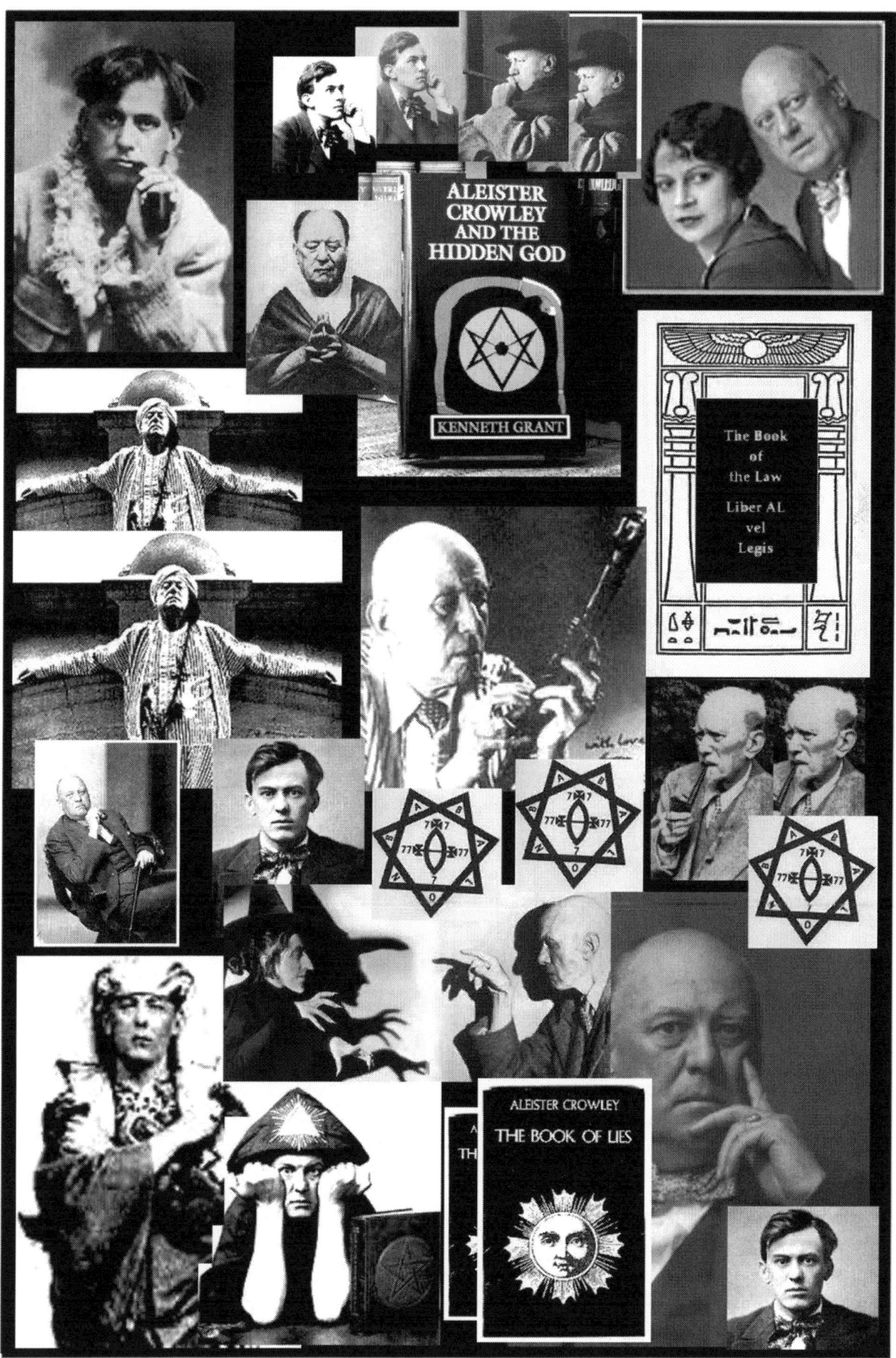

Queen Elizabeth the First, in particular to her advisor and astronomer royal, known as Dr. John Dee (1527-1608). Dee was also a mathematician, occultist and an English spy. When he worked abroad as a spy for Elizabeth, he used the code number 007.

Dee was the first James Bond – no doubt Ian Fleming, along with his friends, such as Crowley, knew of Dee's number.

Dee claimed to have contacted angelic beings that are mentioned in the Book of Enoch. The angelic beings provided him with the Enochian alphabet and a series of magical squares, each of which was divided into four, like the four faces of a pyramid.

Interestingly, where Dr. Dee once lived there now stands a business tower in Canary Wharf, London, simply known as The Pyramid Building because it is topped by a black pyramid. Much like a tower now stands above a place where The Golden Dawn performed their rituals. The tower at the cross-roads of Tottenham Court Road and Oxford Street is called Centre Point; it is built upon what used to be Hangman's Hill.

Enochian magic was not practiced after Dee's death until almost 300 years later – as luck would have it, by members of the Golden Dawn, including Crowley, who did some wild experimentation with Enochian during his travels across the deserts of Morocco, resulting in his book 'The Vision and The Voice'.

One pub I drink in several times a week with various pals is called 'The Sir Christopher Hatton' – back in his time, Sir Christopher Hatton, whatever else he happened to be or do, was a financial sponsor of Dr. John Dee.

It all means something I'm sure, and like Professor Lemming used to say; 'It's all connected.'

*

To help Gary out with the charges of theft that he was facing I decided to use a talisman (in the form of a magical square), found in a very old occult text known as 'The Sacred Magic of Abra-Melin the Mage', dating back to at least 1378. The Book of Abra-Melin outlines a lengthy magical procedure which lasts for 18 months and is designed to enable the magician/priestess to obtain 'the knowledge and conversation' with their Holy Guardian Angel.

The book also contains dozens of talismans whose various purposes include causing spirits to 'appear in the shape any animal', for obtaining visions in wax, in fire, in the Moon, in water, or in the hand, retaining Familiar Spirits, to 'excite tempests' (curiously, Dr. Dee invoked a tempest to defeat the Spanish Armada – perhaps that's why Sir Walter Raleigh calmly played a game of bowls before the battle?), 'to transform animals into men, and men into animals', to heal various ailments, and also the talisman I selected to help out Gary, namely – 'To acquire the affection of a Judge'.

I devised a ceremony that Gary could use, and also suggested that he paint the talisman green – a colour associated with Venus/love/affection. A few days later, Gary phoned. He said that just as he'd started to paint the talisman, he received a phone call from the police. They informed him that they were dropping all charges.

Over the years I've found that talismans are highly effective tools for harnessing the powers of the mind, of focusing them upon a given intention, capable of causing changes to occur in the external reality of this world. I've used talisman's several times to aid other

A PUNK ROCK FLASHBACK

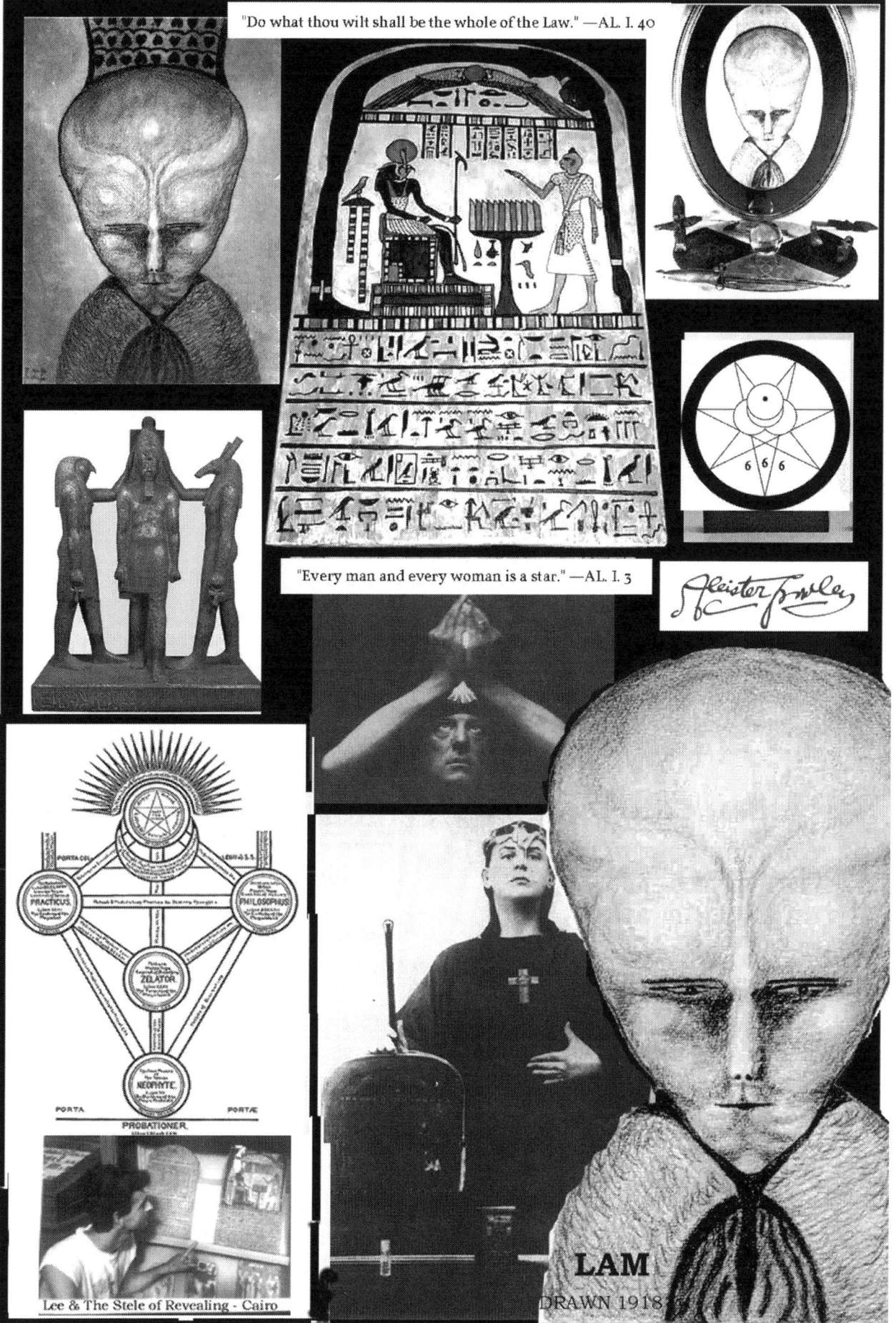

people, including family members.

*

While Gary was living with his father in Birmingham, shortly before his father died, he asked me to assist him in structuring a ritual. He was finding caring for his father increasingly difficult and he wanted to perform a ritual in the place of his childhood and upbringing as an act of self-empowerment; he wanted to rise above the restrictions of his past and the boxed-in, straight-laced, regulated environment that was bringing him down.

We spent some time devising the ritual, using astrology to work out the most appropriate time to perform the rite, taking note of the positions of the Sun and the Moon. The rite was performed on a full Moon. I can't recall in which zodiacal sign the Moon occupied. We decided that the ritual would take place in the back garden at midnight and would terminate at the rising of the Sun; from darkness into light.

Gary had read a few books by Aleister Crowley, and due to our inherent natures, it was agreed that wine and drugs would be freely used in order, to use a Crowley phrase, 'loosen the girders of the soul'.

For the symbolic ritual weapons of Wand, Cup, Sword and Disc, regular house-hold items were to be selected and used. For example, the Wand was a fire poker; the Cup was an old silver chalice from the kitchen cupboard. Gary also wanted to document the rite and I agreed to take some photographs, standing outside the magical circle that would serve to protect Gary from malignant forces, but not me; I would be hanging in the wind. I was confident enough to feel safe being on the outside; being on the outside is the story of my life.

For some unknown reason, ever since I turned up at the house in Birmingham and Gary introduced me to his father, his father refused to call me Lee. He always called me Murgatroyd – this was very peculiar, tho' obviously Gary's father was suffering from dementia and he could have mistaken me for anyone, but Gary was equally baffled. As a child I recall being somewhat fascinated with the name for no reason that I can recall. However, a little Google search has helped me recall the phrase 'Heaven's to Murgatroyd'. The source of this name is unknown – the country or ethnicity of its origin is unknown.

(The name is a sir name, not a first name – a few things I found on the net regarding Murgatroyd: 'Heavens to Murgatroyd' is American in origin and dates from the mid 20th century. The expression was popularized by the cartoon character Snagglepuss - a regular on the Yogi Bear Show in the 1960s. However, the first use of the phrase wasn't by Snagglepuss but comes from the 1944 film Meet the People. It was spoken by Bert Lahr, best remembered for his role as the Cowardly Lion in The Wizard of Oz. Also, no fewer than ten of the characters in Gilbert and Sullivan's comic opera Ruddigore, 1887, are baronets surnamed "Murgatroyd", eight of whom are ghosts. Anyhow, that's enough research into the name for me – we've got Yogi Bear, the Wizard of Oz and several ghosts from 1887.)

On some level I became increasingly convinced that Gary's father's dementia, and his nearness to the gates of death, were opening up the veil of Isis, that he was seeing through the veil, glimpsing into beyond, and his latent psychic powers were opening like a lotus flower in summer heat.

Once his father had gone to bed we began making final preparations such as taking wine and drugs, creating the magical circle in the garden, collecting the magical weapons of Wand, Cup, Sword and Disc and preparing the talismanic clay tablet that would later be consecrated and inscribed with ritual intent during the rite, before being buried beneath a tree in the garden as an offering to the Elemental forces; forces older than the human race.

The ritual had a full and complete structure; Gary understood every aspect, such as the Purification, the Banishings, the Invocation, etc – while I helped him with the structure, he wrote each part of the ritual himself, as it should be. We were sitting in the kitchen, looking out over the garden, drinking wine and smoking herb, when Gary's father suddenly appeared.

He seemed to be in a trance and completely unaware of our presence, like we were ghosts. Without saying a single word, he began to gather up the household items that Gary had chosen to use as his magical weapons. This was really strange. Like his father knew, on some other level, that Gary was trying to rise above certain limitations to do with his past – to do with his father. Gary and I looked at each other – we knew this was weird behaviour.

"Gary," I said, "You have to take them back from him."

Before we'd even started the ritual, it had begun.

It seemed like some aspect of his father's consciousness was making a determined effort to thwart the ritual intent.

Gently, Gary took each of the four items from the crook of his frail father's arms, and then he escorted him back upstairs to bed.

Gary performed the ritual, from midnight and full Moon to dawn and first sunlight. During the high point of the ritual, while I was standing outside the protection of the magical circle, a very loud scratching and clawing noise sounded against the fence behind me. I didn't dare to turn around – it could have been a cat, it could have been a demonic entity, or it could have been a sign that the intended force had truly arrived as bidden.

Of all the photographs I took, the one Gary liked best was taken at the very instant of sunrise, at the climax of the operation – a distinct and vivid beam of light appears to shoot out, directly from the Sun, passing straight through his forehead, as if he is being illuminated by a divine force.

The next day, out of curiosity, Gary wanted to see if the Talisman was still buried beneath the tree.

With bare hands, he dug down into the soil.

The Talisman was gone – the Elementals had accepted his offering.

A few months later, Gary's father passed over to the other side, a side I'm certain he was already glimpsing at the time of the ritual.

Gary said afterwards that the ritual helped, more than anything, for him to deal with the loss of his father.

*

The last time I created a talisman had a very specific purpose - northing sordid, dear, sordid reader.

I was out of work. Paul C. was talking about going trekking through the mountains of the Himalayas in Nepal. He was thinking of going for about 3 months. I decided to do a ritual to obtain money. I'd never used Magick to obtain money before, or since. Usually, my rituals were designed to invoke creative energy, wisdom, and cosmic tickles! From what I'd read, I knew that doing rituals for personal gain could always make you hic-cup and puke in your own lap, or shit on your own doorstep, so to speak. Same with putting a hex on someone – fail, and the powers set-forth come back three-fold. I'd heard the story of someone using an Abra-Melin talisman to obtain gold. The ritual was a success and true to its word. The magician received his wealth, in the form of a will from the sudden, unexpected death of his parents. BE CAREFUL WHAT YOU ASK FOR – YOU JUST MIGHT GET IT.

The talisman I created was very specific and the ritual fine tuned – the more fine tuned and focused a thought is, the clearly it manifests its word. I intended to acquire 'gold to travel East', no more, no less, just enough to fulfil my will, or intention, of travelling half way around the world, to India, travelling over 600 miles across her northern regions to reach Nepal and the city of Kathmandu, and then onwards into the mountains for real.

*

OPUS X
Saturday 25th of July, 1987.
New Moon in Leo.
Sun in Leo.
Intention: Gold to Travel East.
Perform Banishing Ritual of the Pentagram
Perform Banishing Ritual of the Hexagram
The Confession of the Adept
The Lion and The Hawk – Ritual using meditation & sexual energy
(OTO formula)
The Consecration of the Talisman
Perform Banishing Ritual of the Pentagram
Perform Banishing Ritual of the Hexagram

This Ritual is an invocation of a solar-phallic god-form in the guise of Horus, the ancient Egyptian son of Isis and Osiris.

Upon the altar. Built a small truncated pyramid, symbolic of Horus. Yellow candles; the Sun, light, Leo. Also Horus incense. A dagger – Tarot cards, XIX and XI – Thoth deck. Three 4-leaf'd clovers that I pasted onto a fish-eye lens, all found within the space of a few weeks. A crystal pyramid standing upon a truncated pyramid.

*

As a result of Opus X, I received an offer of work at the start of August, when the Sun still occupied the zodiacal sign of Leo the Lion. The job was in a west end office block in London. Basically they were knocking every plasterboard wall down, and then re-building them one foot from their previous location. Obviously this was some kind of refurbishing tax-scam. I think the job cost the nameless company £5,000,000 for 10 weeks of labour and materials, no-one knows what they got back off that from tax, or what kind of scams these people can play in the game of Monopoly. It didn't matter to me. Everyone runs scams, from the bottom of the pyramid to the top. I found out the job would last until the time we planned to go away. I was more than happy to work for my coin (aware of spooky Abra-Melin tales and such like). Paul, like me, knew how to make the best out of a situation.

I had my ritual intention in mind – I was earning gold for travel East. The 'coincidences' and 'synchronicities' came on like a tsunami of magical symbolism. Certain numbers began to appear, like an insistent force, numbers such as 6, 666, 2, 3, 5. 23, 253. I recall that the CEO, the Chief Executive Officer of the company travelled in a red chauffeur-driven Bentley. It had the license plate number 666 AWB. I recall thinking, 'Who the fuck are we working for, really?'

Some evenings, basically whenever I saw the CEO leaving the building, heading toward his blood-red (the colour of blood just as it starts to dry when it's exposed to the air), chosen mode of transport, I would open an office window, and shout loud enough to cause him to pause, 'Hey, Beelzebub! Satan! 6! 6! 6!'

On the site Paul and I worked happily alongside a guy who instantly made you think of Timothy Leary and Andy Warhol, perhaps in the same body! The guy was lovely, sporting peroxide blonde hair, his brainwaves were totally out there, yet totally clued-up, switched on and bang-on tune. He was a self proclaimed 'Truth Reality Activist – T.R.A.' I think it was his own 'order'. He used to sing songs and ballads all day long, every song questioning our place in reality, with all the wit and magical charm of a renegade leprechaun. He was another one of those weird yet helpful Elemental Spirits that sometimes hold us up by the elbow when we can scarcely sense their presence or their love.

During that time of working the final stretch of the year, a year where Paul and I would work a 93 hour week, sleeping in metal on-site cabins, smoking more dope than Lord Shiva hisself, I noted in my comments to the 'gold for East' ritual that I happened to work through one of those weird dates;1/10/1987. Written in reverse; 7, 8, 9, 10, 11. This only occurs every 800 years, the last in this sequence took place in 2/1/1101; reversed – 10/11/12.

My magical record contains more details that I could add, but I'd sooner get to the ritual's end-

Close-up shot of hand-written dairy-

'Just finished ten weeks of labour. 23's have been visible without fail. Flight number is 235. We leave the UK for India-Nepal on Wednesday, November 4th, 1987. We return on January 23rd, 1988.'

Fade to black ;-)

*

Fade up from black –

A screaming face!

Ha...no....seriously-

Taking off from a Heathrow Terminal on magical-flight number 235, ready to travel over 4,000 miles, bracing myself for a 9 hour flight; this was my first time on a plane. Nervous and thrilled by the prospect of the Great Unknown that would soon unfurl before us, we had nothing to hide behind – no home, no job, just a rucksack, a few maps, first aid kit, malaria tablets, military style water bottle, survival blanket, a bundle of traveller's cheques and documents sealed in a water-tight plastic jiffy-bag, and on my part, a few books by Uncle Crowley for company on dark Himalayan nights, plus my tarot cards and a small statue of

Buddha as an extra blanket;-) We both brought with us far too much luggage, and within weeks of the trek we'd traded or given away most of our belongings. Doing a high altitude Himalayan trek, the last thing that you need are 'things'.

If we could have, we'd probably have taken night-vision goggles, AK-47's or some such, equipped with silencers, and Flash-Bang's, of course. We'd already decided that an RPG would be too much hassle, and a tank was out of the question due to our budget limitations as we headed for the 4th poorest nation on our planet.

When you travel in this fashion, I think that karmic forces begin to accelerate. Crowley once wrote that drugs 'loosened the girders of the soul'. I would apply the same to travel and also to the practice of magical rituals. The further into the abyss of the unknown one throws oneself, the more accelerated the resulting karma is going to be; it has to compensate for your sudden shift, and fill in the void you created, with flames if necessary. If it can, the resultant force of the 'travel demon' might slap one in the face. I think you are more likely to get hit with twists, swerves and sometimes vicious curve balls by muggers, robbers, rapists and killers as you arc likely to encounter pure friends, helpful people, strange smiling faces, loving embraces, and even a subtle glimpse of the holy glow whilst in this state of 'transience'. Travel - you step out of your routine bubble and venture into 'the spaces between the spaces'. At the mercy of gods that might not even exist – skirting beyond the fringes of your own imagination (or lack-of), – not to mention crossing other people's orbits and their intentions toward you.

When Paul C. and I left the house we'd been sharing with Poison Girls, Vi gave us some hash-cake to eat when we got to Heathrow; something to help alleviate the tedium of the long flight to India; 'get high while you fly'. Thank god it started to kick-in. Taking-off was a rush, a total blast, but I find long flights are tedious and dehydrating, unless you happen to see a UFO!

*

We touched down at New Delhi airport in the early hours of morning – a strange silver light was breaking the sky. Stepping down from the aircraft and walking into the airport, we entered a new world. Nothing looked familiar. Birds of all sorts were flying free above the desks of ticket clerks and foreign exchange offices. The clerks had huge books laid out on the counters before them, many of them adorned with a swastika; a Hindu/Buddhist symbol of peace, reversed by Hitler in Kraut Times. There were a few typewriters. No computers.

(Note on technology: we are always ten years behind what the military are working on, at the real Cutting Edge. If we're lucky, 60 years from now, they might even show us aspects of their technology that they were busy creating and back-programming, back when we were children. Philip K. Dick would be with me on this one. The future is Delhi.)

We headed for the exit and were confronted by a huge glass wall, with dozens of people on the other side, pressing themselves against the glass, like zombies wanting to eat us alive. George Romero would be with me on that one; our first impression of India was like a scene from 'The Walking Dead'. However, 3 months later, it felt equally strange to be returning to the cold grey climate of a submissive, January UK.

We took stock of the situation.

We'd travelled halfway around the planet, and now here we were, spooked and afraid to venture forth into the abyss.

The situation in India is never what it seems.

A mob pressed against a wall of glass, sweltering beneath a wall of heat, waiting for us – I recall a water truck driving past as if it was filmed in slow motion, leaking its vital contents onto the dusty ground. The water truck helped me understand the way of India, to a degree. We figured that the 'zombies' pressed against the glass waiting to eat us alive were actually taxi drivers looking for business; they were going to eat us alive in their own fashion. We had no choice, we had to step out of the airport and trust on absolute blind luck and confused, jet-lagged intuitions. Can we trust the driver? Will he rip us off? Has he killed many tourists before? Maybe he's a nice bloke, with a family and kids? Maybe he won't rip us off? How much do they sell organs for in the East? Did we just pick the best driver in the world? Is he capable of killing us both? You get the sense of paranoia?

The taxi driver was a placid bloke who took us directly where we wanted to go. No real hassle, we already knew we'd been over-charged and stiffed. Getting ripped-off is the traveller's lot – as time passes and the traveller 'settles in', things get cheaper, the traveller starts to feel like a local, but they're still getting ripped-off. Why not? People got to make a living...mouths to feed.

We took a cheap hotel in Old Delhi; we were fish out of water, strangers dancing in a strange land...the shock of poverty and child-deformity were overwhelmed by the 'scent' that inhabits the air like a living creature. The first night in Delhi, we couldn't sleep. Who can sleep on their first night in an alien-nation? Outside, to our ears, it sounded as though a riot or civil uprising was taking place, us thinking it would be just our luck to travel all this way and then get killed in a fucking revolution we knew nothing about.

India was such a shock to my senses and my psyche that I didn't eat anything for three days. I'd never seen so many flies buzzing around food...

*

We travelled across the northern state of Uttar Pradesh, a journey of 600 miles or so, heading for a Nepalese border crossing. We staggered the journey so that we could stay a few days in various places of interest; there was no time pressure like you get on a two-week summer holiday. Our visa cards for India and Nepal were valid for 3 months. 3 is a Magick number.

Our first stop was Agra, 124 miles south of Delhi. We went there to see the Taj Mahal, 'a wonderful symmetrical building dedicated to love' it says on Wikipedia. I thought it was a bit bland, to be honest, although it did radiate an aura of calm. There's a photo in the press I saw once with Lady Dianna standing where we did in front of the Taj Mahal; that photo captured the vibe perfectly. I prefer the architecture and sculptures of the Hindu and Buddhist temples. The Taj Mahal took 22 years to build and was completed in 1652. Our train journey from Delhi to Agra took about half that time.

Trains and time move differently in India, but they do move faster than trains in Egypt, where sometimes your carriage can be overtaken by a heavily burdened mule. Sorting a train ticket in India was like taking on six missions at once. However, once you've waded through one Q to get a ticket, then another Q to pay for the ticket, and another Q to get it stamped and get your receipt for their receipt and so on, the train and its passengers eventually leave the station.

The toilet was a hole in the floor.

'Welcome to Iceland.'

We also visited Agra Fort, known as the Red Fort, built in 1565, and on the way back to our hotel we managed to score some hashish from our friendly 'Tuk-Tuk' driver. Truth be told, we didn't have much interest in the Red Fort - we had a better time at 'Tuk-Tuk's' house afterwards, getting high with his friends and sharing cultural differences with mutual respect and humour, and buying a little smoke in the process. First days in India would be better if we were stoned was our only real plan.

From Agra we travelled 226 miles to Lucknow; the capital city of Uttar Pradesh, and then another 200 miles to the holiest Hindu city in all of India; Varanasi.

For each train journey we always stocked up on fruit – every train stop confronts you with begging children, thin arms poking through the barred window – we gave them fruit, knowing they would eat it, whereas any coin would no doubt go to an adult or parent or some other exploiter. Outside of every town and city, first thing on a morning, people used the side of the railway tracks as a lavatory – we saw more people taking dumps that you can imagine.

Varanasi is built beside the River Ganges; some of its temples are now half submerged. From a boat on the river it looks like the city is sliding into the waters of death.

Varanasi is a city obsessed with death. Bodies are burned in the open air all day and all night, all year round. We took out a small boat to get a decent view, avoiding the corpses of dead animals, such as a cow, as they drifted in the idle current. The cremation grounds are run by Holy Men, 'Saddhu's'; they live in the cemeteries and smear their skin with the blue-grey ashes of the dead. They are forever surrounded by death; the focus of their meditations. The ashes of the dead are scattered into the sacred river. People bathe in the river, performing ritualistic gestures, praying to higher forces. People drink the water. People bring their beloved dead to Varanasi from all quarters of India. Varanasi is a power centre; the place where soul's are liberated and re-cycled or re-incarnated. Varanasi is a gate to immortality. Varanasi is a City of the Dead.

I have a thing with ancient cities of the dead; the occult mysteries of life. When I was travelling with Neil K. in Morocco we stayed in an area of Marrakesh called 'Djema el fna'; 'The City of the Dead'. I've visited Egypt twice; once with Paul C. and once with Suzette G. (Felix's mum); ancient Egypt is full of cities of the dead, it's the Nation of Death, and re-birth – immortality - starlight.

*

Saddhu's have no source of income. They have few possessions; an orange robe, a staff, a bell, and a cup or bowl from which to feed. As holy men they rely upon the goodwill of human nature. Saddhu's can be very strange, they are said to possess magical abilities, they have power. All true, perhaps, but when you first come face to face with a Saddhu in the street, the words 'creepy' and 'spooky' spring to mind.

Saddhu's wander throughout the continent of India. Some work the cemeteries of Varanasi. Some live in solitude, in a cave. Rumour has it that some murderer's have evaded the law by donning the guise of a Saddhu; free to roam and trusting on other people's generosity of spirit. I don't like rumours. Every Saddhu that I encountered possessed radiant eyes, their very being was so intense, as if they were a Holy Grail, full to the brim with the light of divine rapture and infinite joy. They spoke to me, but we never spoke a word; we didn't speak the other's language.

Paul and I were eating a meal in a restaurant in New Delhi when a guy in an orange robe, with dread-locked hair and a long beard, his face painted in white stripes, suddenly pushed his face to the window and stared right at me, without blinking, for a few minutes, almost like he recognized me from somewhere, like he knew who I was, and then he was gone.

A day or so later, as we were about to begin our journey across northern India, we were standing on New Delhi train platform. It was approaching midnight. The station was busy; backpackers, like Paul and I, trying to figure out how we're supposed to find our seats, plus working people, and people in suits, and boys selling chai, fruit, biscuits, bread, bottled water, and cigarettes, and cops in khaki uniforms holding long bamboo canes or carrying rifles from WWII, and women, half-veiled, keeping a low profile. And a Saddhu.

He was shorter than me, thinner than me, older than me. He wore a dusty orange robe. I figured he must be 70 years old, or more. He had long grey dread-locked hair and a long grey beard. He had a bowl. And the brightest eyes I've seen in an old man. The spark in them made me smile. I gave him some money, just a small bundle of notes (I was still getting used to the currency). Without a word, the Saddhu, this old git, suddenly leapt onto his hands and proceeded to hand-walk up and down the platform, kicking his legs in the air, then he did a body flip and stood before me, smiled and walked away. Paul and I were cracking-up. It was such a funny scene. Unexpected.

A New Delhi business guy in a suit came up to me. He told me that I was very honoured to have a Saddhu 'perform' like that in front of me, and he told me that the money I had just handed over to the Saddhu would enable him to live for the next 3 months. I was instantly reminded of my ritual intention of 'Gold to travel East', and here I was, for 3 months, it all made sense, to me and the Saddhu, at least. The businessman told me that the Saddhu's display would ensure that our journey was blessed and that we would have good fortune. He was right, we did have good fortune, but if that was all down to an old guy walking on his hands, up and down a train platform in front of us at midnight, who could know?

*

We travelled from Varanasi to Gorakhpur and then began a 12 hour coach trip to Kathmandu, a journey designed to test the metal and break the mind.

We made the border crossing from India to Nepal at a small town called Birganj. The place was like a frontier mining town from the Wild West, but this was the Wild East – lizards on the wall of the hotel room, moth's as big as your fist, and not as many mosquitos' as expected. (We had to take anti-malaria pills every day – if you took one before eating something, then you became sick and pale as a junkie).

As we crossed into Nepal we were both feeling exhausted, not just from travelling, but also from the constant assault on our senses that the journey entailed. The roads became narrower as we climbed higher and ever higher. The ceiling on the interior of the coach was padded – we soon found out why! We got bounced around like a rubber ball. We were so exhausted and burned out that we openly began to wonder if we'd made the biggest mistake of our lives. India seemed primeval, but India had nuclear weapons. Now, we were heading for Nepal, the 4th poorest country in the world. What the fuck were we doing?

Every now and then the Full Moon would emerge from behind the clouds and provide a brief spell of illumination. As we bounced along treacherous roads we'd glimpse our surroundings, bathed in a brief flash of silver light; above us, dark and menacing mountains that vanished into the clouds, bigger than any mountain we'd ever seen, and below us, the edge of the road dropped into a fathomless abyss. The glimpses I saw were worthy of a good horror movie...and when night turned into day, we saw the upturned bellies of many a fallen truck and coach laid at the bottom of some crevasse, as if we didn't already know that this journey was a risky endeavour.

Then suddenly we were in Kathmandu. To be more exact, we were on the outside of Kathmandu. They fix it so that you have to get a taxi into town. First taxi fare in a strange place is always an over-priced piss-take.

We knew the hotel we were headed for, selected from a 'Lonely Planet' traveller's guide to Nepal.

'Freak Street', we said.

'Frikky Street?' said the driver.

'Frikky Street!' we agreed.

Freak Street is something of a living leg-end from the dopey 1960's and it is one of the coolest streets in Kathmandu.

It was legend for us. The taxi driver dropped us off and told us to walk through a small alley to reach our hotel. We found the hotel, but in the alley we also managed to score a huge lump of opium for less than the price of a pack of cigarettes.

Hello Kathmandu, we thought, let's get weird.

We knew that we'd got past the dark doubts created by the fucked-up coach journey along Hell's Edges, when we were mocked by the Full Moon. Things were looking up.

The next morning we were both wandering about, looking up at Hindu and Buddhist temples, marvelling at the handiwork, the paintings and sexually explicit tantric carvings made of wood and stone, the harmony of the structures, their beauty, inner power, and timeless radiant energy.

The day after that, Paul fell ill, green as a frog in a swamp, and I bumped into the King of Nepal.

*

Paul was losing it from both ends, suffering from 'Delhi Belly'; a few years later in Egypt I caught 'The Curse of the Pharaoh's'. Trust me; all you can do is puke and shit, sometimes both at once. Not fun, unless P&S is your kind of doggie-bag.

I got stoned and ventured out for a walk; we'd agreed to stay in Kathmandu until Paul felt well enough to begin our planned 100 mile trek through the Himalayas, and we were also waiting for another guy, Phil G. to join us from the UK.

I was wandering through Durbar Square, looking up at the pagoda-temples when I became aware that I was wandering through a huge crowd, and more than half of them were wearing military uniforms and carrying a gun.

As I turned around, I suddenly realized that I was just a few feet from the King of Nepal;

King Birendra. I recognized him immediately; he didn't know me from Adam. Then I looked around me – everyone in Durbar Square, with the exception of the King, his soldiers and I, was bowing or supplicating upon their knees, I instantly followed suit, hands clasped in prayer, bowing and backing away, hoping I wasn't going to be killed for my dopey rudeness because wherever I travel, I try to do so with a genuine sense of mutual respect. I call it harmonious magick in diverse spaces.

I went back to the hotel room and said to Paul, 'Guess what? I just bumped into the King of Nepal. I almost knocked the fucker over; soldier's everywhere, people bowing...the whole works.'

'Bollocks,' he says, 'have we got any opium left? I'm starting to feel better.'

Such was our brief life in Frikky Street.

*

I remember King Birendra's birthday. Paul, Phil and I were guests of honour, but obviously not at the Kings palace in Kathmandu. We were on the last stages of our month long trek, staying in the village of Kusma. After a very early morning rise on the morning of December 28th, we had just returned from a sacred cave and a smoke with a Saddhu (more of that in its place). When we returned to the village we were stoned out of our minds.

The whole village had been freshly painted. Everyone painted their home for the King's birthday. Paul, Phil and I were the only westerners in the village. For some reason, they thought we should be guests of honour.

We were flying Zen kites inside and outside our minds, just struggling to hold it together, the smoke was wicked.

The entire village walked past us in a procession, including several Ghurkhas, wearing their time-worn-out uniforms, their time-worn-out guns and their shining medals...encompassed by their immortal sense of honour.

I remember the King of Nepal's birthday – Ghurkha soldiers and their families were celebrating – I was stoned – slouched on a small podium, feeling humble, small, and hung out to dry.

*

'Namaste,' is a traditional Nepali greeting, it translates as 'I celebrate the divinity within you.'

It sounds so much better than 'Alright geezer', or as they say in Morocco: 'Fuck you and fuck your country!'

*

13 years later King Birendra, aged 55, was murdered, gunned down along with his wife, his brother and his sister. The King was murdered by his own son, Dipendra, who turned up for a royal dinner at the palace in Kathmandu armed to the teeth – he shot his family and then turned the gun on himself. Or so says the Nepalese Govt. report.

*

When Paul had recovered we allowed ourselves a few more days to chill-out before we left Kathmandu. We wanted to see some temples and statues, Buddhist, Hindu and anything in-between. One morning we hired bicycles and made our way six miles from 'Frikky' Street to the outskirts of the city to visit the Boudhanath Stupa; one of the holiest Buddhist sites in Kathmandu, the spherical Stupa is also one of the largest in the world. With flags of prayer fluttering in the breeze, the dome of the Stupa looks like a UFO rising from the star of its mandala-shaped base.

Another ancient temple-complex we visited was Swayambhunath, more commonly known as the Monkey Temple, as there are holy monkeys living in the north-west parts of the temple. The name of Swayambhunath means 'self sprung'. The monkeys abound. They are brazen and unafraid. They can be a threatening pain in the ass – they steal food and objects from people, they jump on people and bite them, before laughing and jumping onto someone else. Holy Monkey!

A steep stone stairway of over 300 steps, some say 365, leads to the top, where the gigantic dome of a white-painted Stupa, painted with Buddha's eyes and a symbol that looks like a question mark or a nose, actually a symbol of 'unity', stares out across the temples and Stupa's and the orb-ended wands known as a Vajra, or a Dorje; a symbolic ritual object whose Sanskrit name translates as both 'Thunderbolt' and 'Diamond'; symbolic representations of ancient weapons of power.

We also stumbled upon a really fascinating statue of Kali, the Hindu goddess of empowerment. Her name means 'black' 'death' and 'time'. Kali is the goddess of Change. She was freshly painted, offerings lay at her feet, her wild black hair coiled like serpents, her eyes were wide, bright and fierce, her tongue dripped blood, a necklace of human skulls hung around her neck. Here was the statue of Kali, vivid, tended to, and worshiped – the statue stood in one corner of a very small square that served as a thoroughfare, where people went about their daily business.

*

Before leaving England we'd already agreed that we didn't want to do the Everest thing. To our minds, Everest had several drawbacks. Number one: too many people. Number two: the popularity of Everest was slowly turning it into a garbage dump; seems like no one wanted to carry their empty plastic water bottles back down to base camp. Number three: we didn't intend to be roping up rock faces, wearing crampons and oxygen masks, ushered by Sherpa's across icy plateau's, we intended to walk for 30 days through what are known as the foothills of the Himalayas, just below the snowline. We settled on a Trek that would take us around the Annapurna mountain region of the Himalayas.

*

We left Kathmandu on a chilly, foggy morning. Nepali men were bustling about as dozens of westerners stood waiting in a coach park area, getting ready to head off into one more unknown. Nepali men usually wore jeans or trousers, with a western-style suit jacket, plus brightly coloured Nepali hats and a scarf. They smoked like Victorian chimneys.

We took the first coach from Kathmandu to the town of Pokhara. Our rucksacks were secured to the roof of the bus by a million helping hands. We climbed aboard, taking note of the padding on the inner-roof above our seats. It was going to be another bumpy, Himalaya rock'n'rolla, but we already sensed that it would be worth it; Nepal was much more chilled-out and spiritually honest than India, in our limited experience. Besides, the lure of the mountains was taking hold and dipping into our very souls.

Pokhara is a popular destination in Nepal, and it has expanded considerably since the time we visited. Three of the ten highest mountains in the world are situated within 30 miles of the town (a city now, I think), and it provides amazing views of the snow-covered, ice-capped Himalayan Titans that claw their way through the clouds and into the very sky.

Seriously, I never knew mountains could be so…vast.

*

As it turned out, the journey to Pokhara was luxury compared to the coach journey from India to Kathmandu. That's not to say we didn't bump our heads on the ceiling or see more than our fair share of upturned trucks and coaches that had slipped off the road and fallen down a treacherous mountainside, or fallen off a bridge into a river or a dry-riverbed.

The drivers in Nepal and India adorn their rear-view mirrors with dangling pennants and holy relics, they burn incense, they always have a full box of tissues in a flashy tissue-box holder on display, (I never did suss-out the cult of the flashy tissue-box holder on display), and once they've invoked their gods, they proceed to drive like complete suicidal maniacs, so certain are they of their divine protection.

*

We spent a few days in Pokhara, enjoying the last bastion of civilisation - the final frontier town of western Nepal. After Pokhara we knew that things would be very different; small villages and settlements with no electricity, unless a generator was rigged-up, and maybe one source of fresh water per village. Not to mention the hiking and spiralling up mountains all day to reach the next village and finding a place to stay. Then rising at sunset the next day and hiking and spiralling all the way down the mountain, sometimes heading through a valley, sometimes crossing rope and timber bridges that looked ready to drop you into the river 1,000 feet below if your number was up.

So we took a few days out.

We checked our maps and our route, we stocked up on our last supplies; food, cigarettes, dope.

We hired a boat early one morning and went rowing on Phewa Lake, the second largest lake in Nepal.

The surface of the fresh water lake was covered in a creeping mist. We rowed out and eventually the mist began to clear. The view from the middle of the lake was truly astounding. We were surrounded, not only by 360 degrees of white capped mountains, their peaks snapping at the sky like the ragged teeth of a shark, we were also surrounded by their reflections in still water.

I jumped off the boat and into the water. I think I managed to swim for about a minute before the icy cold water numbed me out. Getting back onto the boat was a struggle –
'Dude, that water was the coldest I ever saw.'

We also went to see a movie…even tho' we didn't speak the lingo.

Paul and I went out of curiosity. It was our first full-on Bollywood experience. We didn't know a damn thing about the only film showing in the only cinema in town, but like everyone else in this one horse town, we wanted to see it, we too wanted to dissolve and vanish into the silver screen, even in the middle of such powerful natural monuments.

We paid for the most expensive tickets (which were not really expensive, not like West End theatre tickets, more like the difference between two pence and five pence, back then). We weren't trying to be clever. We'd never been to a cinema in Nepal. As north-eastern guys, it made sense to stay out of view and keep a low profile. However, the cinema, like everything else in the East, worked on a different level. In this cinema, the more you paid for a ticket, the closer you got to sit in front of the screen. It kinda made sense. Paul and I ended up sitting right at the front on a narrow wooden bench. Before long the 'cinema' was crammed, and then the long film began. We were in the front line. Many eyes were upon us. We were stuck in the front line. We watched the entire crazy movie, all three hours of it.

Lights – camera - action – what the fuck is this film about?

People were singing, a lot, people were crying, a lot, people were dancing, even more. This tragic song and dance movie involved a couple who were not permitted to be with one another. The girl, for some reason beyond me then and beyond me now, got put into a mental asylum. A mental asylum with very nice grounds and wonderful fountains and a dance crew on hand at every turn of the unfathomable plot. The best bit for me was the whole cast singing in the asylum grounds, swirling their umbrella's in the rain. The audience were enraptured. I only mention this because the next day, when we left Pokhara, our young driver, who looked like he was wearing blocks of wood on his feet, like that brat from Indiana Jones – he just wore very thick-soled sandals. Our young driver began singing a song. I recognised it and asked him if it was from the movie. He told me it was. He beamed a smile of healthy young teeth and then sang the song in full. He'd seen the movie in Pokhara, and now he knew that particular song by heart – I liked his sense of cinematic obsession; I could relate. If you can't compare something to a movie then it obviously has no counterpart in your reality. If it doesn't exist in a movie, then it simply doesn't exist. We are all smoke and mirrors.

*

Our 'cinemaniac' driver steered the jeep toward Nagdanda; the first village we had to reach before darkness fell. The Jeep only went as far as the end of the road. After driving for almost three hours he pulled to a halt. We were at the end of the road. From here on in, our only mode of transport, and hence the speed of our lives, and perhaps the undulating rhythm of our brain frequencies, was based on footsteps, altitude, the rise and fall of sun and moon and the swirl of the stars, we didn't give a damn about dollars, minutes or hours - forget the hours, this was it; the sweet Abyss.

*

We hiked from Nagdanda to Birethanti, from Tirkhedhunga to Ghorapani, where we encountered our worst weather, wet for two days, surrounded by, and literally walking through the clouds. Walking the day after the rain had stopped we came to the place by a river where a village was supposed to exist. All that remained was a huge scoop that had been washed away by the swollen river. We met someone who told us that during the night they heard a great roaring sound. They managed to evacuate before a torrent of water washed their village away. As we approached the village we were pretty high up the side of a slope, but much of our path had been destroyed. At times, we had to press our faces against the rock and with our arms outstretched step slowly, sideways, until safety was reached. If we slipped and fell, we would have smashed on the rocks far below, or we would have drowned in the relentless force of the river.

Eventually we reached Tatopani, a place known for its hot springs that are situated right next to the roaring Kali Gandaki River. The name Tatopani translates as 'hot water'. We were advised by locals not to continue with our proposed plan to trek around the Annapurna region due to heavy snow fall. So we spent a few days there, before heading off in a different direction, slowly curving our way back toward Pokhara; a place of cars and electricity, shops and crowds of people, a place of noise compared to the silence of the immense mountains.

*

Sometimes hiking steep trails uphill all day, or bracing against steep trails downhill all day, was real hard work; a test of stamina. We had a daily routine, waking up at dawn, having a breakfast of Tibetan bread and honey, and a glass of hot chocolate. The mornings were cold. The daytimes were generally sunny and comfortable. The nights were always cold and the stars were awesome.

We always set off hiking early in the morning in order to make the most of the daylight, making our way to the next stop of human habitation to obtain food and shelter. We usually stayed in simple lodges; Spartan rooms with a narrow mattress on a wooden bed, and a candle for a light. The rooms we rented were often part of a family's home; it's a way that the people make extra income. We also took lots of pens with us, because we heard that writing materials for children in such areas were scarce, but that proved to be a bullshit myth.

We would hike for most of the day, sometimes for seven hours or more, winding our way around a mountain, or as many hours hiking downwards the next day. The walks were hard. At every pit-stop we would check through our gear, wanting to lose the lot, trying to thin it out and lighten the load on our backs. We started with full rucksacks. We ended up carrying very little, though I still had my Crowley books and a small statue of Buddha, and a chillum. All our western clothing, besides our boots, was replaced with Indian cotton. We also lost a lot of weight. I lost two stone in weight during our 120 miles trek; I wasn't much beyond slim when I started, but I was way below slim when I finished. I recall that when we got back to Pokhara, we hadn't seen a mirror or a reflected image of ourselves for 30 days; it was something of a shock.

At some point we lost our minds. Letters home to family and friends became exercises in dope-fog surrealism sent from a land whose snow-capped mountains pierced the purity of the sky like primeval blades.

The population was Buddhist and Hindu, mainly vegetarians, tho' I did see a guy chopping up a dog with a cleaver, presumably to eat. We met a lot of Tibetans who were fleeing across the Tibetan border to escape from Chinese tyranny.

A shadow was cast over Nepal, but we barely noticed it. It came in the form of Maoist, (Chinese backed), violence that was spreading over from Tibet and directly into Nepal. Every town or village we entered we had to deal with a military official, checking our papers, visas, faces and passport stamps, and the fact that not all areas of Nepal were accessible to westerner's, made it perfectly clear that the country was lurking on the brink of an impending civil war.

*

We spent Christmas week in the small town of Beni. We stayed in a fair sized lodge; we had a room upstairs. Every morning we would stay in our heavy duty sleeping bags until the morning's breakfast guests had left the dining room downstairs. The breakfast guests were two soldiers who manned the village – they were freeloaders, said the nice lady who ran the lodge. She advised us to stay clear of them. We soon found out that her son grew marijuana in a nearby valley. We agreed to buy some and her son set off to get it. He returned later the next day. The dope was truly amazing quality. The price was insanely cheap. What we bought lasted us right until the end of our eastern expedition.

One morning we were woken at dawn by the land Lady's husband. He spoke little English, and we only spoke enough Nepali to be polite. He wanted us to go with him. We sensed no ill will and so got up and followed him by torchlight to a small Hindu temple. We'd been invited to worship Lord Shiva; known as the Destroyer, or the Transformer.

There were half a dozen other people there. We smoked marijuana and then the ritual began. It was more like a crazy party, so unlike the piety of a church sermon. They were singing and chanting, dancing, playing goat-skinned bongo drums, crashing split cymbals, chiming bells, burning incense, and making offerings to a trident-bearing image of Shiva. We were given yellow flowers to place before him. One of the men walked up to me and anointed my forehead, between the eyebrows with a red dot; a Bindi. The Bindi is placed in the region of the 6th chakra, or wheel of energy, called the Ajna; the seat of concealed wisdom, what we call the Third Eye. The Bindi is said to protect against demons and bad luck. In my side-notes on the map I was carrying at that time, I commented- 'Allowed into the Shiva temple for a ritual; got stamped'.

On December 21st 1987, the day of the Winter Solstice, and thus the day with the shortest amount of daylight, Paul and I decided to storm Poon Hill. We were going to climb to the top in order to gain what was supposed to be a spectacular panoramic view of the Annapurna mountain range, including the top of Machapuchare; also known a 'Fish Tail Mountain because it's double summits resemble the tail of a fish. It is forbidden by State and Holy Law to climb Machapuchare; the mountain is sacred to the god Shiva and it remains unclimbed to this day. We would also need to get back to the village before dark because the only things we carried were hip flasks of water, a few hard boiled eggs and our cameras. I also took with me a small statue of Buddha We were not equipped for night walking. If it got dark, we'd be stuck, and in risk of freezing or falling to our stupid deaths.

The reason for our decision to storm Poon Hill was due to the fact that it rained when we were at one of the highest altitudes of our trek. The clouds obscured the view, but Poon Hill would grant us the same view, if we were prepared to make the effort.

Poon Hill has an altitude of 3,232 metres/10,531 ft. The term 'Hill' is ironic; Ben Nevis in Scotland, for example, has an elevation of 1,344 metres/4,409 ft.

The climb was hard and steep. For much of it we splashed upward through a cold stream. By the time we were close to the summit I was starting to feel dizzy and a bit sleepy; altitude sickness, caused by ascending too rapidly and not giving the body enough chance to adapt to the harsher environmental conditions, the cause of many deaths in the world of mountain climbing. I could hear Paul shouting from somewhere higher up, 'Keep going. It's worth it!'

I dragged my sorry ass to the top of that cursed 'hill'. The climb took us five and a half hours. It was the shortest day of the year and the Sun had just entered the sign of Capricorn;

sign of the Goat/Devil. Time was getting tight.

When I reached the top I was gobsmacked. My eyes filled with a rush of tears and I sank to my knees. We were standing alone on Poon Hill, surrounded by an amazing 360 panoramic view of the ice covered giants. I placed my little Buddha on a rock and took some photo's of the statue, with the mountains and the blue sky as backdrop. The view, and having earned it, was probably one of the peak experiences of my life. I knew then why they called Nepal 'The Roof of the World'.

We took our photographs, then just sat down, smoked a doobie, and stared in silence at the immense beauty that surrounded us. We drank some water and ate the boiled eggs, getting some energy back. Then we had to start the downward journey on legs made of rubber.

It only took us two and a half hours to descend. As the light began to fade, we half-ran down that 'hill' and we made it safely back before sunset; we knew by then that darkness always came in real fast.

Unfortunately progress also moves in real fast. Now they have guides taking people to Poon Hill, from Ghoropani, the opposite side to that which we climbed. The isolated peak of Poon Hill has now been built upon and disfigured with observation towers for the tourists.

*

It was Christmas day. We didn't care, apart from thinking of our families and how far away we were. It was cool to be spending the xmas period somewhere so remote and free from all the commercial crap that Christmas usually entails.

Our land Lady had other ideas. She brought us a wonderful decorated bowl of fruit as a seasonal gift, but then expected us to start singing and dancing around because it Christmas, thinking we would be joyous and merry in our devotions as the people of Nepal were in their celebrations of the gods. We were something of a letdown. We thanked her profusely for the fruit and explained that we had no real interest in Christianity. At that time, I was more interested in Horus, the ancient Egyptian star-god.

*

On the morning of Boxing Day we set off at dawn and hiked along the Kali Gandaki River - I made a note at the side of my map, it simply says: 'Saw three UFOs'. We reached the village of Kusma on the 28th, just in time for the next stage of our initiation into the cult of Shiva.

*

Kusma was built at the top of a ravine that looked down upon the raging forces of the Kali Gandaki River. One morning the guy who owned the lodge we were staying in promised to take us to the local Shiva temple, he would awaken us just before dawn. The next day, before the rays of the sun had begun to touch or brighten the horizon, we were led away from the village to a level area of ground, not too far from a precipice. As the sunlight broke the sky, we made offerings to Lord Shiva.

The following morning, we were again awoken at dawn, and this time we were sworn to secrecy. We were going to see another part of the temple, but one that was kept away from general tourists. He was going to take us to the hidden aspect of the temple, deep underground, despite the risk of facing two years in prison for taking westerners to a place outlawed by State Law. We agreed to tell no-one until we left Nepal.

We were guided out of the village and down into the ravine. The descent was steep and we climbed down until we were almost level with the river. Our guide led us to a rock face, where a solitary Saddhu, wearing the customary orange robe, lived beneath a simple lean-to shelter covered in rags. We were introduced to the Saddhu, tho' none of us spoke a single word of the other's language. We shared a holy smoke, inhaled the Holy Spirit, and created a holy moment of peace and peace everywhere.

Beyond the Saddhu's shelter stood the black entrance to a cave.

The Saddhu gestured for us to enter. We removed our shoes and our voluntary guide led the way.

There were four of us, Paul, Phil, me and the dude who seemed hell-bent on showing us stuff. We only had two torches between us and had to keep passing them around.

We reached what appeared to be the end of what is now known as the mysterious cave of Gupteswor.

The cave was warm, with water dripping everywhere. Then the guide pulled out a narrow ladder from behind a rock. The ladder was a thin piece of wood with triangle foot-holds nailed to it. He leaned the narrow, four inches wide, ladder against the wall of the cave, and then shone his torch higher.

The beam of torchlight revealed a small dark slit in the wall. Our guide climbed up the ladder and then pulled himself upwards, before vanishing into the slit. We followed, taking it in turn. Phil was the last to go. He got real frightened as he faced the small hole we had to wriggle through; it was so narrow, and half flooded with warm flowing water that we had to lie on our sides and wriggle through that way. Phil only came with us when he realized that we had the torches.

We wriggled through a very scary tunnel. Fuck it, we were potholing! Passing the torch back and forth, our guide, who we couldn't understand, warned us sharp low hanging rock, or when we were wriggling along on our bellies he would point out a hole in the oncoming ground that was big enough for two of us to fall into at the same time. We dropped rocks down the hole and never heard them hit. Then suddenly we emerged in a huge dome-shaped cave. We stood upright, our torch beams could barely reach the side walls, and the cavern was huge. Our guide explained, in his peculiar way, that we were now in a sacred centre. Indeed, in the centre of the cave, there stood a huge stalagmite, shaped like a Shiva Lingham. This huge phallic symbol lay directly beneath the temple of Shiva that we had been introduced to the day before. Now it stood thousands of feet above us. We smoked a tribute to Shiva, turned off the torches and listened to water trickle down the walls, surrounded by a heavy black density that reminds me of the energy-field in the King's Chamber of the Great Pyramid in Egypt.

Every time we were invited, by total strangers, into the mysteries of Shiva, I couldn't help but think about that old Saddhu I encountered at midnight on the platform of Delhi train station, doing his hand-walks and acrobatics, his eyes full of wicked delight.

*

From Kusma it was a 57 km hike back to Pokhara. In one village, we were in our shared lodge room when three soldiers entered the room and began searching about, rummaging through our things.

I turned and looked at Phil, 'Should I put this out?' I was smoking a joint. I'd watched the soldiers come into the room. I was watching as they began to rummage about. Was something happening?

Phil was silently frantic, silently screaming 'YES!'

I killed the joint. I thought I was invisible to the soldiers and I had no interaction with them at all. The soldiers never found our dope. That was weird. The air was full of it. We didn't even get hit for a bribe.

We spent New Year's Eve, crossing from 1987 into 1988, staying in a tiny village that only had access to a single collective water-tap, and as usual, we were probably crashed out by eight O'clock at night. Once it got dark there wasn't much to do, either watch the black night sky as it filled with diamonds, or write or read by candlelight, or crash-out in preparation for another grueling hike.

*

The return to Pokhara was something of a culture shock, perhaps even more of a shock than when we first arrived at Delhi airport; we'd been so out of everything.

The mountains of Nepal are scarcely populated, their trails always gently flowing with human traffic climbing and descending the stone pathways. Nepali people ferrying various goods, either carrying them in huge woven baskets that they carried on their backs, baskets so big that the carrier needed a strap around his forehead to hold it in place, or ferrying goods on mule-trains; the mules all fully loaded, brightly decorated and adorned with bells that rang as they navigated the pathways and stepping stones.

*

Then we were back in the world - from Pokhara we travelled back to Kathmandu, then across the border into India, carrying dope. I think Phil and I were having a bit of a genuine row when we approached the military checkpoint; the soldiers just waved us through as quickly as they could.

In Delhi we had a day or two to kill before flying back to the UK. For want of anything much better to do, we visited the nightmare that is New Delhi Zoo (unless it's improved since then). Animals like black panthers were confined in strait-jacket sized cages. A solitary gorilla stood on a small hill in the confines of his open prison. The crowd were constantly jeering and tormenting the gorilla. Every now and then, the gorilla would pick up a rock or a stone, then spin, and hurl the rock or stone directly at the crowd. The crowd would cheer. The gorilla obviously wanted to kill everyone in the crowd, and I don't blame him. That gorilla was in serious need of an Uzi sub-machine pistol. Even the Hippo's were pissed-off. They would face away from the crowd, and then spin their tails. Paul saw this one coming and pulled me out of the way, just in time. The Hippo's were shitting at the crowd, using their spinning tails to spread their shit as far as they could. These animals were showing amazing moments of blatant revolt. The place was terrible, and if I ever watch Planet of the Apes, or alien invasion movies, I always side against the humans.

*

We'd chopped up the dope and shaped it into dozens of capsules, wrapped in cling-film and sealed with a flame, ready to swallow before the flight.

Easy money; Nepali dope is probably the best in the world...then something strange happened - A simple, little thing; a spiritual test.

The night before the 23rd, when we were due to fly back, I lost my magical ring; a five-pointed star in a circle.

I took this as symbolic, like a sign or an omen, a word from the hidden forces that surround us, warning of impending bad luck.

I listened to the voice and expressed my concerns about swallowing drugs for profit, especially after such a magical time.

We hired a tuk-tuk and visited several hostels that catered for trekkers, most of whom were inspired by Jack Kerouac's novel 'On the Road', and sold the smoke we'd brought from Nepal for a fair price in less than an hour – sharing the love and getting rid of the gear.

*

London - Heathrow airport - January 23rd, 1988.

We were all wearing clothes made in Nepal; bright coloured jackets, collarless striped cotton shirts, deep-knit patterned pullovers, baggy cotton trousers, hefty boots, carrying just a few possessions and a few gifts for friends and family.

I was carrying a handmade drum with goatskin-skins, plus a fragile statue of Ganesha, some paintings created in fine detail by novice Buddhist Monks, and a set of ceremonial bells made from a combination of 7 different metals, including gold and silver - when struck together the bells create a magical, resonating chime.

As we walked through customs I was called over to the customs desk.

The guy at the desk looked at me.

'Okay, son,' he said, 'put your drugs on the counter.'

I laughed, and in that instant the customs guy read me like an open book; he knew that I was clean.

He waved me through the barrier and I laughed like a fool.

THE END

Printed in Great Britain
by Amazon